EARLY AMERICAN POETRY

SELECTIONS FROM
Bradstreet, Taylor, Dwight,
Freneau, and Bryant

EDITED BY
Jane Donahue Eberwein

THE UNIVERSITY OF WISCONSIN PRESS

The University of Wisconsin Press
114 North Murray Street
Madison, Wisconsin 53715

3 Henrietta Street
London WC2E 8LU, England

10   9   8   7   6   5   4   3

Printed in the United States of America

Library of Congress Cataloging in Publication Data
Main entry under title:
Early American poetry.
    Includes bibliographical references and index.
    1. American poetry—1783–1850.   2. American
poetry—Colonial period, ca. 1600–1775.   I. Eberwein,
Jane Donahue, 1943–   .
PS609.E2   811'.1'08   77-91051
ISBN 0-299-07440-4
ISBN 0-299-07444-7 pbk.

Contents

Preface

THIS IS a major-figure anthology of American poetry in the colonial and early national periods. It examines the changing patterns of our literature through the work of five poets, each representative of a period in America's cultural development but distinctive as well, speaking in a personal voice on a variety of themes. Discovering Anne Bradstreet, Edward Taylor, Timothy Dwight, Philip Freneau, and William Cullen Bryant, the reader will notice changing literary forms, varying personalities, and drastically differing attitudes toward man's place in the universe. Even within the supposedly rigid theology of New England Puritanism, he will find surprisingly different ideas and expressions; a pattern of belief uniting Bradstreet with Taylor and Dwight could hardly be called constrictive. Nor did the republican spirit of the Revolution force Dwight and Freneau to sing in patriotic harmony. The reader will find great differences in the poetic voices introduced here, but will recognize continuities as well in the spiritual searching and literary adventuring of these artistic pilgrims.

In choosing the poems to represent each writer, I have tried to illustrate the range of the poet's interests and forms. I have attempted, also, to let these five voices speak for various periods of our cultural history: successive generations of Puritanism, two aspects of neoclassicism, and several approaches to romanticism. Each writer is, in some sense, both typical and transitional. Continuities and changes may readily be studied by comparing poems by different writers confronting shared themes: nature, religion, human destiny, death, and poetry itself. Believing as I do, however, that these five major poets were all fine writers and made enduring contributions to American literature, I have tried to select and emphasize their best poems, confident that literary value transcends historical considerations.

To make the poems useful to college students in colonial literature courses and surveys of American poetry, I have provided introductory essays on each writer, annotation to clarify the poems, and bibliographic suggestions to facilitate further inquiry. The poets are presented chronologically, as are the poems, which I have arranged by order of publication or, in Taylor's case, in probable order of composition. The first date following each poem indicates when the work was written; the second date when it was *first* published in book form. The texts of the poems follow the most recent scholarly editions, if available, or the best text prepared in the author's lifetime.

A brief appendix offers three historically significant poems by three other authors, Michael Wigglesworth, Ebenezer Cook, and Joel Barlow; these expand the reader's sense of the range of early American verse and the variety of its voices. Vast numbers of persons wrote poetry during the more than two hundred years surveyed in this anthology; many achieved a few memorable poems, though few rivaled the five featured here in their total literary achievement.

I hope that this anthology will encourage students to read more deeply and widely in American poetry before the nineteenth century and in the prose of William Bradford, Cotton Mather, Samuel Sewall, John Woolman, Jonathan Edwards, Benjamin Franklin, and Charles Brockden Brown, which provides the literary context in which the poetry can best be understood. There is much to be enjoyed; this book is only an introduction.

I wish to acknowledge my gratitude to the English Department of Oakland University for frequent opportunities to teach early American literature and to two people whose help has been particularly valuable in preparing this book: to Marian Wilson for her advice and editorial assistance and to my husband, Robert Eberwein, for his consistent helpfulness. Without them, this book would surely have run "more hobbling than is meet."

Acknowledgments

I ACKNOWLEDGE, gratefully, the cooperation of editors and publishers who have permitted me to include their materials in this anthology. Selections from Anne Bradstreet are reprinted by permission of the publishers from *The Works of Anne Bradstreet*, ed. Jeannine Hensley (Cambridge, Mass.: The Belknap Press of Harvard University Press, [c] 1967 by the President and Fellows of Harvard College). Edward Taylor's poems follow the text of *The Poems of Edward Taylor*, ed. Donald Stanford (New Haven, Conn.: Yale University Press, 1960), with the permission of Donald Stanford and the Yale University Press. "A Fragment of Bion," from *The Last Poems of Philip Freneau*, ed. Lewis Leary (Westport, Conn.: Greenwood Press, 1945), appears with Lewis Leary's permission.

EARLY AMERICAN POETRY

ONE

Anne Bradstreet
(1612-1672)

LONDON READERS of 1650 must have been startled by the title of an otherwise unimposing volume: *The Tenth Muse, Lately Sprung Up in America.* The name, perhaps, suggested such marvelous thoughts as the image of an Indian princess leaping from the forest with her poems stained by berry juice on birchbark or even the prospect of a wholly new art form, presided over by a successor to the nine Greek Muses. Sobering second thoughts would have come as they read the extended title which explained that these were "several poems compiled with great variety of wit and learning . . . by a gentlewoman in New-England." Even the addendum left questions enough. What sort of "gentlewoman" inhabited the American colonies? How could she find time to write or nerve to publish? What, in any case, had "wit and learning" to do with any woman, with the possible exception of a few court ladies with unusual opportunities? And yet the poems clearly showed intellectual achievement; they showed respect for the Muses of lyric poetry, love poetry, epic, and history even though the author promptly disclaimed any pretension to "tenth Muse" status. Perhaps she would have been better pleased with a later and almost equally memorable title, "the mother of American poetry," but even that would no doubt have troubled her. She prided herself on her maternity and probably, in private, on her verse (referring to it as yet another child in "The Author to Her Book"), but she would hardly have described herself as an American or conceived of an enduring New World literary tradition.

Anne Bradstreet had been born in England in 1612 and had grown up in the household of the Earl of Lincoln, whom her father, Thomas Dudley, served as steward. The Dudley children enjoyed the pleasures of the Lincolnshire countryside and benefited as well from the stimulation of the earl's library and the spiritual discipline of family prayer and Puritan preaching. They belonged to that reforming branch of the Church of England which tried to return to the simplicity of early Christianity by ridding the Anglican church of all vestiges of Roman Catholicism and by attempting to reconstruct the patterns of congregational church governance they found in the Bible. The young Dudleys also enjoyed the companionship of their father's well-educated, upright, and adventurous friends, including his one-time assistant, Simon Bradstreet, whom Anne married when she was sixteen and he twenty-five. Two years later, in 1630, in response to political pressures from the king against the Earl of Lincoln, persecution of Puritan ministers, and fear of coming disaster in their own country, the Dudleys and Bradstreets left their old life behind them and joined John Winthrop's party aboard the *Arbella* for the hazardous journey to New England, where they would found the Massachusetts Bay colony with Winthrop as governor and Dudley his assistant. In time, Thomas Dudley would serve as governor also, and Simon Bradstreet, always active in colonial affairs, would become the last governor of Massachusetts Bay under its original charter.

Life was challenging in America; Anne Bradstreet told her children years later that "I found a new world and new manners, at which my heart rose," but she resigned herself to God's will, joined the church at Boston, and accepted the changes of frontier life.[1] There were many moves—from Salem, to Charlestown, to Cambridge, to Ipswich, and finally to what is now Andover, Massachusetts, where the burning of one house forced a move to yet another. After an extended and troubling period of childless-

1. Bradstreet's autobiography may be found in "To My Dear Children," a grouping of prose and verse meditations and personal reminiscence, which offers an invaluable complement to her poems. See *The Works of Anne Bradstreet*, ed. Jeannine Hensley (Cambridge, Mass.: Belknap Press of Harvard University Press, 1967), pp. 240-293.

ness, she became the mother of four boys and four girls, whose progress she recalled delightfully in "I had eight birds hatched in one nest" (1659). She devoted herself to ordering her successive households, caring for her husband and her children, and often handling household responsibilities alone for substantial periods while Simon Bradstreet traveled to Boston, Connecticut, and even England on colonial business. Despite recurring periods of illness, a problem since her childhood, she lived the life of a New England gentlewoman and probably impressed her neighbors as the ideal matron she described in her 1643 elegy for her own mother:

> Here lies,
> A worthy matron of unspotted life,
> A loving mother and obedient wife,
> A friendly neighbor, pitiful to poor,
> Whom oft she fed and clothed with her store;
> To servants wisely awful, but yet kind,
> And as they did, so they reward did find.
> A true instructor of her family,
> The which she ordered with dexterity.
> The public meetings ever did frequent,
> And in her closet constant hours she spent;
> Religious in all her words and ways,
> Preparing still for death, till end of days:
> Of all her children, children lived to see,
> Then dying, left a blessed memory.[2]

The difference, of course, is that Anne Bradstreet distilled her experience into poetry, which her brother-in-law and first editor, John Woodbridge, excused as "the fruit but of some few hours, curtailed from her sleep and other refreshments." [3]

Paralleling the life which can be summarized in conventional

---

2. "An Epitaph on my dear and ever-honoured Mother Mrs. Dorothy Dudley, who deceased December 27, 1643, and of her age, 61," in *Works of Anne Bradstreet*, p. 204.

3. John Woodbridge, "Epistle to the Reader," in *Works of Anne Bradstreet*, p. 3. This letter, prefaced to the original edition of *The Tenth Muse*, provides a warm introduction to Anne Bradstreet as a person even while showing ambivalence toward the idea of a woman writer.

biography—birth, education, marriage, maternity, and writing—was the life of the spirit which Bradstreet valued more and which she eventually recorded for her children. As a young girl of six or seven, she had come to an awareness of her sinful nature and had striven to amend her ways until adolescence directed her mind toward carnality. A serious attack of smallpox, however, restored her thoughts to God, and the responsibilities of marriage helped her to live the pious, serviceable life of the good Puritan despite recurring doubts about the validity of her religion and the assurance of her own conversion experience. She saw the repeated sicknesses of her adult life and the sorrows of losing homes, friends, and even grandchildren as trials sent by God to test and confirm her faith. In many ways, hers was a typical Puritan autobiography; she had heard others record their trials, doubts, failures, and awakenings in similar terms, and she watched anxiously over the spiritual odyssey of each child. Life, for the Puritans, was a pilgrimage toward heaven, an adventurous quest on which the individual soul would be tested to the limits of its endurance and on which only God's few elect would be successful. The New England pilgrim[4] used whatever assistance he could—his family, his church, the community structure which reinforced the religious, and even poetry, which could be employed to order experiences and search them for meaning, to beg for grace, and to celebrate God's mercy. Many early colonists wrote verses with this intention, mostly flat, conventional pieces more expressive of piety than aesthetic judgment. Anne Bradstreet's distinction is that she went beyond the conventions of her society to write poems which still give pleasure, still speak to the modern reader of valid emotional and intellectual perceptions.

Like any literature, her poems reflect the culture of her time, specifically that of post-Elizabethan England. Her British educa-

4. The word *pilgrim* is used here in a generalized sense to designate the spiritual quester on the way to heaven. It was a common Puritan metaphor, as witness John Bunyan's *Pilgrim's Progress* (1675) and Jonathan Edwards's undated sermon, "The Christian Pilgrim." American usage applies the term, in a specialized meaning, to the community of Puritan separatists who colonized Plymouth in 1620; Anne Bradstreet, of course, had no connection with that group.

tion and her readings from her father's and husband's libraries
in England and Massachusetts exposed her to English literature
and literary fashions. She had read Raleigh, Sidney, Spenser, and
possibly Shakespeare, and she studied books of astronomy, anat-
omy, history, and religion as eagerly as she read her favorite poets.
Her early writings show the strong influence of the amazingly
learned and surprisingly popular French Calvinist poet, Guillaume
de Salluste Sieur Du Bartas, as translated by Joshua Sylvester,
though her later work reveals more confidence in her own style
and subject matter. Her most important literary resource, however,
was always the Bible, both the Geneva translation printed by
English Puritan exiles in Switzerland in 1560 and the Authorized
Version of 1611. Her poetry also reflects its period in its early
preference for intellectual and even academic subject matter and
in its use of wit and fun with wordplay, its adventurousness with
language.
  It also shows Bradstreet's delight in being English while her
native country asserted itself politically and militarily as the world
champion of Protestantism against the Catholic forces of France
and the Pope. She rejoiced in the recent memory of Sir Philip
Sidney. She reveled in the glory of Queen Elizabeth, whose ac-
complishments continued to illuminate her country and vindicate
her sex:

> Now say, have women worth? or have they none?
> Or had they some, but with our Queen is't gone?
> Nay masculines, you have thus taxed us long,
> But she, though dead, will vindicate our wrong.
> Let such as say our sex is void of reason,
> Know 'tis a slander now but once was treason.[5]

The poems reveal Bradstreet's enthusiasm for military glory and
her hopefulness with regard to Britain's future as a world power
committed to reformed religion. Her "Dialogue Between Old
England and New" (1643) and Old Age's speech in "Of the Four

  5. This passage comes from Bradstreet's extended elegy, "In Honour of that
High and Mighty Princess Queen Elizabeth of Happy Memory," in *Works of
Anne Bradstreet*, pp. 197-198, lines 100-105.

Ages of Man" (1642) reflect her continuing political interest in her native country, her sorrow for its internal discord, which she attributed to the latent influence of popery, and her anticipation of moral and political awakening, even at the cost of violence.

Critics, in fact, have often faulted Bradstreet for her lack of explicit interest in America, for her tendencies to describe a biblical or literarily British rather than Massachusetts landscape and to ignore the Indians, the forest, and other wilderness observations later Americans find significant. This is a limitation which she shared with Winthrop, Bradford, and our other early writers. They recorded experience in their own terms, without anticipating the sensibilities of unborn readers who would be influenced more by the romantic poets than the Bible and whose minds would be formed by Turner's frontier thesis and by modern research in anthropology. The American quality of Bradstreet's work lies in something more subtle than imagery or choice of subject matter. It is her sensitive recording of the Puritan people who colonized New England, with their values, their psychology, their blind spots, and their distinctive insights. Her poetry expresses, better than any other colonial verse, the human experience of Puritanism and helps us to see its influence on the early settlers and their descendants.

The Puritan, like the Anglican, Catholic, or almost any other seventeenth-century man, lived with a constant awareness of God. He saw God as the originator and end of his existence and profoundly believed that everything in life was ordered by divine purpose. Puritans, in fact, tended to stress God's participation in human existence by emphasizing surprising though often trivial happenings as special providences, signs of God's action and indications of His pleasure or displeasure with man's behavior. Life, as mentioned earlier, took the shape of a quest or pilgrimage through this world to an eternity in heaven or hell. Bradstreet's final poem, "As Weary Pilgrim" (1669), beautifully expresses this understanding as it tells how the pilgrim appreciates the refreshments of his journey but constantly directs his steps toward heaven and looks for signs that he is moving in the most direct path. By his own efforts alone, of course, the pilgrim will wander toward damnation. He depends on divine grace and on the special help

of Christ, by whose covenant of faith the Christian may hope
for salvation.

The path to salvation led through this world of ordinary human
experience, and the Puritan involved himself actively in the duties
of family life, citizenship, and his trade. Material achievements
could hardly earn his way to heaven, he realized, but success
in earthly responsibilities was commonly recognized as a probable
sign of election. In any case, there was much practical work to
be done in building Winthrop's hoped-for "Citty upon a Hill,"
which was to show Europe the fruits of reformed Protestantism.
This commitment to material duties reflects itself in Bradstreet's
poetry as does the emphasis on family for which Puritans were
known in England and the joy in sexual love which made pleasur-
able the obligation to increase and multiply and people the wilder-
ness with saints. Her poems for Simon Bradstreet, especially "To
My Dear and Loving Husband" (1641-1643?), and the series of
warm, witty verse letters she sent to cheer his travels give eloquent
testimony to the Puritan's capacity for physical love even as they
advise that the fulfillment of that love can only be found in eternal
life.

The dominant feeling of Bradstreet's poetry, in fact, is that
of tension between temporal and eternal values. This conflict
emerges most painfully in her elegies for her three dead grand-
children and her lament for the Andover house, the destruction
of which by fire deprived the poet of family treasures, valued
for their sentimental associations more than for their material
worth. It is obvious from her writing that Anne Bradstreet loved
this life intensely and clung passionately to such real though
temporal values as beautiful objects, friendship, and health. She
knew, however, that she must always be prepared to yield these
goods in favor of eternal ones, and her poetry records the painful
effort of will it took her to echo Job in blessing "His Name that
gave and took"; sometimes she could only repeat the sentiments
she knew the Christian ought to feel: "Let's say He's merciful
as well as just."

The tension between flesh and spirit would have been less
terrible, certainly, if man were naturally good or if grace trans-
formed his human nature directly to a state of perfection. Puritans

knew that God's ways were different, however, and that He had made man a "sinful creature, frail and vain,/This lump of wretchedness, of sin and sorrow"—a creature forced to struggle blindly toward a heaven he could only imperfectly imagine and perhaps did not even want, while foregoing those earthly comforts which distracted him too readily from his pilgrimage. Childhood's speech in "Of the Four Ages of Man" startles the modern reader with its assertion of man's inherent sinfulness, and Bradstreet's poetry in general shows her belief that human beings, even when not exactly evil, are always severely limited in their capacities for good.

Her poems reflect the psychological dilemma caused by such beliefs. Knowing herself radically flawed, she hoped for salvation; loving this life powerfully, she wanted to desire the next life more; always struggling to understand God's purpose in her life, she tried to discipline her often stubborn will to His. Obviously, she struggled with God, but she seems to have fought with Him as a daughter with her father, who is sure to overpower her eventually but can be counted upon to forgive her and continue in his love.

Everything else was subordinate to this fundamental drama of the pilgrim's quest for God. Nature, for instance, was more useful as a sign of its creator than as a value in itself. "Contemplations" (1664-1665?), her most successful extended poem, celebrates the power and beauty of the natural world, indicating that Anne Bradstreet could and did respond powerfully to the rivers, trees, and wildlife of her environment. She meditates on nature in this poem, however, only as a means of revealing, over and over, man's limitations in his own natural state and his need of grace by which God offers him the immortality that sets him above all other creatures.

Poetry, too, like reflection on nature and performance of duties in this world, had an instrumental rather than a final value. It could be used to order the meditations of the poet and to express his prayer and praise in the clearest, most pleasing terms, but the Puritan valued literature for its didactic value more than its aesthetic charm, treated with suspicion any excessively sensuous imagery or artistic embellishment, and felt that wit should be kept subservient to devotion except, at times, in verses written for private circulation. New Englanders wrote a great deal of poetry for pious reasons and exchanged it with friends for their mutual improvement and enjoyment. Anne Bradstreet originally wrote in the same way and offered her verses to her immediate family circle with no thought of the book with which her brother-in-law surprised her in 1650. After seeing *The Tenth Muse* she revised her early poems and wrote others with greater confidence in her poetic vocation, but her writing still seems more a personal and familial spiritual resource than a display of artistry intended to win fame from a large, sophisticated audience.

This perception of poetry as a useful, pleasant, but potentially dangerous art governed Anne Bradstreet's choice of subject matter and style. Many poems took the form of prayers—of intercession, praise, or thanksgiving—and generally found expression in simple lyric forms she might have noticed in her hymnal. "Contemplations" called for a more complex but regularly repeated form, a variation of the Spenserian stanza, to draw out the cyclically interrelated pattern of its meditations and to lend added emphasis to the conclusion of each thought. Her early poems, like the debates of the four elements, four humors, four seasons, and four ages of man and the histories of four ancient monarchies, which formed the bulk of *The Tenth Muse,* were academic in their purpose and were intended to arrange and display her knowledge for the amusement of her father, to whom they were dedicated, and a few friends who might sympathize with her seemingly desperate impulse to recall and use her education even in the wilderness. These take the form of iambic couplets, a dreary choice of form but suited to discursive material. She experimented with a variety of poetic conventions to suit her various subjects and audiences, but she seldom let language and style dominate her verses or call attention to themselves. Only in such a private exchange as "A Letter to Her Husband, Absent Upon Public Employment" (1641-1643?) did she indulge in wit and verbal dexterity mainly for entertainment—her own and Simon Bradstreet's. In this poem she drew cleverly from the stiff erudition of the quaternions to present herself as the melancholy earth waiting for the quickening heat of her loving sun in a world where the seasons have been reversed by his travels southward. Despite her humble disclaimers in "The Author to Her Book" (1650-1670?) and "The Prologue" to the quaternions (1642?), she knew she could use the poetic conventions of her metaphysical literary era successfully and with imagination. That she so often chose clarity over complexity and simplicity over sophistication tells us much about the Puritan's ambivalence toward art.

The inherent Puritanism of Anne Bradstreet's style and themes, coupled with the metaphysical conventions of seventeenth-century English poetry, helps to explain her shifting reputation. Welcomed in her own time as a gifted poet though something of a curiosity because of her sex and situation, she found readers in England and America well into the eighteenth century, as long as conservative Calvinism still provided an audience. The nineteenth century found her less attractive; critics reacted against the rough baroque quality of her poetry as they rejected Donne, Herbert, and Crashaw, and readers looked in vain for the love of nature, the sentimental view of man, and the comforting philosophy which they expected in poetry. The rediscovery of English metaphysical verse in the early twentieth century which revitalized interest in American Puritanism and the later enthusiasm for confessional poetry of psychological interest have established her again as our first important American poet and as a compelling, attractive person whose humanity speaks to us and whose qualities of sensitivity, balance, openness, and even toughness still have the power to encourage and sustain.

BIBLIOGRAPHIC NOTE

The most complete and accurate edition of Bradstreet's poetry is *The Works of Anne Bradstreet,* ed. Jeannine Hensley (Cambridge, Mass.: Belknap Press of Harvard University Press, 1967). Still valuable for its inclusiveness and its introduction, though out of date in terms of scholarship, is *The Works of Anne Bradstreet in Prose and Verse,* ed. John Harvard Ellis (Charlestown, Mass.: Abram E. Cutter, 1867; reprinted, New York: Peter Smith, 1932; Gloucester, Mass.: Peter Smith, 1962). Another item of interest to the modern reader, though necessarily limited to her early poems, is the facsimile edition of *The Tenth Muse,* ed. Josephine K. Piercy (Gainesville, Fla.: Scholars' Facsimiles & Reprints, 1965).

Anyone interested in the poet's life or cultural environment should consult Elizabeth Wade White's exceptionally thorough biography, *Anne Bradstreet: "The Tenth Muse"* (New York: Oxford University Press, 1971). Other book-length studies of her life and work include Josephine K. Piercy's *Anne Bradstreet*, Twayne's United States Authors Series (New York: Twayne Publishers, 1965), and Ann Stanford's *Anne Bradstreet, the Worldly Puritan: An Introduction to Her Poetry* (New York: Burt Franklin & Co., 1974).

As the "mother of American poetry," Anne Bradstreet has also inspired creative tributes. Her admirers will find memorable and revealing insights into her experiences as woman and artist, as seen through the eyes of a modern poet, in John Berryman's *Homage to Mistress Bradstreet* (New York: Farrar, Straus & Giroux, 1956).

THE TEXT

This text follows Jeannine Hensley's edition of *The Works of Anne Bradstreet*, published in 1967 by the Belknap Press of Harvard University Press. For poems first published in 1650 in *The Tenth Muse* ("The Prologue," "Of the Four Ages of Man," "A Dialogue," and "The Vanity of All Worldly Things") Hensley uses the posthumous *Several Poems* text of 1678 on the theory that the revised versions of the poems more nearly reflect Bradstreet's own editorial preferences than the much-flawed first edition published without her supervision. Readers interested in the changes Bradstreet made between editions, some quite substantive, should consult Hensley's detailed appendix. "Contemplations," "The Author to Her Book," "Before the Birth of One of Her Children," "To My Dear and Loving Husband," "A Letter to Her Husband," "In Reference to Her Children," and the elegies for Elizabeth and Simon Bradstreet appeared first in the 1678 edition. The remaining poems were originally included in the Andover Manuscript, given by the poet to her son Simon and first printed in 1867. The ordering of poems in this anthology is, then, roughly chronological and follows the order of publication. Dates of composition can sometimes be determined accurately but are more often conjectural; they are indicated here according to the chronology suggested by Ann Stanford in *Anne Bradstreet, the Worldly Puritan: An Introduction to Her Poetry* (New York: Burt Franklin & Co., 1974), pp. 125-127.

From *The Tenth Muse*

THE PROLOGUE

1

[handwritten: constructs of history]

[handwritten left margin: posture of humility]

To sing of wars, of captains, and of kings,
Of cities founded, commonwealths begun,
For my mean pen are too superior things:
Or how they all, or each their dates have run
Let poets and historians set these forth,
My obscure lines shall not so dim their worth.

[handwritten right margin: transience of glory] 5

2

But when my wond'ring eyes and envious heart
Great Bartas'[1] sugared lines do but read o'er,
Fool I do grudge the Muses did not part
'Twixt him and me that overfluent store;
A Bartas can do what a Bartas will
But simple I according to my skill.

[handwritten: ?]

[handwritten right margin: more lyric]

10

[handwritten right margin: heroic couplet undermines Bartas]

3

From schoolboy's tongue no rhet'ric we expect,
Nor yet a sweet consort from broken strings,
Nor perfect beauty where's a main defect:
My foolish, broken, blemished Muse so sings,
And this to mend, alas, no art is able,
'Cause nature made it so irreparable.

[handwritten left margin: Herbert (Easter?)]

15

4

Nor can I, like that fluent sweet tongued Greek,[2]
Who lisped at first, in future times speak plain.

20

1. Guillaume de Salluste Sieur Du Bartas, author of *La Sepmaine* (1578) and *La Seconde Sepmaine* (1584), translated by Joshua Sylvester as *Divine Weekes and Workes* (1621). Du Bartas, much admired in England during Bradstreet's youth, popularized a style of poetry known for its encyclopedic display of information and its Calvinistic didacticism. Bradstreet was strongly influenced by his work and was saluted by Nathaniel Ward, another New England author, as "a right Du Bartas girl."
2. Demosthenes.

By art he gladly found what he did seek,
A full requital of his striving pain.
Art can do much, but this maxim's most sure:
A weak or wounded brain admits no cure.

      5

I am obnoxious to each carping tongue
Who says my hand a needle better fits,
A poet's pen all scorn I should thus wrong,
For such despite they cast on female wits:
If what I do prove well, it won't advance,
They'll say it's stol'n, or else it was by chance.

      6

But sure the antique Greeks were far more mild
Else of our sex, why feigned they those nine
And poesy made Calliope's[3] own child;
So 'mongst the rest they placed the arts divine:
But this weak knot they will full soon untie,
The Greeks did nought, but play the fools and lie.

      7

Let Greeks be Greeks, and women what they are
Men have precedency and still excel,
It is but vain unjustly to wage war;
Men can do best, and women know it well.
Preeminence in all and each is yours;
Yet grant some small acknowledgement of ours.

      8

And oh ye high flown quills that soar the skies,
And ever with your prey still catch your praise,
If e'er you deign these lowly lines your eyes,
Give thyme or parsley wreath, I ask no bays;
This mean and unrefined ore of mine
Will make your glist'ring gold but more to shine.

      (1642?; 1650)

3. The Muse of epic poetry.

[Handwritten marginal annotations: "Combination of Christian and Neoclassical elements"; "25"; "Feminist — Defines poetic voice / Female in Puritan society"; "30"; "Greeks more liberated about roles of women"; "35"; "10th muse's tongue will be untied"; "Greeks / Women acknowledge women writers?"; "40"; "Condescending?"; "poet"; "45"; "poetry"; "Domestic role"; "art gender"]

16 Anne Bradstreet

OF THE FOUR AGES OF MAN

Lo now four other act upon the stage,[1]
Childhood and Youth, the Manly and Old Age;
The first son unto phlegm, grand-child to water,
Unstable, supple, cold, and moist's his nature.
The second, frolic, claims his pedigree   5
From blood and air, for hot and moist is he.
The third of fire and choler is composed
Vindicative and quarrelsome disposed.
The last of earth, and heavy melancholy,
Solid, hating all lightness and all folly.   10
Childhood was clothed in white and green to show[2]
His spring was intermixed with some snow:
Upon his head nature a garland set
Of primrose, daisy and the violet.
Such cold mean flowers the spring puts forth betime   15
Before the sun hath thoroughly heat the clime.
His hobby striding, did not ride but run,
And in his hand an hour-glass new begun,
In danger every moment of a fall,
And when 'tis broke then ends his life and all: 20
But if he hold till it have run its last,
Then may he live out threescore years or past.
Next Youth came up in gorgeous attire,
(As that fond age doth most of all desire).
His suit of crimson and his scarf of green,   25
His pride in's countenance was quickly seen;

Use of reason to order world?

Powerful natural imagery

1. This debate is the third of Bradstreet's four quaternions and may best be
appreciated in light of the debates among the elements, humors, and seasons.
All four debates interrelate according to a medieval system of correspondences:

Element	Humor	Age	Season
fire	choler	middle age	summer
earth	melancholy	old age	autumn
air	sanguine	youth	spring
water	phlegmatic	childhood	winter

2. In the following lines note the emblematic portrayals of the characters, each
of whom is garbed and posed to clarify his allegorical function.

Garland of roses, pinks and gilliflowers
Seemed on's head to grow bedewed with sh wers:
His face as fresh as is Aurora[3] fair,
When blushing she first 'gins to light the air.   30
No wooden horse, but one of mettle tried,

Middle Age?

He seems to fly or swim, and not to ride.
Then prancing on the stage, about he wheels,
But as he went, death waited at his heels.
The next came up in a much graver sort,   35
As one that cared for a good report,
His sword by's side, and choler in his eyes,
But neither used as yet, for he was wise:
Of autumn's fruits a basket on his arm,
His golden god in's purse, which was his charm.   40
And last of all to act upon this stage
Leaning upon his staff came up Old Age,
Under his arm a sheaf of wheat he bore,
An harvest of the best, what needs he more?
In's other hand a glass even almost run,   45
Thus writ about: This out then am I done.
His hoary hairs, and grave aspect made way,
And all gave ear to what he had to say.
These being met each in his equipage
Intend to speak according to their age;   50
But wise Old Age did with all gravity
To childish Childhood give precendency,
And to the rest his reason mildly told,
That he was young before he grew so old.
To do as he, each one full soon assents,   55
Their method was that of the Elements,
That each should tell what of himself he knew,
Both good and bad, but yet no more than's true.
With heed now stood three ages of frail man,
To hear the child, who crying thus began.   60

Childhood

Ah me! conceived in sin and born with sorrow,

3. The dawn.

public confession

A nothing, here today and gone tomorrow,
Whose mean beginning blushing can't reveal,
But night and darkness must with shame conceal.
My mother's breeding sickness I will spare,   65
Her nine months weary burthen not declare.
To show her bearing pains, I should do wrong,
To tell those pangs which can't be told by tongue:
With tears into the world I did arrive;
My mother still did waste as I did thrive,   70
Who yet with love and all alacrity,
Spending, was willing to be spent for me.
With wayward cries I did disturb her rest,
Who sought still to appease me with the breast:
With weary arms she danced and "By By" sung,   75
When wretched I, ingrate, had done the wrong.
When infancy was past, my childishness
Did act all folly that it could express,
My silliness did only take delight
In that which riper age did scorn and slight.   80
In rattles, baubles, and such toyish stuff,
My then ambitious thoughts were low enough:
My highborn soul so straitly was confin'd,
That its own worth it did not know nor mind:
This little house of flesh did spacious count,   85
Through ignorance all troubles did surmount;
Yet this advantage had mine ignorance,
Freedom from envy and from arrogance.
How to be rich or great I did not cark,
A baron or a duke ne'er made my mark,   90
Nor studious was kings' favours how to buy,
With costly presents or base flattery:
No office coveted wherein I might
Make strong myself and turn aside weak right:
No malice bear to this or that great peer,   95
Nor unto buzzing whisperers gave ear:
I gave no hand nor vote for death or life,
I'd nought to do 'twixt King and people's strife.
No statist I, nor martialist in th' field;

Where e'er I went, mine innocence was shield. 100
My quarrels not for diadems did rise,
But for an apple, plum, or some such prize:
My strokes did cause no blood, no wounds or scars,
My little wrath did end soon as my wars:
My duel was no challenge nor did seek 105
My foe should welt'ring in his bowels reek.
I had no suits at law neighbours to vex,
Nor evidence for lands did me perplex.
I feared no storms, nor all the wind that blows,
I had no ships at sea, nor freights to lose. 110
I feared no drought nor wet, I had no crop,
Nor yet on future things did set my hope.
This was mine innocence, but ah! the seeds
Lay raked up of all the cursed weeds
Which sprouted forth in mine ensuing age, 115
As he can tell that next comes on the stage:
But yet let me relate before I go
The sins and dangers I am subject to.
Stained from birth with Adam's sinful fact,
Thence I began to sin as soon as act: 120
A perverse will, a love to what's forbid,
A serpent's sting in pleasing face lay hid:
A lying tongue as soon as it could speak,
And fifth commandment[4] do daily break.
Oft stubborn, peevish, sullen, pout and cry, 125
Then nought can please, and yet I know not why.
As many are my sins, so dangers too;
For sin brings sorrow, sickness, death, and woe:
And though I miss the tossings of the mind,
Yet griefs in my frail flesh I still do find. 130
What grippes of wind mine infancy did pain,
What tortures I in breeding teeth sustain?
What crudities my stomach cold hath bred,
Whence vomits, flux, and worms have issued?

4. "Honour thy father and thy mother . . ." (Exod. 20:12). Bradstreet's biblical citations refer to the Geneva version, and I have used that Bible in annotating her poems.

Autobiographical?

20 Anne Bradstreet   *caused by humors*

What breaches, knocks and falls I daily have,   135
And some perhaps I carry to my grave;
Sometimes in fire, sometimes in water fall,
Strangely preserved, yet mind it not at all:
At home, abroad my danger's manifold,
That wonder 'tis, my glass till now doth hold.   140
I've done; unto my elders I give way,
For 'tis but little that a child can say.

Youth

My goodly clothing, and my beauteous skin
Declare some greater riches are within:
But what is best I'll first present to view,   145
And then the worst in a more ugly hue:
For thus to do we on this stage assemble,
Then let not him that hath most craft dissemble.
My education and my learning such,
As might myself and others profit much;   150
With nurture trained up in virtue's schools,
Of science, arts, and tongues I know the rules,
The manners of the court I also know,
And so likewise what they in th' country do.
The brave attempts of valiant knights I prize,   155
That dare scale walls and forts reared to the skies.
The snorting horse, the trumpet, drum I like,
The glitt'ring sword, the pistol, and the pike:
I cannot lie intrenched before a town,
Nor wait till good success our hopes doth crown: 160
I scorn the heavy corslet, musket-proof;
I fly to catch the bullet that's aloof.
Though thus in field, at home to all most kind,
So affable, that I can suit each mind.
I can insinuate into the breast,   165
And by my mirth can raise the heart depressed.
Sweet music raps my brave harmonious soul,
My high thoughts elevate beyond the pole:
My wit, my bounty, and my courtesy
Make all to place their future hopes on me.   170

military imagery

This is my best; but Youth is known, alas!
To be as wild as is the snuffing ass:
As vain as froth, or vanity can be,
That who would see vain man, may look on me.

disillusioned?

My gifts abused, my education lost;   175
My woeful parents' longing hopes are crossed;
My wit evaporates in merriment;
My valour in some beastly quarrel's spent;
My lust doth hurry me to all that's ill:
I know no law nor reason but my will.   180
Sometimes lay wait to take a wealthy purse,
Or stab the man in's own defence (that's worse).
Sometimes I cheat (unkind) a female heir
Of all at once, who not so wise as fair
Trusteth my loving looks and glozing tongue,   185
Until her friends, treasure, and honour's gone.
Sometimes I sit carousing others' health,
Until mine own be gone, my wit and wealth.
From pipe to pot, from pot to words and blows,
For he that loveth wine wanteth no woes.   190
Whole nights with ruffins, roarers, fiddlers spend,
To all obscenity mine ears I lend;
All counsel hate (which tends to make me wise,)   *?*
And dearest friends count for mine enemies.
If any care I take 'tis to be fine,   195
For sure my suit more than my virtues shine
If time from lewd companions I can spare,
'Tis spent to curl, and pounce my new-bought hair.[5]
Some new Adonis[6] I do strive to be;
Sardanapalus[7] now survives in me.   200
Cards, dice, and oaths concomitant I love,
To plays, to masques, to taverns still I move.
And in a word, if what I am you'd hear,
Seek out a British brutish cavalier:

Cavalier / Puritan

5. Bradstreet's sarcastic reference to the new fashion of powdered wigs, which particularly offended the Puritans, long known for the simplicity of their dress and hairstyles.
6. Mythical Greek youth destroyed by his vanity.
7. Mythical last king of Assyria, said to have been brave though effete.

Such wretch, such monster am I, but yet more,   205
I have no heart at all this to deplore,
Wigglesworth Rememb'ring not the dreadful day of doom,
Nor yet that heavy reckoning soon to come.
Though dangers do attend me every hour,
And ghastly Death oft threats me with his power,   210
Sometimes by wounds in idle combats taken,
Sometimes with agues all my body shaken:
Sometimes by fevers all my moisture drinking,
My heart lies frying and mine eyes are sinking,
Sometimes the quinsy, painful pleurisy,   215
With sad affrights of death doth menace me:
Sometimes the twofold pox me sore be-mars
With outward marks and inward loathsome scars,
Sometimes the frenzy strangely mads my brain,
That oft for it in bedlam I remain.   220
Too many my diseases to recite,
That wonder 'tis, I yet behold the light,
That yet my bed in darkness is not made,
And I in black oblivion's den now laid.
Of aches full my bones, of woe my heart,   225
Clapt in that prison, never thence to start.
Ecclesiastes Thus I have said, and what I've been, you see,
Childhood and Youth are vain, yea vanity.

Middle Age

Childhood and Youth (forgot) I've sometimes seen
And now am grown more staid who have been green: 230
What they have done, the same was done by me,
As was their praise or shame, so mine must be.
Now age is more; more good you may expect,
But more mine age, the more is my defect.
When my wild oats were sown and ripe and mown,   235
I then received an harvest of mine own.
My reason then bad judge how little hope
Such empty seed should yield a better crop;
Then with both hands I grasped the world together.
Thus out of one extreme into another,   240

But yet laid hold on virtue seemingly;
Who climbs without hold climbs dangerously.
Be my condition mean, I then take pains
My family to keep, but not for gains.
A father I, for children must provide;
But if none, then for kindred near allied.
If rich, I'm urged then to gather more,
To bear a port i' th' world, and feed the poor.
If noble, then mine honour to maintain,
If not, riches nobility can gain.
For time, for place, likewise for each relation
I wanted not, my ready allegation.
Yet all my powers for self ends are not spent,
For hundreds bless me for my bounty lent,
Whose backs I've clothed, and bellies I have fed
With mine own fleece, and with my household bread;
Yea, justice have I done, was I in place,
To cheer the good, and wicked to deface.
The proud I crushed, th' oppressed I set free,
The liars curbed, but nourished verity.
Was I a pastor, I my flock did feed,
And gently lead the lambs as they had need.
A captain I, with skill I trained my band,
And showed them how in face of foes to stand.
A soldier I, with speed I did obey,
As readily as could my leader say.
Was I a labourer, I wrought all day
As cheerfully as e'er I took my pay.
Thus hath mine age in all sometimes done well,
Sometimes again, mine age been worse than hell.
In meanness, greatness, riches, poverty,
Did toil, did broil, oppressed, did steal and lie.
Was I as poor as poverty could be,
Then baseness was companion unto me,
Such scum as hedges and highways do yield,
As neither sow, nor reap, nor plant, nor build.
If to agriculture I was ordained,
Great labours, sorrows, crosses I sustained.

245

250

255

260

265

270

275

The early cock did summon but in vain
My wakeful thoughts up to my painful gain: 280
My weary beast rest from his toil can find,
But if I rest the more distressed my mind.
If happiness my sordidness hath found,
'Twas in the crop of my manured ground,
My thriving cattle and my new-milch-cow,   285
My fleeced sheep, and fruitful farrowing sow:
To greater things I never did aspire,
My dunghill thoughts or hopes could reach no higher.
If to be rich or great it was my fate,
How was I broiled with envy and with hate?   290
Greater than was the great'st was my desire,
And thirst for honour, set my heart on fire:
And by ambition's sails I was so carried,
That over flats, and sands, and rocks I hurried,
Oppressed and sunk and staved all in my way   295
That did oppose me, to my longed bay.
My thirst was higher than nobility,
I oft longed sore to taste on royalty:
Then kings must be deposed or put to flight,
I might possess that throne which was their right;   300
There set, I rid my self straight out of hand
Of such competitors as might in time withstand.
Then thought my state firm founded sure to last,
But in a trice 'tis ruined by a blast,
Though cemented with more than noble blood,   305
The bottom nought, and so no longer stood.
Sometimes vainglory is the only bait
Whereby my empty soul is lured and caught.
Be I of wit, of learning, and of parts,
I judge I should have room in all men's hearts.   310
And envy gnaws if any do surmount,
I hate not to be held in high'st account.
If Bias[8] like I'm stripped unto my skin,

8. One of the Seven Wise Men of Greece, Bias refused to pack his goods for
flight from his war-torn city, explaining, "I carry everything with me."

I glory in my wealth I have within.
Thus good and bad, and what I am you see,
Now in a word, what my diseases be.
The vexing stone in bladder and in reins,[9]
The strangury[10] torments me with sore pains.
The windy colic oft my bowels rend,
To break the darksome prison where it's penned.
The cramp and gout doth sadly torture me,
And the restraining, lame sciatica.
The asthma, megrim, palsy, lethargy,
The quartan ague, dropsy, lunacy:
Subject to all distempers, that's the truth,
Though some more incident to Age or Youth.
And to conclude, I may not tedious be,
Man at his best estate is vanity.

Old Age

What you have been, ev'n such have I before:
And all you say, say I, and somewhat more.
Babe's innocence, youth's wildness I have seen,
And in perplexed Middle Age have been;
Sickness, dangers, and anxieties have past,
And on this stage am come to act my last.
I have been young, and strong and wise as you:
But now *"Bis pueri senes"* [11] is too true.
In every age I've found much vanity,
An end of all perfection now I see.
It's not my valour, honour, nor my gold
My ruined house now falling can uphold.
It's not my learning, rhetoric, wit so large,
Hath now the power, death's warfare to discharge.
It's not my goodly state nor bed of down
That can refresh, or ease, if conscience frown.
Nor from alliance can I now have hope,
But what I have done well, that is my prop;

9. Kidneys.
10. Painful urination.
11. "Old men are children twice over."

He that in youth is godly, wise, and sage,
Provides a staff then to support his age. *good deeds*
Mutations great, some joyful and some sad,
In this short pilgrimage I oft have had.   350
Sometimes the Heavens with plenty smiled on me[12]
Sometime again rained all adversity.
Contingency Sometimes in honour, sometimes in disgrace,
Sometime an abject, then again in place.
Such private changes oft mine eyes have seen,   355
In various times of state I've also been.
tree imagery I've seen a kingdom flourish like a tree, *testimonial*
When it was ruled by that celestial she;[13]
And like a cedar, others so surmount
That but for shrubs they did themselves account.   360
Then saw I France and Holland saved, Callais[14] won,
And Philip and Albertus half undone.
I saw all peace at home, terror to foes,
But ah, I saw at last those eyes to close,
(Good Friday) And then methought the day at noon grew dark   365
When it had lost that radiant sun-like spark: *(Son)*
In midst of griefs I saw our hopes revive,
(For 'twas our hopes then kept our hearts alive)
We changed our queen for king[15] under whose rays
We joyed in many blest and prosperous days.   370
I've seen a prince,[16] the glory of our land,
In prime of youth seized by heaven's angry hand,
Which filled our hearts with fears, with tears our eyes,
No medical Wailing his fate, and our own destinies.
I've seen from Rome an execrable thing,   375
A plot[17] to blow up nobles and their king,

12. The references to English history in the following lines parallel the experiences and observations of Thomas Dudley from the reign of Queen Elizabeth to the Restoration.
13. Queen Elizabeth I.
14. Cadiz, Spain, its harbor burned by Sir Francis Drake in 1587 and the city itself destroyed in 1596 by the Earl of Essex and Lord Charles Howard.
15. James I.
16. Henry, Prince of Wales.
17. The Gunpowder Plot of Catholic insurgents to blow up the Houses of Parliament and murder King James, November 5, 1605.

But saw their horrid fact soon disappointed,
And land and nobles saved with their anointed.
I've princes[18] seen to live on other's lands;
A royal one[19] by gifts from strangers' hands,   380
Admired for their magnanimity,
Who lost a princedom and a monarchy.
I've seen designs for Ree and Rochelle[20] crossed,
And poor Palatinate[21] forever lost.
I've seen unworthy men advanced high,   385
(And better ones suffer extremity)
But neither favour, riches, title, state,
Could length their days or once reverse their fate;
I've seen one stab'd, and some to lose their heads,
And others fly, struck both with guilt and dread.   390
I've seen, and so have you, for 'tis but late,
The desolation of a goodly state,
Plotted and acted so that none can tell
Who gave the counsel, but the prince of hell,
Three hundred thousand slaughtered innocents,[22]   395
By bloody Popish, hellish miscreants:
Oh may you live, and so you will I trust
To see them swill in blood until they burst.   *defiles sacrament?*
I've seen a king[23] by force thrust from his throne,
And an usurper[24] subtly mount thereon.   400
I've seen a state unmoulded, rent in twain,
But yet may live to see't made up again.
I've seen it plundered, taxed, and soaked in blood,
But out of evil you may see much good.
What are my thoughts, this is no time to say.   405

18. Noble European Protestant exiles.
19. Frederick V, the Elector Palatine.
20. The Isle of Rhé and La Rochelle, scenes of British military disasters in 1625 and 1627.
21. The Elector Palatine, husband of England's Princess Elizabeth, was defeated and exiled from his kingdom in 1625 despite British military support for his Protestant regime.
22. Protestant victims of the Irish rebellion of 1641.
23. Charles I.
24. Oliver Cromwell; Bradstreet's invidious term for him indicates a surprisingly negative judgment by a Puritan poet.

Men may more freely speak another day.[25]
These are no old-wives' tales, but this is truth,
We old men love to tell what's done in youth.
But I return from whence I stepped awry,
My memory is bad, my brain is dry: 410
Mine almond tree,[26] grey hairs, do flourish now,
And back once straight, apace begins to bow:
My grinders now are few, my sight doth fail,
My skin is wrinkled, and my cheeks are pale,
No more rejoice at music's pleasing noise,   415
But waking glad to hear the cock's shrill voice:
I cannot scent savours of pleasant meat,
Nor sapors find in what I drink or eat:
My arms and hands once strong have lost their might;
I cannot labour, much less can I fight.   420
My comely legs as nimble as the roe
Now stiff and numb, can hardly creep or go,
My heart sometimes as fierce as lion bold,
Now trembling is, all fearful sad and cold;
My golden bowl and silver cord e'er long   425
Shall both be broke, by racking death so strong:
Then shall I go whence I shall come no more,
Sons, nephews, leave my farewell to deplore.
In pleasures and in labours I have found
That earth can give no consolation sound;   430
To great, to rich, to poor, to young, to old,
To mean, to noble, fearful, or to bold:
From king to beggar, all degrees shall find
But vanity, vexation of the mind.
Yea, knowing much, the pleasant'st life of all,   435
Hath yet among those sweets some bitter gall;
Though reading others' works doth much refresh,

25. Perhaps a reference to pressure felt by the poet, whether from English
politicians or Massachusetts community sentiment, against full expression of her
opinions.
26. A sign of old age in Eccles. 12:5. This concluding chapter of Ecclesiastes,
with its assertion that "all is vanitie," forms the basis of Old Age's remaining
speech.

Yet studying much brings weariness to th' flesh:
My studies, labours, readings all are done,
And my last period now ev'n almost run.   440
Corruption my father I do call,
Mother and sisters both, the worms that crawl
In my dark house, such kindred I have store,
Where I shall rest till heavens shall be no more,
And when this flesh shall rot and be consumed,   445
This body by this soul shall be assumed:
And I shall see with these same very eyes,
My strong Redeemer coming in the skies.
Triumph I shall o'er sin, o'er death, o'er hell,
And in that hope I bid you all farewell.   450

(1642; 1650)

A DIALOGUE BETWEEN OLD ENGLAND AND NEW; CONCERNING THEIR PRESENT TROUBLES, ANNO, 1642

New England

Alas, dear Mother, fairest queen and best,
With honour, wealth, and peace, happy and blest;
What ails thee hang thy head and cross thine arms?
And sit i' th' dust, to sigh these sad alarms?
What deluge of new woes thus overwhelm   5
The glories of thy ever famous realm?
What means this wailing tone, this mournful guise?
Ah, tell thy daughter, she may sympathize.

Old England

Art ignorant indeed of these my woes?
Or must my forced tongue these griefs disclose? 10
And must myself dissect my tattered state,
Which 'mazed Christendom stands wond'ring at?
And thou a child, a limb, and dost not feel
My fainting weak'ned body now to reel?

30 Anne Bradstreet

This physic purging potion I have taken   15
Will bring consumption or an ague quaking,
Unless some cordial thou fetch from high,
Which present help may ease my malady.
If I decease, doth think thou shalt survive? *(irony?)*
Or by my wasting state dost think to thrive?   20
Then weigh our case, if't be not justly sad;
Let me lament alone, while thou art glad.

New England

And thus (alas) your state you much deplore
In general terms, but will not say wherefore.
What medicine shall I seek to cure this woe,   25
If th' wound's so dangerous I may not know.
But you perhaps, would have me guess it out:[1]   *History*
What hath some Hengist like that Saxon stout
By fraud or force usurped thy flow'ring crown,
Or by tempestous wars thy fields trod down?   30
Or hath Canutus, that brave valiant Dane,
The regal, peaceful scepter from thee ta'en?
Or is't a Norman, whose victorious hand
With English blood bedews thy conquered land?
Or is't intestine wars that thus offend?   35
Do Maud and Stephen for the crown contend?
Do barons rise and side against their king,
And call in foreign aid to help the thing?
Must Edward be deposed? or is't the hour
That second Richard must be clapt in th' tower?   40
Or is't the fatal jar, again begun,
That from the red white pricking roses sprung?
Must Richmond's aid, the nobles now implore,
To come and break the tushes of the boar?
If none of these, dear mother, what's your woe?   45

1. In lines 28-44 New England sketches in a quick review of England's history and problems from Anglo-Saxon wars and foreign invasions through the Norman Conquest, Plantagenet quarrels, and the Wars of the Roses, which had ended with the ascent of the Tudor dynasty. Old England echoes her catalogue in lines 68-79.

Pray do you fear Spain's bragging Armado?
Doth your ally, fair France, conspire your wrack,
Or do the Scots play false behind your back?
Doth Holland quit you ill for all your love?
Whence is the storm from earth or heaven above? 50
Is't drought, is't famine, or is't pestilence?
Doth feel the smart, or fear the consequence?
Your humble child entreats you, show your grief,
Though arms, nor purse she hath for your relief,
Such is her poverty, yet shall be found 55
A suppliant for your help, as she is bound.

Old England

I must confess some of those sores you name,
My beauteous body at this present maim;
But foreign foe, nor feigned friend I fear,
For they have work enough (thou know'st) elsewhere. 60
Nor is it Alcie's son, nor Henry's daughter,
Whose proud contention cause this slaughter,
Nor nobles siding to make John no king,
French Lewis unjustly to the crown to bring;
No Edward, Richard, to lose rule and life, 65
Nor no Lancastrians to renew old strife;
No Duke of York, nor Earl of March to soil
Their hands in kindred's blood whom they did foil;
No crafty tyrant now usurps the seat,
Who nephews slew that so he might be great; 70
No need of Tudor roses to unite,
None knows which is the red, or which the white;
Spain's braving fleet, a second time is sunk;
France knows how oft my fury she hath drunk
By Edward Third and Henry Fifth of fame, 75
Her lilies in mine arms avouch the same.
My sister Scotland hurts me now no more
Though she hath been injurious heretofore;
What Holland is I am in some suspense,
But trust not much unto his excellence. 80
For wants, sure some I feel, but more I fear,

And for the pestilence, who knows how near;
Famine and plague,[2] two sisters of the sword,
Destruction to a land doth soon afford;
They're for my punishment ordained on high,   85
Unless our tears prevent it speedily.
But yet I answer not what you demand,
To show the grievance of my troubled land.
Before I tell th' effect, I'll show the cause
Which are my sins, the breach of sacred laws.   90
Idolatry, supplanter of a nation,[3]
With foolish superstitious adoration,
Are liked and countenanced by men of might,
The Gospel trodden down and hath no right;
Church offices were sold and bought for gain,   95
That Pope had hope to find Rome here again.
For oaths and blasphemies, did ever ear
From Belzebub himself such language hear?
What scorning of the saints of the Most High?
What injuries did daily on them lie?   100
What false reports, what nick-names did they take
Not for their own, but for their master's sake?
And thou, poor soul,[4] wert jeered among the rest,
Thy flying for the truth was made a jest.
For Sabbath-breaking and for drunkenness,   105
Did ever land profaneness more express?
From crying blood yet cleansed am not I,
Martyrs and others, dying causelessly.
How many princely heads on blocks laid down
For nought but title to a fading crown?   110

2. Like other natural disasters, these were often interpreted by the Puritans
as God's punishment for the nation's sin.

3. In lines 91-102 reference is made to the impending civil war in England,
with Puritan pressure against the king and the bishops, whose efforts to enforce
High Church practice seemed to Bradstreet and her sect a return to Roman
Catholicism. Persecution of Puritan ministers by Archbishop Laud struck New
Englanders as especially menacing.

4. New England Puritans found mockery rather than admiration the result
of their colonizing ventures. Even English Puritans sometimes accused them of
escapism.

'Mongst all the cruelties by great ones done
Oh, Edward's youths, and Clarence hapless son,[5]
O Jane,[6] why didst thou die in flow'ring prime?
Because of royal stem, that was thy crime.
For bribery, adultery, and lies,   115
Where is the nation, I can't paralyze.
With usury, extortion, and oppression,
These be the Hydras[7] of my stout transgression.
These be the bitter fountains, heads, and roots,
Whence flowed the source, the springs, the boughs
    and fruits   120
Of more than thou canst hear or I relate,
That with high hand I still did perpetrate,
For these were threatened the woeful day
I mocked the preachers, put it far away;
The sermons yet upon record do stand   125
That cried destruction to my wicked land;
I then believed not, now I feel and see,
The plague of stubborn incredulity.
Some lost their livings, some in prison pent,
Some fined, from house and friends to exile went.   130
Their silent tongues to heaven did vengeance cry,
Who saw their wrongs and hath judged righteously
And will repay it sevenfold in my lap:
This is forerunner of my afterclap.
Nor took I warning by my neighbour's falls.   135
I saw sad Germany's[8] dismantled walls,
I saw her people famished, nobles slain,
Her fruitful land, a barren heath remain.
I saw, unmoved, her armies foiled and fled,
Wives forced, babes tossed, her houses calcined.   140
I saw strong Rochelle[9] yielded to her foe,

5. Innocent victims of the Wars of the Roses.
6. Lady Jane Grey.
7. Many-headed and almost invincible monsters, associated in Greek mythology with the labors of Hercules.
8. The Protestant Palatinate, defeated in the Thirty Years War.
9. Defeat of the Huguenots at La Rochelle.

34 Anne Bradstreet

Thousands of starved Christians there also.
I saw poor Ireland[10] bleeding out her last,
Such cruelties as all reports have past;
Mine heart obdurate stood not yet aghast.   145
Now sip I of that cup, and just 't may be
The bottom dregs reserved are for me.

New England

To all you've said, sad Mother, I assent,
Your fearful sins great cause there's to lament,
My guilty hands, in part, hold up with you,   150
A sharer in your punishment's my due.
But all you say amounts to this effect,
Not what you feel, but what you do expect,
Pray in plain terms, what is your present grief?
Then let's join heads and hearts for your relief.   155

Old England

Well to the matter then, there's grown of late
'Twixt king and peers a question of state,
Which is the chief, the law, or else the king.
One said, "It's he," the other no such thing.
'Tis said, my better part in Parliament[11]   160
To ease my groaning land, showed their intent,
To crush the proud, and right to each man deal,
To help the Church and stay the commonweal.
So many obstacles came in their way,
As puts me to a stand what I should say;   165
Old customs, new prerogatives stood on,
Had they not held law fast, all had been gone,
Which by their prudence stood them in such stead
They took high Strafford[12] lower by the head.

10. Massacre of Protestants in the Irish Rebellion of 1641.
11. Dominated by Puritans, Parliament represented their interests against the king and Archbishop Laud.
12. Thomas Wentworth, Earl of Strafford, chief adviser to Charles I, was accused of treason by parliamentary enemies and executed in 1641 after failing to put down a Scottish insurrection.

And to their Laud[13] be't spoke, they held i'th' tower   170
All England's metropolitan[14] that hour;
This done, an act they would have passed fain,
No prelate should his bishopric retain;
Here tugged they hard, indeed, for all men saw
This must be done by Gospel, not by law.   175
Next the militia they urged sore,
This was denied (I need not say wherefore).
The King,[15] displeased, at York himself absents,
They humbly beg return, show their intents;
The writing, printing, posting to and fro,   180
Shows all was done, I'll therefore let it go.
But now I come to speak of my disaster,
Contention grown, 'twixt subjects and their master;
They worded it so long, they fell to blows,
That thousands lay on heaps, here bleeds my woes,   185
I that no wars so many years have known,
Am now destroyed and slaught'red by mine own;
But could the field alone this strife decide,
One battle two or three I might abide,
But these may be beginnings of more woe.   190
Who knows, but this may be my overthrow.
Oh pity me in this sad perturbation,
My plundred towns, my houses' devastation,
My weeping virgins and my young men slain;
My wealthy trading fall'n, my dearth of grain,   195
The seedtime's come, but ploughman hath no hope
Because he knows not who shall in his crop.
The poor they want their pay, their children bread,
Their woeful mothers' tears unpitied.

13. Pun on Archbishop Laud, imprisoned in 1640 and executed in 1645.

14. Principal bishop. The Puritans opposed bishoprics in principle, regarding congregational or presbyterian church governance as the forms approved by the Bible.

15. Charles I, retiring to York, rejected the advice of Puritan representatives, including the Reverend John Woodbridge, Bradstreet's brother-in-law. The king's obstinacy in clinging to royal prerogatives exacerbated the tension between his supporters and Parliament and hastened the civil war in which Charles was beheaded.

If any pity in thy heart remain,   200
Or any childlike love thou dost retain,
For my relief, do what there lies in thee,
And recompense that good I've done to thee.

   New England

Dear Mother, cease complaints and wipe your eyes,
Shake off your dust, cheer up, and now arise;   205
You are my mother nurse, and I your flesh,
Your sunken bowels gladly would refresh;
Your griefs I pity, but soon hope to see,
Out of your troubles much good fruit to be,
To see those latter days of hoped for good,   210
Though now beclouded all with tears and blood.
After dark Popery the day did clear,
But now the sun in's brightness shall appear.
Blest be the nobles of thy noble land,
With ventured lives for truth's defence that stand.   215
Blest be thy commons, who for common good,
And thy infringed laws have boldly stood.
Blest be thy counties, who did aid thee still,
With hearts and states to testify their will.
Blest be thy preachers, who do cheer thee on,   220
O cry, "the sword of God and Gideon";[16]
And shall I not on them wish Mero's curse,[17]
That help thee not with prayers, arms, and purse?
And for myself let miseries abound,
If mindless of thy state I e'er be found.   225
These are the days the Church's foes to crush,
To root out Popelings head, tail, branch, and rush;
Let's bring Baal's [18] vestments forth to make a fire,
Their miters, surplices, and all their tire,

---

16. Biblical hero who led Israel against the Midianites (Judg. 6:11ff).
   17. "Curse ye Meroz: (said the Angel of the Lord) curse the inhabitants thereof, because they came not to helpe the Lord, to helpe the Lord against the mightie" (Judg. 5:23).
   18. A heathen idol.

Copes, rochets, crosiers, and such empty trash,   230
And let their names consume, but let the flash
Light Christendom, and all the world to see
We hate Rome's whore with all her trumpery.
Go on brave Essex[19] with a loyal heart,
Not false to king, nor to the better part;   235
But those that hurt his people and his crown,
As duty binds, expell and tread them down.
And ye brave nobles chase away all fear,
And to this hopeful cause closely adhere;
O Mother, can you weep, and have such peers?   240
When they are gone, then drown yourself in tears.
If now you weep so much, that then no more
The briny ocean will o'erflow your shore.
These, these are they I trust, with Charles our King,
Out of all mists such glorious days shall bring;   245
That dazzled eyes beholding much shall wonder
At that thy settled peace, thy wealth and splendor.
Thy Church and weal established in such manner,
That all shall joy, that thou displayed'st thy banner;
And discipline erected so I trust,   250
That nursing kings shall come and lick thy dust.
Then justice shall in all thy courts take place,
Without respect of person or of case;
Then bribes shall cease, and suits shall not stick long,
Patience and purse of clients oft to wrong.   255
Then high commissions shall fall to decay,
And pursuivants and catchpoles want their pay.
So shall thy happy nation ever flourish,
When truth and righteousness they thus shall nourish,
When thus in peace, thine armies brave send out   260
To sack proud Rome and all her vassals rout;
There let thy name, thy fame, and glory shine,

19. Robert Devereux, third Earl of Essex, commander of the Parliamentary
army, 1642-1645. A moderate, Essex refused to march against King Charles.
Bradstreet's reference to him shows her sympathy with those whose desire for
reform stopped short of regicide.

As did thine ancestors' in Palestine;
And let her spoils full pay with interest be,
Of what unjustly once she polled from thee.   265
Of all the woes thou canst let her be sped,
And on her pour the vengeance threat'ned;
Bring forth the beast[20] that ruled the world with's beck,
And tear his flesh and set your feet on's neck;
And make his filthy den so desolate,   270
To th' 'stonishment of all that knew his state.
This done, with brandished swords to Turkey[21] go,
For then what is't but English blades dare do,
And lay her waste for so's the sacred doom,
And do to Gog as thou hast done to Rome.   275
Oh Abraham's seed,[22] lift up your heads on high,
For sure the day of your redemption's nigh;
The scales shall fall from your long blinded eyes,
And Him you shall adore who now despise.
Then fullness of the nations in shall flow,   280
And Jew and Gentile to one worship go;
Then follows days of happiness and rest;
Whose lot doth fall to live therein is blest:
No Canaanite shall then be found i' th' land,
And holiness on horses' bells[23] shall stand.   285
If this make way thereto, then sigh no more,
But if at all, thou didst not see't before;
Farewell, dear Mother, rightest cause prevail,
And in a while, you'll tell another tale.

(1643; 1650)

20. Many Puritans believed that the overthrow of the beast, understood by
them as the Pope, would soon lead to the completion of the prophecies in
Revelation.

21. The conquest of Islam by Protestant Christianity.

22. The conversion of the Jews, sometimes thought to be the last episode of
history before the millennium.

23. "In that day shal there be *writen* upon the bridels of ye horses, The holines
unto the Lord, and the pottes in the Lords House shal be like the bowles before
the altar" (Zech. 14:20).

THE VANITY OF ALL WORDLY THINGS

As he[1] said vanity, so vain say I,
Oh! vanity, O vain all under sky;
Where is the man can say, "Lo, I have found
On brittle earth a consolation sound"?
What is't in honour to be set on high?   5
No, they like beasts and sons of men shall die,
And whilst they live, how oft doth turn their fate;
He's now a captive that was king of late.
What is't in wealth great treasures to obtain?
No, that's but labour, anxious care, and pain.   10
He heaps up riches, and he heaps up sorrow,
It's his today, but who's his heir tomorrow?
What then? Content in pleasures canst thou find?
More vain than all, that's but to grasp the wind.
The sensual senses for a time they please,   15
Meanwhile the conscience rage, who shall appease?
What is't in beauty? No that's but a snare,
They're foul enough today, that once were fair.
What is't in flow'ring youth, or manly age?
The first is prone to vice, the last to rage.   20
Where is it then, in wisdom, learning, arts?
Sure if on earth, it must be in those parts;
Yet these the wisest man of men did find
But vanity, vexation of mind.
And he that knows the most doth still bemoan   25
He knows not all that here is to be known.
What is it then? to do as stoics tell,
Nor laugh, nor weep, let things go ill or well?
Such stoics are but stocks, such teaching vain,
While man is man, he shall have ease or pain.   30
If not in honour, beauty, age, nor treasure,
Nor yet in learning, wisdom, youth, nor pleasure,
Where shall I climb, sound, seek, search, or find
That *summum bonum*[2] which may stay my mind?

1. Solomon, in the last chapter of Ecclesiastes.
2. The highest good.

There is a path no vulture's eye hath seen,   35
Where lion fierce, nor lion's whelps have been,
Which leads unto that living crystal fount,
Who drinks thereof, the world doth nought account.
The depth and sea have said " 'tis not in me,"
With pearl and gold it shall not valued be.   40
For sapphire, onyx, topaz who would change;
It's hid from eyes of men, they count it strange.
Death and destruction the fame hath heard,
But where and what it is, from heaven's declared;
It brings to honour which shall ne'er decay,   45
It stores with wealth which time can't wear away.
It yieldeth pleasures far beyond conceit,
And truly beautifies without deceit.
Nor strength, nor wisdom, nor fresh youth shall fade,
Nor death shall see, but are immortal made.   50
This pearl of price, this tree of life, this spring,
Who is possessed of shall reign a king.
Nor change of state nor cares shall ever see,
But wear his crown unto eternity.
This satiates the soul, this stays the mind,   55
And all the rest, but vanity we find.

(1647-1648?; 1650)

From *Several Poems*

BEFORE THE BIRTH OF ONE OF HER CHILDREN

All things within this fading world hath end,
Adversity doth still our joys attend;
No ties so strong, no friends so dear and sweet,
But with death's parting blow is sure to meet.
The sentence past is most irrevocable,   5
A common thing, yet oh, inevitable.
How soon, my Dear, death may my steps attend,
How soon't may be thy lot to lose thy friend,

We both are ignorant, yet love bids me
These farewell lines to recommend to thee,
That when that knot's untied that made us one, 10
I may seem thine, who in effect am none.
And if I see not half my days that's due,[1]
What nature would, God grant to yours and you;
The many faults that well you know I have 15
Let be interred in my oblivious grave;
If any worth or virtue were in me,
Let that live freshly in thy memory
And when thou feel'st no grief, as I no harms,
Yet love thy dead, who long lay in thine arms. 20
And when thy loss shall be repaid with gains
Look to my little babes, my dear remains.
And if thou love thyself, or loved'st me,
These O protect from step-dame's injury.
And if chance to thine eyes shall bring this verse, 25
With some sad sighs honour my absent hearse;
And kiss this paper for thy love's dear sake,
Who with salt tears this last farewell did take.

(1640-1652?; 1678)

1. Reference to possible death in childbirth before age thirty-five, half of the "threscore yeres & ten" described in Psalm 90 as the typical human lifespan.

TO MY DEAR AND LOVING HUSBAND

If ever two were one, then surely we.
If ever man were loved by wife, then thee;
If ever wife was happy in a man,
Compare with me, ye women, if you can.
I prize thy love more than whole mines of gold 5
Or all the riches that the East doth hold.
My love is such that rivers cannot quench,
Nor ought but love from thee, give recompense.
Thy love is such I can no way repay,
The heavens reward thee manifold, I pray. 10
Then while we live, in love let's so persevere
That when we live no more, we may live ever.

(1641-1643?; 1678)

A LETTER TO HER HUSBAND, ABSENT UPON PUBLIC EMPLOYMENT

My head, my heart, mine eyes, my life, nay, more,
My joy, my magazine[1] of earthly store,
If two be one, as surely thou and I,
How stayest thou there, whilst I at Ipswich lie?
So many steps, head from the heart to sever,   5
If but a neck, soon should we be together.
I, like the Earth this season, mourn in black,
My Sun is gone so far in's zodiac,
Whom whilst I 'joyed, nor storms, nor frost I felt,
His warmth such frigid colds did cause to melt.   10
My chilled limbs now numbed lie forlorn;
Return, return, sweet Sol, from Capricorn;[2]
In this dead time, alas, what can I more
Than view those fruits which through thy heat I bore?
Which sweet contentment yield me for a space,   15
True living pictures of their father's face.
O strange effect! now thou art southward gone,
I weary grow the tedious day so long;
But when thou northward to me shalt return,
I wish my Sun may never set, but burn   20
Within the Cancer[3] of my glowing breast,
The welcome house of him my dearest guest.
Where ever, ever stay, and go not thence,
Till nature's sad decree shall call thee hence;
Flesh of thy flesh, bone of thy bone,   25
I here, thou there, yet both but one.

(1641-1643?; 1678)

1. Warehouse.
2. The southernmost sign of the zodiac; mid-winter.
3. The northernmost constellation; mid-summer.

THE AUTHOR TO HER BOOK

Thou ill-formed offspring of my feeble brain,
Who after birth didst by my side remain,
Till snatched from thence by friends,[1] less wise than true,
Who thee abroad, exposed to public view,
Made thee in rags, halting to th' press to trudge,   5
Where errors were not lessened (all may judge).
At thy return my blushing was not small,
My rambling brat (in print) should mother call,
I cast thee by as one unfit for light,
Thy visage was so irksome in my sight;   10
Yet being mine own, at length affection would
Thy blemishes amend,[2] if so I could:
I washed thy face, but more defects I saw,
And rubbing off a spot still made a flaw.
I stretched thy joints to make thee even feet,   15
Yet still thou run'st more hobbling than is meet;
In better dress to trim thee was my mind,
But nought save homespun cloth i' th' house I find.
In this array 'mongst vulgars may'st thou roam.
In critic's hands beware thou dost not come,   20
And take thy way where yet thou art not known;
If for thy father asked, say thou hadst none;
And for thy mother, she alas is poor,
Which caused her thus to send thee out of door.

(1650-1670?; 1678)

1. John Woodbridge and those who helped him arrange publication of *The Tenth Muse* in London without Bradstreet's knowledge.
2. After seeing her book, Bradstreet revised the poems, substantially in some cases, and apparently hoped to publish them later in corrected form. The revised version and most of the shorter poems on which her modern reputation rests were published posthumously as *Several Poems* in 1678.

IN REFERENCE TO HER CHILDREN, 23 JUNE, 1659

birds as children

I had eight birds hatched in one nest,
Four cocks there were, and hens the rest.
I nursed them up with pain and care,
Nor cost, nor labour did I spare,
Till at the last they felt their wing,   5
Mounted the trees, and learned to sing.
→ Chief of the brood [1] then took his flight
To regions far and left me quite.
My mournful chirps I after send,
Till he return, or I do end: 10
Leave not thy nest, thy dam and sire,
Fly back and sing amidst this choir.
→ My second bird [2] did take her flight,
And with her mate flew out of sight;
Southward they both their course did bend,   15
And seasons twain they there did spend,
Till after blown by southern gales,
They norward steered with filled sails.
A prettier bird was no where seen,
Along the beach among the treen.   20
→ I have a third [3] of colour white,
On whom I placed no small delight;
Coupled with mate loving and true,
Hath also bid her dam adieu;
And where Aurora first appears,   25
She now hath perched to spend her years.
→ One to the academy flew [4]
To chat among that learned crew;
Ambition moves still in his breast
That he might chant above the rest,   30
Striving for more than to do well,

1. Samuel Bradstreet, then studying medicine in England.
2. Dorothy, wife of the Reverend Seaborn Cotton, who lived for two years in Connecticut before settling in Hampton, New Hampshire.
3. Sarah, wife of Richard Hubbard, who lived in Ipswich, Massachusetts.
4. Simon, then a student at Harvard.

That nightingales he might excel.
My fifth,[5] whose down is yet scarce gone,
Is 'mongst the shrubs and bushes flown,
And as his wings increase in strength,   35
On higher boughs he'll perch at length.
My other three[6] still with me nest,
Until they're grown, then as the rest,
Or here or there they'll take their flight,
As is ordained, so shall they light.   40
If birds could weep, then would my tears
Let others know what are my fears
Lest this my brood some harm should catch,   *Dangers*
And be surprised for want of watch,
Whilst pecking corn and void of care,   45
They fall un'wares in fowler's snare,
Or whilst on trees they sit and sing,
Some untoward boy at them do fling,
Or whilst allured with bell and glass,
The net be spread, and caught, alas.   50
Or lest by lime-twigs they be foiled,
Or by some greedy hawks be spoiled.
O would my young, ye saw my breast,
And knew what thoughts there sadly rest,
Great was my pain when I you bred,   55
Great was my care when I you fed,
Long did I keep you soft and warm,
And with my wings kept off all harm,
My cares are more and fears than ever,
My throbs such now as 'fore were never.   60
Alas, my birds, you wisdom want,
Of perils you are ignorant;
Oft times in grass, on trees, in flight,
Sore accidents on you may light.
O to your safety have an eye,   65
So happy may you live and die.
Meanwhile my days in tunes I'll spend,   ?

Shift

5. Dudley, a grammar school pupil in Ipswich.
6. Hannah, Mercy, and John.

Poet?
vs.
Mother?

Heaven

Till my weak lays with me shall end.
In shady woods I'll sit and sing,
And things that past to mind I'll bring.   70
Once young and pleasant, as are you,
But former toys (no joys) adieu.
My age I will not once lament,
But sing, my time so near is spent.
And from the top bough take my flight   75
Into a country beyond sight,
Where old ones instantly grow young,
And there with seraphims set song;
No seasons cold, nor storms they see;
But spring lasts to eternity.   80
When each of you shall in your nest
Among your young ones take your rest,

Poems—
instructive

In chirping language, oft them tell,
You had a dam that loved you well,
That did what could be done for young,   85
And nursed you up till you were strong,
And 'fore she once would let you fly,
She showed you joy and misery;
Taught what was good, and what was ill,
What would save life, and what would kill.   90
Thus gone, amongst you I may live,
And dead, yet speak, and counsel give:
Farewell, my birds, farewell adieu,
I happy am, if well with you.

(1659; 1678)

spiritual autobiography

CONTEMPLATIONS

Some time now past in the autumnal tide,
When Phoebus[1] wanted but one hour to bed,
The trees all richly clad, yet void of pride,
Where gilded o'er by his rich golden head.
Their leaves and fruits seemed painted, but was true,   5
Of green, of red, of yellow, mixed hue;
Rapt were my senses at this delectable view.

must be
tasted

1. Apollo, the sun god.

2

I wist not what to wish, yet sure thought I,
If so much excellence abide below,
How excellent is He that dwells on high,
Whose power and beauty by his works we know?
Sure he is goodness, wisdom, glory, light,
That hath this under world so richly dight;
More heaven than earth was here, no winter and no night.

nature as reflection of heaven

10

3

Then on a stately oak I cast mine eye,
Whose ruffling top the clouds seemed to aspire;
How long since thou wast in thine infancy?
Thy strength, and stature, more thy years admire,
Hath hundred winters past since thou wast born?
Or thousand since thou brakest thy shell of horn?
If so, all these as nought, eternity doth scorn.

15

20

4

Then higher on the glistering Sun I gazed,
Whose beams was shaded by the leavie tree;
The more I looked, the more I grew amazed,
And softly said, "What glory's like to thee?"
Soul of this world, this universe's eye,
No wonder some made thee a deity;
Had I not better known, alas, the same had I.

25

Sun

5

Thou as a bridegroom from thy chamber rushes,
And as a strong man, joys to run a race;
The morn doth usher thee with smiles and blushes:
The Earth reflects her glances in thy face.
Birds, insects, animals with vegative,
Thy heat from death and dullness doth revive,
And in the darksome womb of fruitful nature dive.

?

30

Benevolence of nature

35

6

Thy swift annual and diurnal course,
Thy daily straight and yearly oblique path,
Thy pleasing fervor and thy scorching force,

cycle of nature

All mortals here the feeling knowledge hath.
Thy presence makes it day, thy absence night,   40
Quaternal seasons caused by thy might:
Hail creature, full of sweetness, beauty, and delight.

     7

Art thou so full of glory that no eye
Hath strength thy shining rays once to behold?
And is thy splendid throne erect so high,   45
As to approach it, can no earthly mould?
How full of glory then must thy Creator be,
Who gave this bright light luster unto thee?
Admired, adored for ever, be that Majesty.

     8

Silent alone, where none or saw, or heard,   50
In pathless paths I lead my wand'ring feet,
My humble eyes to lofty skies I reared
To sing some song, my mazed Muse thought meet.
My great Creator I would magnify,
That nature had thus decked liberally;   55
But Ah, and Ah, again, my imbecility!

     9

I heard the merry grasshopper then sing.
The black-clad cricket bear a second part;
They kept one tune and played on the same string,
Seeming to glory in their little art.   60
Shall creatures abject thus their voices raise
And in their kind resound their Maker's praise,
Whilst I, as mute, can warble forth no higher lays?

     10

When present times look back to ages past,
And men in being fancy those are dead,   65
It makes things gone perpetually to last,
And calls back months and years that long since fled.
It makes a man more aged in conceit

Than was Methuselah, or's grandsire great,
While of their persons and their acts his mind doth treat. 70

11

Sometimes in Eden fair he seems to be,
Sees glorious Adam there made lord of all,
Fancies the apple, dangle on the tree,
That turned his sovereign to a naked thrall.
Who like a miscreant's driven from that place, 75
To get his bread with pain and sweat of face,
A penalty imposed on his backsliding race.

12

Here sits our grandame in retired place,
And in her lap her bloody Cain new-born;
The weeping imp oft looks her in the face, 80
Bewails his unknown hap and fate forlorn;
His mother sighs to think of Paradise,
And how she lost her bliss to be more wise,
Believing him that was, and is, father of lies.

13

Here Cain and Abel come to sacrifice, 85
Fruits of the earth and fatlings each do bring,
On Abel's gift the fire descends from skies,
But no such sign on false Cain's offering;
With sullen hateful looks he goes his ways,
Hath thousand thoughts to end his brother's days, 90
Upon whose blood his future good he hopes to raise.

14

There Abel keeps his sheep, no ill he thinks;
His brother comes, then acts his fratricide;
The virgin Earth of blood her first draught drinks,
But since that time she often hath been cloyed. 95
The wretch with ghastly face and dreadful mind
Thinks each he sees will serve him in his kind,
Though none on earth but kindred near then could he find.

15

Who fancies not his looks now (at the bar,) ?
His face like death, his heart with horror fraught,   100
Nor malefactor ever felt like war,
When deep despair with wish of life hath fought,
Branded with guilt and crushed with treble woes,
A vagabond to Land of Nod[2] he goes.
A city builds, that walls might him secure from foes.   105

16

Who thinks not oft upon the father's ages,
Their long descent, how nephews' sons they saw,
The starry observations of those sages,
And how their precepts to their sons were law,
How Adam sighed to see his progeny,   110
Clothed all in his black sinful livery,
Who neither guilt nor yet the punishment could fly.

17

Our life compare we with their length of days
Who to the tenth of theirs doth now arrive?
And though thus short, we shorten many ways,   115
Living so little while we are alive;
In eating, drinking, sleeping, vain delight
death So unawares comes on perpetual night,
And puts all pleasures vain unto eternal flight.

18

When I behold the heavens as in their prime,   120
And then the earth (though old) still clad in green,
cycle The stones and trees, insensible of time,
Nor age nor wrinkle on their front are seen;
If winter come and greenness then do fade,
A spring returns, and they more youthful made;   125
But man grows old, lies down, remains where once
      he's laid.

2. Wilderness east of Eden to which Cain was exiled.

19

By birth more noble than those creatures all,
Yet seems by nature and by custom cursed,
No sooner born, but grief and care makes fall
That state obliterate he had at first;   130
Nor youth, nor strength, nor wisdom spring again,
Nor habitations long their names retain,
But in oblivion to the final day remain.

20

Shall I then praise the heavens, the trees, the earth
Because their beauty and their strength last longer?   135
Shall I wish there, or never to had birth,
Because they're bigger, and their bodies stronger?
Nay, they shall darken, perish, fade and die,
And when unmade, so ever shall they lie,
But man was made for endless immortality.   140

Mutability of nature—also fallen

21

Under the cooling shadow of a stately elm
Close sat I by a goodly river's side,
Where gliding streams the rocks did overwhelm,
A lonely place, with pleasures dignified.
I once that loved the shady woods so well,   145
Now thought the rivers did the trees excel,
And if the sun would ever shine, there would I dwell.

22

While on the stealing stream I fixt mine eye,
Which to the longed-for ocean held its course,
I marked, nor crooks, nor rubs that there did lie
Could hinder ought, but still augment its force.
"O happy flood," quoth I, "that holds thy race
Till thou arrive at thy beloved place,
Nor is it rocks or shoals that can obstruct thy pace,

journey imagery (life to heaven)   150

23

Nor is't enough, that thou alone mayst slide,   155
But hundred brooks in thy clear waves do meet,
So hand in hand along with thee they glide
To Thetis' house,[3] where all embrace and greet.
Thou emblem true of what I count the best,
O could I lead my rivulets to rest,   160
So may we press to that vast mansion, ever blest."

24

Ye fish, which in this liquid region 'bide,
That for each season have your habitation,
Now salt, now fresh where you think best to glide
To unknown coasts to give a visitation,   165
In lakes and ponds you leave your numerous fry;
So nature taught, and yet you know not why,
You wat'ry folk that know not your felicity.

25

Look how the wantons frisk to taste the air,
Then to the colder bottom straight they dive;   170
Eftsoon to Neptune's glassy hall [4] repair
To see what trade they great ones there do drive,
Who forage o'er the spacious sea-green field,
And take the trembling prey before it yield,
Whose armour is their scales, their spreading fins
   their shield.   175

26

While musing thus with contemplation fed,
And thousand fancies buzzing in my brain,
The sweet-tongued Philomel[5] perched o'er my head
And chanted forth a most melodious strain

3. The sea.
4. Ocean depths.
5. Nightingale.

Which rapt me so with wonder and delight,   180
I judged my hearing better than my sight,
And wished me wings with her a while to take my flight.

    27

"O merry Bird," said I, "that fears no snares,
That neither toils nor hoards up in thy barn,
Feels no sad thoughts nor cruciating cares   185
To gain more good or shun what might thee harm.
Thy clothes ne'er wear, thy meat is everywhere,
Thy bed a bough, thy drink the water clear,
Reminds not what is past, nor what's to come dost fear."

    28

"The dawning morn with songs thou dost prevent,   190
Sets hundred notes unto thy feathered crew,
So each one tunes his pretty instrument,
And warbling out the old, begin anew,
And thus they pass their youth in summer season,
Then follow thee into a better region,   195
Where winter's never felt by that sweet airy legion."

    29

Man at the best a creature frail and vain,
In knowledge ignorant, in strength but weak,
Subject to sorrows, losses, sickness, pain,
Each storm his state, his mind, his body break,   200
From some of these he never finds cessation,
But day or night, within, without, vexation,
Troubles from foes, from friends, from dearest, near'st
    relation.

    30

And yet this sinful creature, frail and vain,
This lump of wretchedness, of sin and sorrow,   205
This weatherbeaten vessel wracked with pain,

Animal Doesn't Desire? Heaven.

54 Anne Bradstreet

Joys not in hope of an eternal morrow;
Nor all his losses, crosses, and vexation,
In weight, in frequency and long duration
Can make him deeply groan for that divine translation.   210

Sailing metaphor

31

The mariner that on smooth waves doth glide
Sings merrily and steers his bark with ease,
As if he had command of wind and tide,
And now become great master of the seas:
But suddenly a storm spoils all the sport,   215
And makes him long for a more quiet port,
Which 'gainst all adverse winds may serve for fort.

32

So he that saileth in this world of pleasure,
Feeding on sweets, that never bit of th' sour,
That's full of friends, of honour, and of treasure,   220
Fond fool, he takes this earth ev'n for heav'n's bower.   *Spenserian*
But sad affliction comes and makes him see
Here's neither honour, wealth, nor safety;
Only above is found all with security.

33

Ozymandias O Time the fatal wrack of mortal things,   225
That draws oblivion's curtains over kings;
Their sumptuous monuments, men know them not,   *4 couplets*
Their names without a record are forgot,
Their parts, their ports, their pomp's all laid in th' dust
Christ Nor wit nor gold, nor buildings scape times rust;   230
But he whose name is graved in the white stone[6]
Shall last and shine when all of these are gone.

left us victims of time

(1664-1665?; 1678)

6. "To him that overcometh, wil I give to eat of the Manna that is hid, and wil give him a white stone, and in the stone a new name writen, which no man knoweth saving he that receiveth it" (Rev. 2:17).

IN MEMORY OF MY DEAR GRANDCHILD ELIZABETH BRADSTREET, WHO DECEASED AUGUST, 1665, BEING A YEAR AND HALF OLD

Farewell dear babe, my heart's too much content,
Farewell sweet babe, the pleasure of mine eye,
Farewell fair flower that for a space was lent,
Then ta'en away unto eternity.
Blest babe, why should I once bewail thy fate,   5
Or sigh thy days so soon were terminate,
Sith thou art settled in an everlasting state.

2

By nature trees do rot when they are grown,
And plums and apples thoroughly ripe do fall,
And corn and grass are in their season mown,   10
And time brings down what is both strong and tall.
But plants new set to be eradicate,
And buds new blown to have so short a date,
Is by His hand alone that guides nature and fate.

(1665; 1678)

ON MY DEAR GRANDCHILD SIMON BRADSTREET, WHO DIED ON 16 NOVEMBER, 1669, BEING BUT A MONTH, AND ONE DAY OLD

No sooner came, but gone, and fall'n asleep,
Acquaintance short, yet parting caused us weep;
Three flowers, two scarcely blown,[1] the last i' th' bud,
Cropt by th' Almighty's hand; yet is He good.

1. Two of Simon's sisters, Elizabeth and Anne, had also died in early childhood. Anne Bradstreet wrote elegies for all three grandchildren and one for their mother, Mercy Bradstreet, Samuel's wife, who died in 1670 after giving birth to a premature and short-lived daughter. Only one child of this marriage, Mercy, lived to adulthood.

With dreadful awe before Him let's be mute,   5
Such was His will, but why, let's not dispute,
With humble hearts and mouths put in the dust,
Let's say He's merciful as well as just.
He will return and make up all our losses,
And smile again after our bitter crosses   10
Go pretty babe, go rest with sisters twain;
Among the blest in endless joys remain.

(1669; 1678)

From the Andover Manuscript

MEDITATION

May 13, 1657

As spring the winter doth succeed
And leaves the naked trees do dress,
The earth all black is clothed in green.
At sunshine each their joy express.

My sun's returned with healing wings,   5
My soul and body doth rejoice,
My heart exults and praises sings
To Him that heard my wailing voice.

My winter's past, my storms are gone,
And former clouds seem now all fled,   10
But if they must eclipse again,
I'll run where I was succored.

I have a shelter from the storm,
A shadow from the fainting heat,

I have access unto His throne,   15
Who is a God so wondrous great.

O hath Thou made my pilgrimage
Thus pleasant, fair, and good,
Blessed me in youth and elder age,
My Baca [1] made a springing flood.   20

O studious am what I shall do
To show my duty with delight;
All I can give is but Thine own
And at the most a simple mite.

 (1657; 1867)

1. A barren place made fertile by grace (Ps. 84:6).

UPON MY DEAR AND LOVING HUSBAND HIS GOING INTO ENGLAND JAN. 16, 1661 [1]

O thou Most High who rulest all
And hear'st the prayers of thine,
O hearken, Lord, unto my suit
And my petition sign.

Into Thy everlasting arms   5
Of mercy I commend
Thy servant, Lord. Keep and preserve
My husband, my dear friend.

At Thy command, O Lord, he went,
Nor nought could keep him back.   10
Then let Thy promise joy his heart,
O help and be not slack.

1. Simon Bradstreet and John Norton represented Massachusetts at the time of the Restoration, when King Charles II raised questions about the colony's charter and its increasingly independent habits of governance.

58   Anne Bradstreet

Uphold my heart in Thee, O God.
Thou art my strength and stay,
Thou see'st how weak and frail I am,   15
Hide not Thy face away.

I in obedience to Thy will
Thou knowest did submit.
It was my duty so to do;
O Lord, accept of it.   20

Unthankfulness for mercies past
Impute Thou not to me.
O Lord, Thou know'st my weak desire
Was to sing praise to Thee.

Lord, be Thou pilot to the ship   25
And send them prosperous gales.
In storms and sickness, Lord, preserve.
Thy goodness never fails.

Unto Thy work he hath in hand
Lord, grant Thou good success   30
And favour in their eyes to whom
He shall make his address.

Remember, Lord, Thy folk whom Thou
To wilderness hast brought;
Let not Thine own inheritance   35
Be sold away for nought.

But tokens of Thy favour give,
With joy send back my dear
That I and all Thy servants may
Rejoice with heavenly cheer.   40

Lord, let my eyes see once again
Him whom Thou gavest me
That we together may sing praise
Forever unto Thee.

And the remainder of our days   45
Shall consecrated be
With an engaged heart to sing
All praises unto Thee.

      (1661; 1867)

HERE FOLLOWS SOME VERSES UPON THE BURNING OF OUR HOUSE JULY 10TH, 1666. COPIED OUT OF A LOOSE PAPER

In silent night when rest I took
For sorrow near I did not look
I wakened was with thund'ring noise
And piteous shrieks of dreadful voice.
That fearful sound of "Fire!" and "Fire!"   5
Let no man know is my desire.
I, starting up, the light did spy,
And to my God my heart did cry
To strengthen me in my distress
And not to leave me succorless.   10
Then, coming out, beheld a space   — house
The flame consume my dwelling place.
And when I could no longer look,
I blest His name that gave and took,   paradox?
That laid my goods now in the dust.   15
Yea, so it was, and so 'twas just.
It was His own, it was not mine,
Far be it that I should repine;
He might of all justly bereft
But yet sufficient for us left.   paradox?   20
When by the ruins oft I past
My sorrowing eyes aside did cast,
And here and there the places spy
Where oft I sat and long did lie:
Here stood that trunk, and there that chest,   25
There lay that store I counted best.
My pleasant things in ashes lie,

And them behold no more shall I.
Under thy roof no guest shall sit,
Nor at thy table eat a bit.   30
No pleasant tale shall e'er be told,
Nor things recounted done of old.
No candle e'er shall shine in thee,
Nor bridegroom's voice e'er heard shall be.
In silence ever shall thou lie,   35
Adieu, Adieu, all's vanity.
Then straight I 'gin my heart to chide,   *human house*
And did thy wealth on earth abide?
Didst fix thy hope on mold'ring dust?
The arm of flesh didst make thy trust?   40
Raise up thy thoughts above the sky
That dunghill mists away may fly.
Thou hast an house on high erect,[1]   — *spiritual body*
Framed by that mighty Architect,
With glory richly furnished,   45
Stands permanent though this be fled.
It's purchased and paid for too
By Him who hath enough to do.
A price so vast as is unknown
Yet by His gift is made thine own;   50
There's wealth enough, I need no more,
Farewell, my pelf, farewell my store.
The world no longer let me love,
My hope and treasure lies above.

(1666; 1867)

1. One of the "many dwelling places" in heaven which Jesus promised his disciples (John 14:2).

AS WEARY PILGRIM

As weary pilgrim, now at rest,
    Hugs with delight his silent nest,
His wasted limbs now lie full soft
    That mirey steps have trodden oft,
Blesses himself to think upon   5
    His dangers past, and travails done.

The burning sun no more shall heat,
    Nor stormy rains on him shall beat.
The briars and thorns no more shall scratch,
    Nor hungry wolves at him shall catch.   10
He erring paths no more shall tread,
    Nor wild fruits eat instead of bread.
For waters cold he doth not long
    For thirst no more shall parch his tongue.
No rugged stones his feet shall gall,   15
    Nor stumps nor rocks cause him to fall.
All cares and fears he bids farewell
    And means in safety now to dwell.
A pilgrim I, on earth perplexed
    With sins, with cares and sorrows vext,   20
By age and pains brought to decay,
    And my clay house mold'ring away.
Oh, how I long to be at rest
    And soar on high among the blest.
This body shall in silence sleep,   25
    Mine eyes no more shall ever weep,
No fainting fits shall me assail,
    Nor grinding pains my body frail,
With cares and fears ne'er cumb'red be
    Nor losses know, nor sorrows see.   30
What though my flesh shall there consume,
    It is the bed Christ did perfume,
And when a few years shall be gone,
    This mortal shall be clothed upon.
A corrupt carcass down it lays,   35
    A glorious body it shall rise.
In weakness and dishonour sown,
    In power 'tis raised by Christ alone.
Then soul and body shall unite
    And of their Maker have the sight.   40
Such lasting joys shall there behold
    As ear ne'er heard nor tongue e'er told.
Lord make me ready for that day,
    Then come, dear Bridegroom, come away.

    (1669; 1867)

TWO

Edward Taylor
(1642?-1729)

LIKE ANNE Bradstreet, Edward Taylor emigrated from England to Massachusetts and found a poetic identity in the wilderness. Coming later, however, to escape the Restoration and King Charles II's Act of Uniformity and settling as a minister on the Connecticut Valley frontier, Taylor articulated the Puritanism of a less political, more theologically oriented, more introspective generation.

Little can be known with certainty about Taylor's early life. He was born in or around Sketchley in Leicestershire, probably in 1642, the son of a Puritan farmer in Cromwell's England. Converted to religion as a child by his sister's account of Adam and Eve, he probably studied at a dissenting academy, may have attended Cambridge briefly, and seems to have taught school in another Leicestershire village until aversion to the required oath of religious conformity forced him and thousands of other displaced Puritans to sail for America in 1668. Introductions to such prominent Bostonians as the Reverend Increase Mather, John Hull (a prosperous merchant), and Charles Chauncy (president of Harvard) facilitated his admission to the college as an advanced student. Although his academic success led to his postgraduate appointment as scholar of the house at Harvard, Taylor quickly left the intellectual stimulus of the New England city and the company of lifelong friends like Samuel Sewall to accept a call to serve as minister at Westfield, a village on the Massachusetts frontier. After an arduous seven-day trek through forest already covered with snow, in November 1671 he reached the unpromising settlement where he would spend the remaining fifty-eight years of his life, serving God in ministerial work and poetry.

Life in Westfield presented quite a contrast to that in Leicestershire or even eastern Massachusetts. Indian attacks still posed a real danger to the settlement, especially during King Philip's War in the 1670s. Taylor held out successfully against abandonment of the town after massacres at Deerfield and neighboring communities, but the townsmen fortified the minister's home just in case. Luckily, Westfield escaped serious damage, and Taylor succeeded in gathering his church officially in 1679 when a small group of elders publicly declared their faith and ordained him their minister. His duties extended beyond preaching and counseling to include the informal practice of medicine, service as a community leader, and management of his family farm. While discharging these responsibilities, Taylor kept up with his scholarship; for years he carefully hand-copied books he borrowed from more prosperous friends. At the time of his death he owned one of the most impressive private libraries in the Connecticut Valley, with books of classical literature, secular and church history, medicine, science, and scriptural commentary. His only volume of English poetry was Anne Bradstreet's *Tenth Muse*, but the books he owned clearly reflected only a small proportion of his actual reading. He wrote extensively and may have intended to publish several series of his sermons and such public poems as *Gods Determinations* and the *Metrical History of Christianity*. The *Preparatory Meditations,* which constitute his main poetic achievement, however, were private documents; family tradition holds that he wanted them destroyed after his death.

Taylor's family reflected the satisfactions and tragedies of colonial life. In 1674 he married Elizabeth Fitch, the daughter of a Connecticut minister. Five of their eight children died very young, and his verses "Upon Wedlock, and Death of Children" (1682-1683) express his grief. Another elegy mourns the poet's wife upon her death in 1689. Three years later, Taylor married Ruth Wyllys, who raised his surviving children and bore six of her own. The memoirs of his grandson Ezra Stiles, president of Yale, show Taylor as a stern but affectionate Puritan father.

The main concerns of Taylor's ministry were the building up of the Westfield church and the protection of its orthodoxy against what he considered the heretical reforms of the Reverend Solomon Stoddard of Northampton. At issue was the status of "half-way" members of the congregations, sons and daughters of the first generation's "visible saints" who had been baptized as infants but had not, as adults, been able to testify to that assurance of personal conversion which would entitle them to the Lord's Supper and full admission to the church. Although the famous Half-Way Covenant of 1662 allowed these persons to present their own children for baptism, Stoddard went beyond the other church leaders in opening even the sacrament of the Lord's Supper to intermediate church members living good lives and wanting to partake of communion. He changed the communion service, in other words, from a sign of conversion to an instrument of conversion. Taylor's reaction was to preach against Stoddard and to emphasize the traditional view of the Lord's Supper in his own community. Sympathetic to the problems of the half-way members, however, he worked steadily to assuage their fears, build up their spiritual self-confidence, and draw them to full union with the church. Taylor anticipated the intensive spiritual self-examination and emphasis on personal conversion which changed the course of American Calvinism in the Great Awakening of the 1740s and which continued to dominate the Connecticut Valley, socially and psychologically, to the lifetime of Emily Dickinson. Unless seen in the context of Puritan conversion awareness and sacramental orthodoxy, his poetry loses much of its force.

Taylor's poetry was an extension of his ministry; it reflected his pastoral concerns. His longest, most labored, and most distasteful poetic effort, for instance, was the undated *Metrical History of Christianity* (so named by Donald E. Stanford, editor of Taylor's recently discovered untitled manuscript), in which he attempted to versify church history and celebrate the triumph of Protestantism over the infidel atrocities of heathens and Catholics. Luckily, this bigoted, barbarous effort stands apart from his other works. More successful propagandizing may be found in *Gods Determinations touching his Elect,* another undated series of poems dramatizing God's method of saving the saints. Although man's sins warrant eternal damnation, God's justice has been satisfied by Christ's mercy in dying for his chosen saints. Yet the saints, already saved, run away from their predestined conversion. Some few enter the coach (church) willingly; most must be pursued and overcome by Justice and Mercy. Even after surrendering, they remain vulnerable to Satan's wily efforts to undermine their hope by pointing to their sinfulness, their lukewarm response to God, and their inborn tendency toward damnation. At various times and in appropriately different ways, Christ comforts his various categories of saints, who finally accept their salvation and ride off to heaven, singing for joy. This work, a sort of affirmative counterpart to Michael Wigglesworth's *Day of Doom* (1662), demonstrates Taylor's concern with attracting half-way members into the church: calming their doubts, buttressing their hopes, emphasizing Christ's redemptive mercy. Even their fears and self-criticism, he shows, might be signs of salvation. Saints would know themselves as sinners.

The *Preparatory Meditations* (1682-1725), Taylor's best poems, served as private reexaminations of his own conversion experience and as preparations for the bimonthly celebration of the Lord's Supper in the Westfield church. The meditations generally paralleled the sermons Taylor delivered on these occasions, and the movements of his thought and associations of his images may often be seen more clearly in the context of the sermons than when the poem stands alone with no introduction beyond the scriptural epigraph.[1] It appears that Taylor generally prepared a scholarly, tightly reasoned sermon on his chosen text, then wrote a poetic meditation on the same text to prepare himself spiritually and psychologically to deliver his sermon. Because the communion service meant so much to Taylor, as a man and as minister of a church symbolically bound by the sacrament, he made himself ready in the most intensive way he could.

These poems belong to an ancient Christian tradition of dis-

1. The interrelationship between Taylor's preaching and poetry is documented in Norman S. Grabo's edition of the *Christographia*, a series of fourteen communion sermons Taylor delivered between October 1701 and October 1703, on the hypostatic union of divine and human natures in Christ, each sermon being prefaced by its accompanying meditation (New Haven, Conn.: Yale University Press, 1962).

ciplined meditation and probably owe much of their inspiration
to Richard Baxter's popular Puritan treatise on meditation, *The
Saints Everlasting Rest*, published in London in 1650. Baxter
advocated meditation as the way to move religious truths from
the believer's head to his heart by a systematic effort to reclaim
a doctrine from memory, submit it to the rational study of the
understanding, summon support from the affections (love, desire,
hope, courage, and joy), and finally motivate the will to take
action on the basis of the emotionally assimilated belief.[2] If Tay-
lor's sermons represent the application of memory and under-
standing to each biblical text, his *Preparatory Meditations* may
be seen as appeals to the affections and will. Some poems follow
Baxter's method in detail, others more loosely, but all fit the
general pattern. Most follow Taylor's personal ordering pattern
as well, moving from stricken awareness of his sin, through hope
in Christ's mercy, to joy in the prospect of salvation. Often he
uses a musical metaphor to express this process of growth from
muteness or dissonance to capacity for song.

Analysis of a typical meditation, "First Series: Number 16"
(1685-1686), may serve to clarify his method. The poet introduces
himself as a fallen creature, having lost the gold-leaf of his original
grace—his share of the divine sun. Blinded by Satan, he "cannot
see, nor Will thy Will aright," and the problem of the poem
becomes that of revitalizing the dead will through restored vision.
For him, the properties of God's fire are fearfully divided: light
streaming from heaven toward his unreceptive eyes; heat emanat-
ing from hell below. Christ's grace, rolled into "a Sunball Shine,"
hurtles toward him from the prophetic pages of scripture and
opens his eyes so that they are again able to receive spiritual
light. So illumined, his affections flame out with the warmth of
religious love, and his rekindled will readies itself for action
expressing his joy.

Taylor's occasional poems, though less clearly related to his
ministry, reveal a mind always alert to find spiritual truths in

2. Louis L. Martz, *The Poetry of Meditation: A Study in English Religious
Literature of the Seventeenth Century* (New Haven, Conn.: Yale University Press,
1954), establishes the intellectual and devotional context in which Taylor's medita-
tions may be read.

ordinary experiences like his wife's spinning or his own observation of a chilled wasp. The Puritan habit of allegorizing incidental happenings displays itself in these poems, as does a constant effort to open himself to God's message and discipline himself to the divine will. All the poems display Taylor's tendency to show his ingenuity in drawing orthodox religious lessons from unconventional stimuli; he rarely opened himself to discovery of new truths, however, by following a perception wherever it might lead. Christ may be seen in the wasp's capacity to break the spider's murderous web, for instance, but the reader should ignore the insect's "froppish, waspish heate" when developing the analogy.

The ritualized pattern by which Taylor guided each line of inquiry to focus on conversion and lead to hope of salvation dramatizes the strength of his interest in conversion and also the assurance he seems to have felt about his own election. Although he had experienced saving grace in childhood, he knew that no person could be sure of salvation, that excessive confidence was a probable sign of damnation (as was, of course, despair); so he perpetually reexamined the state of his soul to convict himself of sin and look for signs of grace. There was only one truly crucial concern for him or any Puritan, and he focused on that one issue of predestination from every possible perspective; yet the issue seems never to have been in doubt. These are the poems of a man who felt himself to have been saved, not of a religious searcher. Although the religious ecstasy of "The Experience" dimmed at times, he never doubted its reality or gave up the effort to reclaim it.

Hopeful of election, Taylor could exult in the contrast between God's infinity and man's nothingness so memorably celebrated in "The Preface" to *Gods Determinations* and echoed in almost every meditation. Man was mud, a crumb of dust, a mite, a worm, the vilest of sinners; God was perfection, creator, king, savior. The human race, fallen into sin with Adam, deserved nothing but destruction; and hell would have been the only satisfaction of God's justice except that Christ, assuming human nature, dignified man above the angels and saved his saints through heroic mercy. Despite Taylor's emphasis on sin and divine wrath, the key words in his theological vocabulary were *glory* and *grace*—the inconceivable glory of God and the grace by which Christ channels saving life to man and draws him to participate in that glory. This stress on Christ, grace, and mercy rather than the Father, power, and justice shows Taylor's alliance with the later genera- tions of American Puritans who, more than Bradstreet, focused attention on human dignity and value in a redeemed universe despite a continuing tendency to weak, sinful behavior.[3]

Although the meditations necessarily concentrated on Taylor's personal relationship with God, he repeatedly emphasized the church's function in salvation history. Most people would travel toward heaven in the ecclesiastical coach of *Gods Determinations*. The church, even more than the individual saint, was Christ's chosen bride foretold in the Canticles. It, after all, dispensed the sacraments linking man to God and preserved the orthodoxy of the Puritan eucharist, which served as man's closest earthly rela- tionship with Christ.

Not surprisingly, Taylor expressed his spiritual insights accord- ing to the metaphysical poetic style favored in seventeenth-century England by writers whom he may have read: Quarles, DuBartas, Crashaw, Donne, Milton, and Herbert. His work never showed the neoclassical influence of Dryden or other Restoration and eighteenth-century writers, though his literary career coincided with theirs. He wrote rough, metrically uneven lines, packed with strong sounds. The writing is forceful, though unpolished, and expresses a tense and active mind. The language is condensed; the thought complex. Taylor chose a startling vocabulary and forced his readers to struggle with archaic diction, Leicestershire colloquialisms, and more or less accessible puns. He felt bound by no rules of decorum requiring exalted or even discreet language to treat sacred topics but enjoyed license to play with whatever words best expressed his feelings. In general, the harshest, strangest language denounces sin ("Hells Nymps with spite their Dog's sticks thereat ding") while the most appealing expresses grace ("Sweet apples mellow so"), but the relationship between style and sense can hardly be considered uniform.

3. The generational conflict in American Puritanism and its effect on literature are clearly analyzed in Emory Elliott's study, *Power and the Pulpit in Puritan New England* (Princeton, N.J.: Princeton University Press, 1975).

The tone of the poems tends toward the exclamatory: cries of anguish, shrieks of desperation, paeans of joy. Particularly in the meditations, where he tried to awaken his will by stirring his affections, Taylor spoke emotionally rather than rationally and voiced even the most abstract theological conceptions in the language of the heart. To emphasize his excitement and sustain a quality of surprise, he made constant use of all the rhetorical structures in the Harvard curriculum: metaphor, synecdoche, paradox, pun, rhetorical question, meiosis, and hyperbole, among others. Hyperbole, in fact, stands out as Taylor's most characteristic device. He delighted in exaggerating man's natural depravity and exalting God's glory by absolutely opposed figures of speech, only to emphasize the paradoxical wonder of Christ's hypostatic union of human and divine and the marvel of grace which lifts hell-deserving man to heaven. He gained even greater dramatic intensity in the meditations and *Gods Determinations* by adopting a uniformly first-person address, so that the speaker himself personally experiences the tension between the diabolical and the divine. His use of the same six-line stanza with interlocking quatrain and final couplet throughout the meditations provided a form calling little attention to itself but allowing tightness of expression within each particular stanza, while the poem as a whole could be readily expanded or contracted.

Drawing his imagery from the Bible, memories of English village life, and everyday domestic occurrences, Taylor cut sharply back and forth across categories of sensate and abstract impressions. The sacramental context of the meditations explains certain repeated patterns of imagery. Food, for instance, represented Christ's banquet but ranged far beyond the conventional bread and wine to include sugar-cake, beer, meat drippings, an egg, anything edible. To express the idea of grace, Taylor chose containers with precious objects (a wicker or gold birdcage, a jewelry box, a punch bowl) or channeling conduits. It is often advisable not to visualize Taylor's images nor to read one image in the context of others from the same poem. Sometimes they link together in one integrated logical pattern, but more often they stand apart, joined only by loose associations. Most of the associations refer to established Christian symbolism by which Christ is king, rose of sharon, bridegroom, artificer, physician, and bread—all in one poem, if imagination suggests. Taylor's allegorizing mind found its own ingenious images for his constant themes of glory, grace, and church so that he could emblemize Christ in the pettish wasp and the earth in a bowling ball as well as in more ennobling symbols; he never hesitated to compare the greater to the less, the real to the artificial, or the conventional to the idiosyncratic. The influence of the Bible, especially the Canticle of Canticles, encouraged him to use frankly erotic imagery, although he adhered to Puritan literary preferences by shifting image patterns and not holding so long any one sensuous image as to distract attention from the argument. Clearly, Taylor enjoyed the interlocking patterns of the universe all pointing out the same truths; he read the Old Testament for types or anticipations of Christ in Isaac, Jonah, and Joseph, and he found related stimuli to devotion wherever he looked.

Like Bradstreet, Taylor accorded poetry or any other art a purely instrumental value; it was a tool for examining the soul and directing it toward God. His poems often spoke harshly of his efforts to write. His best attempts would be "but Inventions Vents or glory/Wits Wantonings, and Fancies frollicks plump." But he felt an obligation to give praise, preferably in words responsive to Christ as the Word, and his meditations frequently moved from acknowledged inability to speak to the promise of grace-inspired song. The act of writing the poem, then, could be perceived as evidence of grace; the process of artistic composition would mean more than the product. Most of his writing, certainly the best of it, served his personal spiritual use. Given his use of poetry as a tool for self-knowledge and religious discipline, it is surprising that Taylor's poetry showed so little change over the years in terms of discernible growth, decline, or spurts of inspiration. A remarkable degree of repetition appears, and there is little evidence of fresh discovery even though each meditation sounds like a new beginning and an independent search.

Edward Taylor never published his poems, although he sent copies of some to friends in Boston and probably shared *Gods Determinations* with his Westfield congregation. When he died in 1729, his papers went to his family and were kept in various private households until most were turned over to libraries in the nineteenth century. Not until early in this century were his poems discovered by literary scholars. Thomas H. Johnson's publication of some poems from the Yale manuscript in 1937 brought him public attention and immediate acclaim as the greatest of America's Puritan poets—our only metaphysical poet who could stand comparison with Donne and Herbert. The coincidence of Taylor's discovery just when aesthetic sensibilities had been reawakened to baroque literature won him intensive, continuing scholarly attention and a steady audience. More of his work has become available in recent years, though some may still be hidden in attics and archives and a few poems elude publication because of his sometimes illegible penmanship.

Taylor's reputation seems today as paradoxical as his poetry. He has been valued for reasons which would have struck him as unimportant or disturbing—for his poetic craftsmanship, for his anticipation of romanticism and modernism, even for the religious heresies some readers profess to find in his verse. And he has been criticized for his rough composition, his departures from "good taste," his lack of Americanness, and even for his orthodoxy. It would be better to read him for what he tried to be: a versifying Puritan minister or even a frontier psalmist, placing emphasis always on the glory which inspired his poetry and the grace which enabled his admittedly "rough Feet" to sing "smooth praises" to his God.

BIBLIOGRAPHIC NOTE

The standard edition of the poems is Donald E. Stanford's *The Poems of Edward Taylor* (New Haven, Conn.: Yale University Press, 1960). Thomas H. Johnson's edition, *The Poetical Works of Edward Taylor* (Princeton, N.J.: Princeton University Press, 1943), remains helpful, though limited to manuscripts found at Yale. Readers interested in the full transcript of *The Metrical History of Christianity* should consult Stanford's edition (Wooster, Ohio: Micro Photo, 1962).

There is no book-length biography of Taylor as yet, but his poetry has received extensive criticism. Two useful introductions to his work are Donald Stanford's pamphlet, *Edward Taylor,*

University of Minnesota Pamphlets on American Writers, no. 52 (Minneapolis, Minn.: University of Minnesota Press, 1965), and his essay, "Edward Taylor," in *Major Writers of Early American Literature*, ed. Everett Emerson (Madison: University of Wisconsin Press, 1972), pp. 59-91. Another helpful introductory study is Norman S. Grabo's *Edward Taylor*, Twayne's United States Authors Series (New York: Twayne Publishers, 1961). Recent critical examinations of Taylor's achievement include Karl Keller's *The Example of Edward Taylor* (Amherst, Mass.: University of Massachusetts Press, 1975), and William J. Scheick's *The Will and the Word: The Poetry of Edward Taylor* (Athens: University of Georgia Press, 1974).

THE TEXT

In compiling these anthology selections, I have used Donald E. Stanford's authoritative edition of *The Poems of Edward Taylor* (New Haven, Conn.: Yale University Press, 1960). Uncertain dating of Taylor's work impedes chronological arrangement, but I have placed poems from *Gods Determinations* first as evidence of his early writing and as a relatively accessible introduction to his theology, followed by the occasional poems and the first and second series of *Preparatory Meditations*, composed at approximately two-month intervals from the early 1680s to the time of his death.

From *Gods Determinations touching his Elect*

Cuplet Form

THE PREFACE

    Infinity, when all things it beheld
In Nothing, and of Nothing all did build,
Upon what Base was fixt the Lath, wherein
He turn'd this Globe, and riggalld [1] it so trim?

1. Marked with ring-like grooves.

pottery.
potter image

Who blew the Bellows of his Furnace Vast?
Or held the Mould wherein the world was Cast?
Who laid its Corner Stone? Or whose Command?
Where stand the Pillars upon which it stands?
Who Lac'de and Fillitted the earth so fine,
With Rivers like green Ribbons Smaragdine? [2]
Who made the Sea's its Selvedge,[3] and it locks
Like a Quilt Ball within a Silver Box?
Who Spread its Canopy? Or Curtains Spun?
Who in this Bowling Alley bowld the Sun?
Who made it always when it rises set
To go at once both down, and up to get?
Who th'Curtain rods made for this Tapistry?
Who hung the twinckling Lanthorns in the Sky?
Who? who did this? or who is he? Why, know
Its Onely Might Almighty this did doe.
His hand hath made this noble worke which Stands
His Glorious Handywork not made by hands.
Who spake all things from nothing; and with ease
Can speake all things to nothing, if he please.
Whose Little finger at his pleasure Can
Out mete ten thousand worlds with halfe a Span:
Whose Might Almighty can by half a looks
Root up the rocks and rock the hills by th'roots.
Can take this mighty World up in his hande,
And shake it like a Squitchen[4] or a Wand.
Whose single Frown will make the Heavens shake
Like as an aspen leafe the Winde makes quake.
Oh! what a might is this Whose single frown
Doth shake the world as it would shake it down?
Which All from Nothing fet,[5] from Nothing, All:
Hath All on Nothing set, lets Nothing fall.
Gave All to nothing Man indeed, whereby
Through nothing man all might him Glorify.

2. Emerald.
3. Border of a woven fabric.
4. Scutcheon; a piece of bark used in tree-grafting.
5. Made.

In Nothing then imbosst the brightest Gem
More pretious than all pretiousness in them.   40
But Nothing man did throw down all by Sin:
And darkened that lightsom Gem in him.
    That now his Brightest Diamond is grown
    Darker by far than any Coalpit Stone.   *assonance*

   (undated; 1939)

GODS SELECTING LOVE IN THE DECREE

    Man in this Lapst Estate at very best,
A Cripple is and footsore, sore opprest,
Can't track Gods Trace but Pains, and pritches[1] prick
Like poyson'd splinters sticking in the Quick.
Yet jims[2] in th'Downy path with pleasures spread   5
As 'twas below him on the Earth to tread.
Can prance, and trip within the way of Sin,
Yet in Gods path moves not a little wing.

    Almighty this foreseing, and withall
That all this stately worke of his would fall   10
Tumble, and Dash to pieces Did in lay
Before it was too late for it a Stay.
Doth with his hands hold, and uphold the same.
Hence his Eternall Purpose doth proclaim.
Whereby transcendently he makes to shine   15
Transplendent Glory in his Grace Divine.
Almighty makes a mighty sumptuous feast:
Doth make the Sinfull Sons of men his guests.
But yet in speciall Grace he hath to some,
(Because they Cripples are, and Cannot come)   20
He sends a Royall Coach forth for the same,
To fetch them in, and names them name by name.
A Royall Coach whose scarlet Canopy

    1. Pricks; grudges; spites.
    2. Jumps(?).

O're silver Pillars, doth expanded ly:
All bottomed with purest gold refin'de,   25
And inside o're with lovely Love all linde.
Which Coach indeed you may exactly spy
All mankinde splits in a Dicotomy.
    For all ride to the feast that favour finde.
    The rest do slite the Call and stay behinde.   30

    O! Honour! Honour! Honours! Oh! the Gain!
And all such Honours all the saints obtain.
It is the Chariot of the King of Kings:
That all who Glory gain, to glory brings.
Whose Glory makes the rest, (when spi'de) beg in.   35
Some gaze and stare. Some stranging at the thing.
Some peep therein; some rage thereat, but all,
Like market people seing on a stall,
Some rare Commodity Clap hands thereon
And Cheapen't hastily, but soon are gone.   40
For hearing of the price, and wanting pay
Do pish thereat, and Coily pass away.
So hearing of the terms, whist, they'le abide
At home before they'l pay so much to ride.
But they to whom its sent had rather all,   45
Dy in this Coach, than let their journey fall.
They up therefore do get, and in it ride
Unto Eternal bliss, while down the tide
The other scull unto eternall woe;
By letting slip their former journey so.   50
For when they finde the Silver Pillars fair
The Golden bottom pav'de with Love as rare,
To be the Spirits sumptuous building cleare,
When in the Soul his Temple he doth reare
And Purple Canopy to bee (they spy)   55
All Graces Needlework and Huswifry;
Their stomachs rise: these graces will not down.
They think them Slobber Sawces: therefore frown.
They loath the same, wamble keck,[3] heave they do:

3. Vomit.

Their Spleen thereat out at their mouths they throw,   60
Which while they do, the Coach away doth high   _Violence_
Wheeling the Saints in't to eternall joy.
    These therefore and their journey now do come
    For to be treated on, and Coacht along.

     (undated; 1939)

THE FROWARDNESS OF THE ELECT IN THE WORK OF CONVERSION

    Those upon whom Almighty doth intend
His all Eternall Glory to expend,
Lulld in the lap of sinfull Nature snugg,
Like Pearls in Puddles cover'd ore with mudd:
Whom, if you search, perhaps some few you'l finde,   5
That to notorious Sins were ne're inclinde.
Some shunning some, some most, some greate, some small.
Some this, that or the other, some none at all.
But all, or almost all you'st easly finde,
To all, or almost all Defects inclinde   10
To Revell with the Rabble rout who say
Let's hiss this Piety out of our Day.
And those whose frame is made of finer twine
Stand further off from Grace than Wash from Wine.
Those who suck Grace from th'breast, are nigh as rare   15
As Black Swans that in milkwhite Rivers are.
Grace therefore calls them all, and sweetly wooes.
Some won come in, the rest as yet refuse,
And run away: Mercy persues apace,
Then some Cast down their arms, Cry Quarter, Grace.   20
Some Chased out of breath drop down with feare
Perceiving the persuer drawing neer.
The rest persude, divide into two rancks
And this way one, and that the other prancks.

    Then in comes Justice with her forces by her,   25

And doth persue as hot as sparkling fire.
The right wing then begins to fly away.
But in the streights strong Baracadoes[1] lay.
They're therefore forc'd to face about, and have
Their spirits Queld, and therefore Quarter Crave.   30
These Captivde thus: justice persues the Game
With all her troops to take the other train.
Which being Chast in a Peninsula
And followd close, they finde no other way
To make escape, but t'rally round about: 35
Which if it faile them that they get not out,
They're forct into the Infernall Gulfe alive
Or hackt in pieces are or took Captive.
But spying Mercy stand with Justice, they
Cast down their Weapons, and for Quarter pray.   40
Their lives are therefore spar'de, yet they are ta'ne
As th'other band: and prisoners must remain.
And so they must now Justice's Captives bee
On Mercies Quarrell: Mercy sets not free.
    Their former Captain[2] is their Deadly foe.   45
    And now, poor souls, they know not what to do.

    (undated; 1939)

1. Barricades.
2. The devil.

CHRISTS REPLY

    I am a Captain to your Will.
You found me Gracious, so shall still,
Whilst that my Will is your Design.
    If that you stick unto my Cause
    Opposing whom oppose my Laws   5
I am your own, and you are mine.

    The weary Soule I will refresh
    And Ease him of his heaviness.

Who'le slay a Friend? And save a Foe?
   Who in my War do take delight,   10
   Fight not for prey, but Pray, and Fight
Although they slip, I'le mercy show.

   Then Credit not your Enemy
   Whose Chiefest daintie is a lie.
I will you comfort sweet extend.   15
   Behold I am a sun and shield
   And a sharp sword to win the field.
I'l surely Crown you in the End.

   His murdering Canons which do roare
   And Engins though as many more   20
Shoot onely aire: no Bullets fly.
   Unless you dare him with your Crest,
   And ope to him the naked breast,
Small Execution's done thereby.

   To him that smiteth hip, and thigh,   25
   My foes as his: Walks warily,
I'le give him Grace: he'st give me praise.
   Let him whose foot doth hit a Stone
   Through weakeness, not rebellion
Not faint, but think on former dayes.   30

     (undated; 1937)

FIRST SATANS ASSAULT AGAINST THOSE THAT FIRST CAME UP TO MERCYS TERMS

   Satan

Soon ripe, soon rot. Young Saint, Old Divell. Loe
Why to an Empty Whistle did you goe?
What Come Uncalld? And Run unsent for? Stay
Its Childrens Bread: Hands off: out, Dogs, away.

Soul

It's not an Empty Whistle: yet withall,   5
And if it be a Whistle, then a Call:
A Call to Childrens Bread, which take we may.
Thou onely art the Dog whipt hence away.

Satan

If I then you: for by Apostasy
You are the Imps of Death as much as I.   10
And Death doth reign o're you through Sin: you see,
As well as Sin doth reign to Death in mee.

Soul

It is deni'd: Gods Mercy taking place,
Prepared Grace for us, and us for Grace.
And Graces Coach in Grace hath fetcht us in,   15
Unto her Feast. We shall not dy in Sin.

Satan

If it be so, your sins are Crucifide:
Which if they be, they struggl'd when they di'de.
It is not so with you: you judge before
You felt them gird, you'de got them out of Doore.   20

Soul

Mercy the Quartermaster speedily,
Did stifle Sin, and still its hidious Cry,
Whose Knife at first stuck in its heart to th'head:
That sin, before it hard did sprunt,[1] fell dead.

Satan

A mere Delusion! Nature shows that Life   25
Will strugle most upon the bloody Knife
And so will Sin. Nay Christ doth onely Call,
And offer ease to such as are in thrall.

1. Struggle, kick.

Soul

He offer'd unto mee, and I receiv'd
Of what hee wrought, I am not yet bereav'd.   30
Though Justice set Amercement[2] on mee
Mercy hath took it off, and set me free.

Satan

Is Mercy impudent? or Justice blinde?
I am to make distraint[3] on thee Designd.
The North must wake before the South proves Kind.   35
The Law must breake before the Gospell binde

Soul

But Giliads Balm,[4] like Balsom heald my wound
Makes not the Patient sore, yet leaves him sound.
The Gospell did the Law prevent: my heart
Is therefore dresst from Sin: and did not smart.   40

Satan

A likely thing! Oh shame! presume on Grace!
Here's Sin in Grain: it hath a Double Face.
Come, Come with mee I'le shew your Outs, and Inns,
Your Inside, and your out: your Holy things.
    For these I will anatomize then see,   45
    Believe your very Eyes, believe not mee.

(undated; 1939)

Faith vs. Sight

2. A fine imposed at the "mercy" of the inflicter; a variable penalty.
3. Legally, the seizure of property to force a debtor to pay his fine.
4. A soothing, fragrant resin from Gilead, a biblical area east of the Jordan.

AN EXTASY OF JOY LET IN BY THIS REPLY RETURND IN ADMIRATION

My Sweet Deare Lord, for thee I'le Live, Dy, Fight,
   Gracious indeed! My Front! my Rear!
   Almighty magnify a Mite:
      O! What a Wonder's here?

Had I ten thousand times ten thousand hearts: 5
    And Every Heart ten thousand Tongues;
    To praise, I should but stut odd parts   *stutter*
       Of what to thee belongs.

If all the world did in Alimbeck[1] ly,
    Bleeding its Spirits out in Sweat;   *God gives* 10
    It could not halfe enlife a Fly   *life*
       To Hum thy Praises greate.

If all can't halfe enlife a Fly to hum,
    (Which scarce an Animall we call)
    Thy Praises then which from me come,   15
       Come next to none at all.

For I have made myselfe ten thousand times
    More naught than nought itselfe, by Sin.
    Yet thou extendst thy Gracious Shines
       For me to bath therein.   20

Oh! Stand amaizd yee Angells Bright, come run
    Yee Glorious Heavens and Saints, to sing:
    Place yee your praises in the sun,
       Ore all the world to ring.

Nay stand agast, ye sparkling Spirits bright!   25
    Shall little Clods of Dust you peere?
    Shall they toote Praises on your pipe?
       Oh! that we had it here.

What can a Crumb of Dust sally such praise
    Which do from Earth all heaven o're ring   30
    Who swaddle up the suns bright rayes
       Can in a Flesh Flie's Wing?

Can any Ant stand on the Earth and spit
    Another out to peer with this?

1. Distilling apparatus.

Or Drink the Ocean up, and yet   35
    Its belly empty is?

Thou may'st this World as easily up hide
    Under the Blackness of thy naile:
    As scape Sins Gulph without a Guide:
      Or Hell without a bale.   40

If all the Earthy Mass were rambd in Sacks
    And saddled on an Emmet small,
    Its Load were light unto those packs
      Which Sins do bring on all.

But sure this burden'd Emmet moves no wing.   45
    Nay, nay, Compar'd with thee, it flies.
    Yet man is easd his weight of Sin.
      From hell to Heav'n doth rise.

When that the World was new, its Chiefe Delight,
    One Paradise alone Contain'de: 50
    The Bridle of Mans Appetite
      The Appletree refrain'de.

The which he robbing, eat the fruit as good,
    Whose Coare hath Chokd him and his race.
    And juyce hath poyson'd all their blood,   55
      He's in a Dismall Case.

None can this Coare remove, Poyson expell:
    He, if his Blood ben't Clarifi'de
    Within Christs veans, must fry in Hell,
      Till God be satisfi'de.   60

Christ to his Father saith, Incarnate make
    Mee, Mee thy Son; and I will doe't:
    I'le purify his Blood, and take
      The Coare out of his Throate.

All this he did, and did for us, vile Clay:
    Oh! let our Praise his Grace assaile.
    To free us from Sins Gulph each way,
        He's both our Bridge, and Raile.

Notice archaic spelling and language throughout

65

Although we fall and Fall, and Fall and Fall
    And Satan fall on us as fast.
    He purgeth us and doth us call
        Our trust on him to Cast.

70

My Lumpish Soule why art thou hamper'd thus
    Within a Crumb of Dust? Arise,
    Trumpet out Praises. Christ for us
        Hath slain our Enemies.

75

Screw up, Deare Lord, upon the highest pin:
    My soul thy ample Praise to sound.
    O tune it right, that every string
        May make thy praise rebound.

Harp image

80

But oh! how slack, slow, dull? with what delay,
    Do I this Musick to, repare,
    While tabernacled in Clay
        My Organs Cottag'de are?

Yet Lord accept this Pittance of thy praise
    Which as a Traveller I bring,
    While travelling along thy wayes
        In broken notes I sing.

85

And at my journies end in endless joyes
    I'l make amends where Angells meet
    And sing their flaming Melodies
        In ravishing tunes most sweet.

90

    (undated; 1939)

THE JOY OF CHURCH FELLOWSHIP RIGHTLY ATTENDED

In Heaven soaring up, I dropt an Eare
   On Earth: and oh! sweet Melody:
And listening, found it was the Saints who were
   Encoacht for Heaven that sang for Joy.
   For in Christs Coach they sweetly sing;   *refrain* 5
   As they to Glory ride therein.

Oh! joyous hearts! Enfir'de with holy Flame!
   Is speech thus tassled with praise?
Will not your inward fire of Joy contain;
   That it in open flames doth blaze?   10
   For in Christ's Coach Saints sweetly sing,
   As they to Glory ride therein.

And if a string do slip, by Chance, they soon
   Do screw it up again: whereby
They set it in a more melodious Tune   15
   And a Diviner Harmony.
   For in Christs Coach they sweetly sing
   As they to Glory ride therein.

In all their Acts, publick, and private, nay
   And secret too, they praise impart.   20
But in their Acts Divine and Worship, they
   With Hymns do offer up their Heart.
   Thus in Christs Coach they sweetly sing
   As they to Glory ride therein.

Some few not in;[1] and some whose Time, and Place   25
   Block up this Coaches way do goe
As Travellers afoot, and so do trace

---

1. Taylor offers hope of salvation to a few saints outside the visible church. It is clearly easier and more typical, however, to travel to heaven in Christ's appointed coach.

The Road that gives them right thereto
While in this Coach these sweetly sing
As they to Glory ride therein.   30

    (undated; 1937)

Occasional Poems

UPON A SPIDER CATCHING A FLY

Thou sorrow, venom Elfe.
    Is this thy play,
To spin a web out of thyselfe
    To Catch a Fly?
      For Why?   5

Satan as spider
web as temptation

I saw a pettish wasp
    Fall foule therein.
Whom yet thy Whorle[1] pins did not clasp
    Lest he should fling
      His sting.

Death (sting)
Pauline 10

But as affraid, remote
    Didst stand hereat
And with thy little fingers stroke
    And gently tap
      His back.   15

Thus gently him didst treate
    Lest he should pet,
And in a froppish,[2] waspish heate
    Should greatly fret
      Thy net.   20

1. Small flywheel on a spinning wheel.
2. Fretful; pettish.

Whereas the silly Fly,
    Caught by its leg
Thou by the throate tookst hastily
    And 'hinde the head
        Bite Dead.   25

This goes to pot, that not
    Nature doth call.
Strive not above what strength hath got
    Lest in the brawle
        Thou fall.   30

This Frey seems thus to us.
    Hells Spider gets
His intrails spun to whip Cords thus
    And wove to nets
        And sets.   35

To tangle Adams race
    In's stratigems
To their Destructions, spoil'd, made base
    By venom things
        Damn'd Sins.   40

But mighty, Gracious Lord
    Communicate
Thy Grace to breake the Cord, afford
    Us Glorys Gate
        And State.   45

We'l Nightingaile sing like
    When pearcht on high
In Glories Cage, thy glory, bright,
    And thankfully,
        For joy.   50

(undated; 1939)

UPON A WASP CHILD WITH COLD

The Bare that breaths the Northern blast
Did numb, Torpedo like, a Wasp
Whose stiffend limbs encrampt, lay bathing
In Sol's warm breath and shine as saving,
Which with her hands she chafes and stands
Rubbing her Legs, Shanks, Thighs, and hands.
Her petty toes, and fingers ends
Nipt with this breath, she out extends
Unto the Sun, in greate desire
To warm her digits at that fire.
Doth hold her Temples in this state
Where pulse doth beate, and head doth ake.
Doth turn, and stretch her body small,
Doth Comb her velvet Capitall.[1]
As if her little brain pan were
A Volume of Choice precepts cleare.
As if her sattin jacket hot
Contained Apothecaries Shop
Of Natures recepts, that prevails
To remedy all her sad ailes,
As if her velvet helmet high
Did turret rationality.
She fans her wing up to the Winde
As if her Pettycoate were lin'de,
With reasons fleece, and hoises sails
And hu'ming flies in thankfull gails
Unto her dun Curld palace Hall
Her warm thanks offering for all.

Lord cleare my misted sight that I
May hence view thy Divinity.
Some sparkes whereof thou up dost hasp
Within this little downy Wasp
In whose small Corporation wee
A school and a schoolmaster see

1. Head.

Where we may learn, and easily finde   35
A nimble Spirit bravely minde
Her worke in e'ry limb: and lace
It up neate with a vitall grace,
Acting each part though ne'er so small
Here of this Fustian[2] animall.   40
Till I enravisht Climb into
The Godhead on this Lather doe. *do*
Where all my pipes inspir'de upraise
An Heavenly musick furrd with praise.

     (undated; 1943)

2. Clothed in thick cloth.

HUSWIFERY

*Man and
Gods combin
efforts*

Make me, O Lord, thy Spining Wheele compleate.
    Thy Holy Worde my Distaff make for mee.
Make mine Affections thy Swift Flyers neate
        And make my Soule thy holy Spoole to bee.
        My Conversation make to be thy Reele   5
        And reele the yarn thereon spun of thy Wheele.

Make me thy Loome then, knit therein this Twine:
        And make thy Holy Spirit, Lord, winde quills:
Then weave the Web thyselfe. The yarn is fine.
        Thine Ordinances make my Fulling Mills.   10
        Then dy the same in Heavenly Colours Choice,
        All pinkt with Varnisht Flowers of Paradise.

Then cloath therewith mine Understanding, Will,
        Affections, Judgment, Conscience, Memory
My Words, and Actions, that their shine may fill   15
        My wayes with glory and thee glorify.
        Then mine apparell shall display before yee
        That I am Cloathd in Holy robes for glory.

     (undated; 1937)

UPON WEDLOCK, AND DEATH OF CHILDREN

A Curious Knot God made in Paradise,
    And drew it out inamled neatly Fresh.
It was the True-Love Knot, more sweet than spice
    And set with all the flowres of Graces dress.
      Its Weddens Knot, that ne're can be unti'de.
      No Alexanders Sword can it divide.

The slips here planted, gay and glorious grow:
    Unless an Hellish breath do sindge their Plumes.
Here Primrose, Cowslips, Roses, Lilies blow
    With Violets and Pinkes that voide perfumes.
      Whose beautious leaves ore laid with Hony Dew.
      And Chanting birds Cherp out sweet Musick true.

When in this Knot I planted was, my Stock
    Soon knotted, and a manly flower[1] out brake.
And after it my branch again did knot
    Brought out another Flowre[2] its sweet breathd mate.
      One knot gave one tother the tothers place.
      Whence Checkling[3] smiles fought in each others face.

But oh! a glorious hand from glory came
    Guarded with Angells, soon did Crop this flowre
Which almost tore the root up of the same
    At that unlookt for, Dolesome, darksome houre.
      In Pray're to Christ perfum'de it did ascend,
      And Angells bright did it to heaven tend.

But pausing on't, this sweet perfum'd my thought,
    Christ would in Glory have a Flowre, Choice, Prime,
And having Choice, chose this my branch forth brought.
    Lord take't. I thanke thee, thou takst ought of mine,

5

10

15

20

25

1. Samuel Taylor (b. 1675).
2. Elizabeth (b. 1676; d. 1677).
3. Chuckling.

It is my pledg in glory, part of mee
Is now in it, Lord, glorifi'de with thee.   30

But praying ore my branch, my branch did sprout
      And bore another manly flower,[4] and gay
And after that another, sweet[5] brake out,
      The which the former hand soon got away.
      But oh! the tortures, Vomit, screechings, groans,   35
      And six weeks Fever would pierce hearts like stones.

Griefe o're doth flow: and nature fault would finde
      Were not thy Will, my Spell Charm, Joy, and Gem:
That as I said, I say, take, Lord, they're thine.
      I piecemeale pass to Glory bright in them.   40
      I joy, may I sweet Flowers for Glory breed,
      Whether thou getst them green, or lets them seed.

      (1682-1683; 1937)

4. James (b. 1678).
5. Abigail (b. 1681; d. 1682).

From *Preparatory Meditations, First Series*

PROLOGUE

Lord, Can a Crumb of Dust the Earth outweigh,
      Outmatch all mountains, nay the Chrystall Sky?
Imbosom in't designs that shall Display
      And trace into the Boundless Deity?
      Yea hand a Pen whose moysture doth guild ore   5
      Eternall Glory with a glorious glore.

If it its Pen had of an Angels Quill,
      And Sharpend on a Pretious Stone ground tite,
And dipt in Liquid Gold, and mov'de by Skill
      In Christall leaves should golden Letters write   10

It would but blot and blur yea jag, and jar
Unless thou mak'st the Pen, and Scribener.[1]

I am this Crumb of Dust which is design'd
    To make my Pen unto thy Praise alone,
And my dull Phancy I would gladly grinde
    Unto an Edge on Zions Pretious Stone.
    And Write in Liquid Gold upon thy Name
    My Letters till thy glory forth doth flame.

Let not th'attempts breake down my Dust I pray
    Nor laugh thou them to scorn but pardon give.
Inspire this Crumb of Dust till it display
    Thy Glory through't: and then thy dust shall live.
    Its failings then thou'lt overlook I trust,
    They being Slips slipt from thy Crumb of Dust.

Thy Crumb of Dust breaths two words from its breast,
    That thou wilt guide its pen to write aright
To Prove thou art, and that thou art the best
    And shew thy Properties to shine most bright.
    And then thy Works will shine as flowers on Stems
    Or as in Jewellary Shops, do jems.

    (undated; 1937)

1. Clerk.

THE EXPERIENCE[1]

Oh! that I alwayes breath'd in such an aire,
    As I suckt in, feeding on sweet Content!
Disht up unto my Soul ev'n in that pray're
    Pour'de out to God over last Sacrament.

1. Donald E. Stanford reads this poem as Taylor's memory of a mystical moment of oneness with God, experienced at communion; the later meditations, then, may be attempts to recreate this central experience of grace ("Edward Taylor," *Major Writers of Early American Literature,* ed. Everett Emerson [Madison: University of Wisconsin Press, 1972], p. 69).

Christ

What Beam of Light wrapt up my sight to finde   5
Me neerer God than ere Came in my minde?

Most strange it was! But yet more strange that shine
    Which filld my Soul then to the brim to spy
My Nature with thy Nature all Divine
    Together joyn'd in Him thats Thou, and I.   10
    Flesh of my Flesh, Bone of my Bone. There's run   *Marriage*
    Thy Godhead, and my Manhood in thy Son.   *imagery*

nasal m
Sound —
lingering

Oh! that that Flame which thou didst on me Cast
    Might me enflame, and Lighten ery where.
Then Heaven to me would be less at last   15
    So much of heaven I should have while here.
    Oh! Sweet though Short! Ile not forget the same.
    My neerness, Lord, to thee did me Enflame.

I'le Claim my Right: Give place, ye Angells Bright.
    Ye further from the Godhead stande than I.
My Nature is your Lord; and doth Unite
    Better than Yours unto the Deity.
    Gods Throne is first and mine is next: to you
    Onely the place of Waiting-men is due.

Herbert?

music

Oh! that my Heart, thy Golden Harp might bee   25
    Well tun'd by Glorious Grace, that e'ry string
Screw'd to the highest pitch, might unto thee
    All Praises wrapt in sweetest Musick bring.
    I praise thee, Lord, and better praise thee would
    If what I had, my heart might ever hold.   30

(undated; 1937)

THE RETURN

Inamoring Rayes, thy Sparkles, Pearle of Price
    Impearld with Choisest Gems, their beams Display
Impoysoning Sin, Guilding my Soule with Choice

allophones

Rich Grace, thy Image bright, making me pray,
    Oh! that thou Wast on Earth below with mee   5
    Or that I was in Heaven above with thee.

Thy Humane Frame, with Beauty Dapled, and
    In Beds of Graces pald with golden layes,
Lockt to thy Holy Essence by thy hand,
    Yields Glances that enflame my Soul, that sayes   10
    Oh! that thou wast on Earth below with mee!
    Or that I was in Heaven above with thee.

All Love in God, and's Properties Divine
    Enam'led are in thee: thy Beauties Blaze
Attracts my Souls Choice golden Wyer to twine   15
    About thy Rose-sweet selfe. And therefore prayes
    Oh! that thou wast on Earth below with mee!
    Or, that I was in Heaven above with thee.

A Magazeen of Love: Bright Glories blaze:
    Thy Shine fills Heaven with Glory; Smile Convayes   20
Heavens Glory in my Soule, which it doth glaze
    All ore with amoring Glory; that she sayes,
    Oh! that thou wast on Earth below with mee!
    Or, that I was in Heaven above with thee!

Heavens Golden Spout thou art where Grace most Choice   25
    Comes Spouting down from God to man of Clay.
A Golden Stepping Stone to Paradise
    A Golden Ladder into Heaven! I'l pray
    Oh! that thou wast on Earth below with mee
    Or that I was in Heaven above with thee.   30

Thy Service is my Freedom Pleasure, Joy,
    Delight, Bliss, Glory, Heaven on Earth, my Stay,
In Gleams of Glory thee to glorify.
    But oh! my Dross and Lets.[1] Wherefore I say

1. Hindrances.

Oh! that thou wast on Earth below with mee: 35
Or that I was in Heaven above with thee.

throw away parts from animal butchering

If off as Offall I be put, if I
Out of thy Vineyard Work be put away:
Life would be Death: my Soule would Coffin'd ly,
Within my Body; and no longer pray   40
Oh! that thou wast on Earth below with mee:
But that I was in Heaven above with thee.

But I've thy Pleasant Pleasant Presence had
In Word, Pray're, Ordinances,[2] Duties; nay,
And in thy Graces, making me full Glad,   45
In Faith, Hope, Charity, that I do say,
That thou hast been on Earth below with mee.
And I shall be in Heaven above with thee.

Herbert

Be thou Musician, Lord, Let me be made
The well tun'de Instrument thou dost assume.   50
And let thy Glory be my Musick plaide.
Then let thy Spirit keepe my Strings in tune,
Whilst thou art here on Earth below with mee   *alters*
Till I sing Praise in Heaven above with thee.   *repetend*

(undated; 1960)

2. Sacraments (baptism and the Lord's Supper).

[6.] ANOTHER MEDITATION AT THE SAME TIME[1]

Are we Gods creation?

Am I thy Gold? Or Purse, Lord, for thy Wealth;
Whether in mine, or mint refinde for thee?
Ime counted so, but count me o're thyselfe,
Lest gold washt face, and brass in Heart I bee.

1. The text of this poem is that of the preceding meditation: "Cant. 2.1. The Lilly of the Vallies." Taylor's biblical citations refer to the King James version, which has been consulted in annotating these poems.

I Feare my Touchstone[2] touches when I try   5
Mee, and my Counted Gold too overly.

Am I new minted by thy Stamp indeed?
    Mine Eyes are dim; I cannot clearly see.
Be thou my Spectacles that I may read
    Thine Image, and Inscription stampt on mee.   10
    If thy bright Image do upon me stand
    I am a Golden Angell[3] in thy hand.

Lord, make my Soule thy Plate: thine Image bright
    Within the Circle of the same enfoile.
And on its brims in golden Letters write   15
    Thy Superscription in an Holy style.
    Then I shall be thy Money, thou my Hord:
    Let me thy Angell bee, bee thou my Lord.

    (undated; 1939)

2. An instrument used to test coins for purity of their gold content.
3. A coin and, of course, a heavenly being.

8. MEDITATION. JOH. 6.51. I AM THE LIVING BREAD

I kening[1] through Astronomy Divine
    The Worlds bright Battlement, wherein I spy
A Golden Path my Pensill cannot line,
    From that bright Throne unto my Threshold ly.
    And while my puzzled thoughts about it pore   5
    I finde the Bread of Life in't at my doore.

When that this Bird of Paradise put in
    This Wicker Cage (my Corps) to tweedle praise
Had peckt the Fruite forbad: and so did fling
    Away its Food; and lost its golden dayes;   10
    It fell into Celestiall Famine sore:
    And never could attain a morsell more.

1. Discovering visually.

Alas! alas! Poore Bird, what wilt thou doe?
    The Creatures field no food for Souls e're gave.
And if thou knock at Angells dores they show   15
    An Empty Barrell: they no soul bread have.
    Alas! Poore Bird, the Worlds White Loafe is done.
    And cannot yield thee here the smallest Crumb.

In this sad state, Gods Tender Bowells run
    Out streams of Grace: And he to end all strife   20
The Purest Wheate in Heaven, his deare-dear Son
    Grinds, and kneads up into this Bread of Life.
    Which Bread of Life from Heaven down came
        and stands
    Disht on thy Table up by Angells Hands.

Protestant view of the Sacramen

Did God mould up this Bread in Heaven, and bake,   25
    Which from his Table came, and to thine goeth?
Doth he bespeake thee thus, This Soule Bread take.
    Come Eate thy fill of this thy Gods White Loafe?
    Its Food too fine for Angells, yet come, take
    And Eate thy fill. Its Heavens Sugar Cake.   30

What Grace is this knead in this Loafe? This thing
    Souls are but petty things it to admire.
Yee Angells, help: This fill would to the brim
    Heav'ns whelm'd-down[2] Chrystall meele Bowle, yea
        and higher.
    This Bread of Life dropt in thy mouth, doth Cry.   35
    Eate, Eate me, Soul, and thou shalt never dy.

    (1684; 1937)

2. Turned downward.

10. MEDITATION. JOH. 6.55. MY BLOOD IS DRINKE INDEED

Stupendious Love! All Saints Astonishment!
    Bright Angells are black Motes in this Suns Light.

Heav'ns Canopy the Paintice[1] to Gods tent
    Can't Cover't neither with its breadth, nor height.
But its Glory doth all Glory else out run,   5
    Beams of bright Glory to't are motes i'th'sun.

My Soule had Caught an Ague, and like Hell
    Her thirst did burn: she to each spring did fly,
But this bright blazing Love did spring a Well
    Of Aqua-Vitae[2] in the Deity,   10
    Which on the top of Heav'ns high Hill out burst
    And down came running thence t'allay my thirst.

But how it came, amazeth all Communion.
    Gods onely Son doth hug Humanity,
Into his very person. By which Union   15
    His Humane Veans its golden gutters ly.
    And rather than my Soule should dy by thirst,
    These Golden Pipes, to give me drink, did burst.

This Liquour brew'd, thy sparkling Art Divine
    Lord, in thy Chrystall Vessells did up tun,   20
(Thine Ordinances,) which all Earth o're shine
    Set in thy rich Wine Cellars out to run.
    Lord, make thy Butlar draw, and fill with speed
    My Beaker full: for this is drink indeed.

Whole Buts of this blesst Nectar shining stand   25
    Lockt up with Saph'rine[3] Taps, whose splendid Flame
Too bright do shine for brightest Angells hands
    To touch, my Lord. Do thou untap the same.
    Oh! make thy Chrystall Buts of Red Wine bleed
    Into my Chrystall Glass this Drink-Indeed.   30

How shall I praise thee then? My blottings Jar
    And wrack my Rhymes to pieces in thy praise.

*Protestant view
of the sacrament*

1. Penthouse; awning.
2. Water of life.
3. Like sapphire.

Thou breath'st thy Vean still in my Pottinger[4]
    To lay my thirst, and fainting spirits raise.
    Thou makest Glory's Chiefest Grape to bleed   35
    Into my cup: And this is Drink-Indeed.

Nay, though I make no pay for this Red Wine,
    And scarce do say I thank-ye-for't; strange thing!
Yet were thy silver skies my Beer bowle fine
    I finde my Lord, would fill it to the brim.   40
    Then make my life, Lord, to thy praise proceed
    For thy rich blood, which is my Drink-Indeed.

(1684; 1943)

4. Small bowl or porringer.

16. MEDITATION. LU. 7.16. A GREATE PROPHET IS RISEN UP

Leafe Gold, Lord of thy Golden Wedge o'relaid
    My Soul at first, thy Grace in e'ry part
Whose peart, fierce Eye thou such a Sight hadst made
    Whose brightsom beams could break into thy heart
    Till thy Curst Foe had with my Fist mine Eye   5
    Dasht out, and did my Soule Unglorify.

I cannot see, nor Will thy Will aright.
    Nor see to waile my Woe, my loss and hew
Nor all the Shine in all the Sun can light
    My Candle, nor its Heate my Heart renew.   10
    See, waile, and Will thy Will, I must, or must
    From Heavens sweet Shine to Hells hot flame be thrust.

Grace then Conceald in God himselfe, did rowle
    Even Snow Ball like into a Sunball Shine
And nestles all its beams buncht in thy Soule
    My Lord, that sparkle in Prophetick Lines.   15
    Oh! Wonder more than Wonderfull! this Will
    Lighten the Eye which Sight Divine did spill.

What art thou, Lord, this Ball of Glory bright?
    A Bundle of Celestiall Beams up bound
In Graces band fixt in Heavens topmost height
    Pouring thy golden Beams thence, Circling round
    Which shew thy Glory, and thy glories Way
    And ery Where will make Celestiall Day.

Lord let thy Golden Beams pierce through mine Eye
    And leave therein an Heavenly Light to glaze
My Soule with glorious Grace all o're, whereby
    I may have Sight, and Grace in mee may blaze.
    Lord ting[1] my Candle at thy Burning Rayes,
    To give a gracious Glory to thy Prayse.

Thou Lightning Eye, let some bright Beames of thine
    Stick in my Soul, to light and liven it:
Light, Life, and Glory, things that are Divine;
    I shall be grac'd withall for glory fit.
    My Heart then stufft with Grace, Light, Life, and Glee
    I'le sacrifice in Flames of Love to thee.

    (1685-1686; 1957)

1. Tinge; color slightly.

21. MEDITATION. PHIL. 2.9. GOD HATH HIGHLY EXALTED HIM

What Glory's this, my Lord? Should one small Point
    Of one small Ray of't touch my Heart 'twould spring
Such joy as would an Adamant[1] unjoynt
    If in't, and tare it, to get out and sing.
    T'run on Heroick golden Feet, and raise
    Heart Ravishing Tunes, Curld with Celestiall praise.

Oh! Bright! Bright thing! I fain would something say:
    Lest Silence should indict me. Yet I feare

1. A hard stone (and possibly a pun on Adam).

To say a Syllable lest at thy day[2]
    I be presented for my Tattling here.   10
    Course Phancy, Ragged Faculties, alas!
    And Blunted Tongue don't Suit: Sighs Soile the Glass.

Yet shall my mouth stand ope, and Lips let run
    Out gliding Eloquence on each light thing?
And shall I gag my mouth, and ty my Tongue,   15
    When such bright Glory glorifies within?
    That makes my Heart leape, dancing to thy Lute?
    And shall my tell tale tongue become a Mute?

Lord spare I pray, though my attempts let fall
    A slippery Verse upon thy Royall Glory.   20
I'le bring unto thine Altar th'best of all
    My Flock affords. I have no better Story.
    I'le at thy Glory my dark Candle light:
    Not to descry the Sun, but use by night.

A Golden Throne whose Banisters are Pearles,   25
    And Pomills[3] Choicest Gems: Carbuncle-Stayes[4]
Studded with Pretious Stones, Carv'd with rich Curles
    Of Polisht Art, sending out flashing Rayes,
    Would him surround with Glory, thron'de therein.
    Yet this is to thy Throne a dirty thing.   30

Oh! Glorious Sight! Loe, How Bright Angells stand
    Waiting with Hat in hand on Him alone
That is Enthron'de, indeed at Gods right hand:
    Gods Heart itselfe being his Happy Throne.
    The Glory that doth from this Person fall,   35
    Fills Heaven with Glory, else there's none at all.

    (1686-1687; 1960)

2. The Day of Judgment.
3. Ornamental knobs on a chair or throne.
4. Supports carved out of red gems.

23. MEDITATION. CANT. 4.8. MY SPOUSE

Would God I in that Golden City were,
    With Jaspers Walld, all garnisht, and made swash,[1]
With Pretious Stones, whose Gates are Pearles most cleare
    And Street Pure Gold, like to transparent Glass.
    That my dull Soule, might be inflamde to see   5
    How Saints and Angells ravisht are in Glee.

Were I but there, and could but tell my Story,
    'Twould rub those Walls of Pretious Stones more bright:
And glaze those Gates of Pearle, with brighter Glory;
    And pave the golden Street with greater light.   10
    'Twould in fresh Raptures Saints, and Angells fling.
    But I poore Snake Crawl here, scarce mudwalld in.

May my Rough Voice, and my blunt Tongue but spell
    My Tale (for tune they can't) perhaps there may
Some Angell catch an end of't up, and tell   15
    In Heaven, when he doth return that way,
    He'l make thy Palace, Lord, all over ring,
    With it in Songs, thy Saint, and Angells sing.

I know not how to speak't, it is so good:
    Shall Mortall, and Immortall marry? nay,   20
Man marry God? God be a Match for Mud?
    The King of Glory Wed a Worm? mere Clay?
    This is the Case. The Wonder too in Bliss.
    Thy Maker is thy Husband. Hearst thou this?

My Maker, he my Husband? Oh! strange joy!   25
    If Kings wed Worms, and Monarchs Mites wed should,
Glory spouse Shame, a Prince a Snake or Fly
    An Angell Court an Ant, all Wonder would.
    Let such wed Worms, Snakes, Serpents, Divells, Flyes.
    Less Wonder than the Wedden in our Eyes.   30

1. Showy, swaggering.

I am to Christ more base, than to a King
    A Mite, Fly, Worm, Ant, Serpent, Divell is,
Or Can be, being tumbled all in Sin,
    And shall I be his Spouse? How good is this?
    It is too good to be declar'de to thee.   35
    But not too good to be believ'de by mee.

Yet to this Wonder, this is found in mee,
    I am not onely base but backward Clay,
When Christ doth Wooe: and till his Spirit bee
    His Spokes man to Compell me I deny.   40
    I am so base and Froward to him, Hee
    Appears as Wonders Wonder, wedding mee.

Seing, Dear Lord, its thus, thy Spirit take
    And send thy Spokes man, to my Soul, I pray.
Thy Saving Grace my Wedden Garment make: 45
    Thy Spouses Frame into my Soul Convay.
    I then shall be thy Bride Espousd by thee
    And thou my Bridesgroom Deare Espousde shalt bee.

    (1687; 1957)

29. MEDITATION. JOH. 20.17. MY FATHER, AND YOUR FATHER, TO MY GOD, AND YOUR GOD

My shattred Phancy stole away from mee,
    (Wits run a Wooling over Edens Parke)
And in Gods Garden saw a golden Tree,
    Whose Heart was All Divine, and gold its barke.
    Whose glorious limbs and fruitfull branches strong   5
    With Saints, and Angells bright are richly hung.

Thou! thou! my Deare-Deare Lord, art this rich Tree
    The Tree of Life Within Gods Paradise.
I am a Withred Twig, dri'de fit to bee
    A Chat Cast in thy fire, Writh off by Vice.   10

Yet if thy Milke white-Gracious Hand will take mee
And grafft mee in this golden stock, thou'lt make mee.

Thou'lt make me then its Fruite, and Branch to spring.
  And though a nipping Eastwinde blow, and all
Hells Nymps with spite their Dog's sticks thereat ding   15
  To Dash the Grafft off, and it's fruits to fall,
  Yet I shall stand thy Grafft, and Fruits that are
  Fruits of the Tree of Life thy Grafft shall beare.

I being grafft in thee there up do stand
  In us Relations all that mutuall are.   20
I am thy Patient, Pupill, Servant, and
  Thy Sister, Mother, Doove, Spouse, Son, and Heire.
  Thou art my Priest, Physician, Prophet, King,
  Lord, Brother, Bridegroom, Father, Ev'ry thing.

I being grafft in thee am graffted here   25
  Into thy Family, and kindred Claim
To all in Heaven, God, Saints, and Angells there.
  I thy Relations my Relations name.
  Thy Father's mine, thy God my God, and I
  With Saints, and Angells draw Affinity.   30

My Lord, what is it that thou dost bestow?
  The Praise on this account fills up, and throngs
Eternity brimfull, doth overflow
  The Heavens vast with rich Angelick Songs.
  How should I blush? how Tremble at this thing,   35
  Not having yet my Gam-Ut,[1] learnd to sing.

But, Lord, as burnish't Sun Beams forth out fly
  Let Angell-Shine forth in my Life out flame,
That I may grace thy gracefull Family
  And not to thy Relations be a Shame.   40
  Make mee thy Grafft, be thou my Golden Stock.
  Thy Glory then I'le make my fruits and Crop.

  (1688; 1939)

1. Musical scale.

32. MEDITATION. 1 COR. 3.22. WHETHER PAUL OR APOLLOS, OR CEPHAS

Thy Grace, Dear Lord's my golden Wrack, I finde
    Screwing my Phancy into ragged Rhimes,
Tuning thy Praises in my feeble minde
    Untill I come to strike them on my Chimes.
    Were I an Angell bright, and borrow could   5
    King Davids Harp, I would them play on gold.

Miltonic

But plung'd I am, my minde is puzzled,
    When I would spin my Phancy thus unspun,   *create words*
In finest Twine of Praise I'm muzzled.

·fallen Language

    My tazzled Thoughts twirld into Snick-Snarls run.   10
    Thy Grace, my Lord, is such a glorious thing,
    It doth Confound me when I would it sing.

Eternall Love an Object mean did smite
    Which by the Prince of Darkness was beguilde,
That from this Love it ran and sweld with spite   15
    And in the way with filth was all defilde
    Yet must be reconcild, cleansd, and begrac'te
    Or from the fruits of Gods first Love displac'te.

Then Grace, my Lord, wrought in thy Heart a vent,
    Thy Soft Soft hand to this hard worke did goe,   20
And to the Milke White Throne of Justice went
    And entred bond that Grace might overflow.
    Hence did thy Person to my Nature ty
    And bleed through humane Veans to satisfy.

Oh! Grace, Grace, Grace! this Wealthy Grace doth lay   25
    Her Golden Channells from thy Fathers throne,
Into our Earthen Pitchers to Convay
    Heavens Aqua Vitae to us for our own.
    O! let thy Golden Gutters run into
    My Cup this Liquour till it overflow.   30

Third party consumption

(substance)

Thine Ordinances, Graces Wine-fats where
    Thy Spirits Walkes, and Graces runs doe ly
And Angells waiting stand with holy Cheere
    From Graces Conduite Head, with all Supply.
    These Vessells full of Grace are, and the Bowls   35
    In which their Taps do run, are pretious Souls.

receivers

Thou to the Cups dost say (that Catch this Wine,)
    This Liquour, Golden Pipes, and Wine-fats plain,
Whether Paul, Apollos, Cephas, all are thine.
    Oh Golden Word! Lord speake it ore again.   40
    Lord speake it home to me, say these are mine.
    My Bells shall then thy Praises bravely chime.

Vehicle of pastort

Power of word

    (1689; 1954)

39. MEDITATION. FROM 1 JOH. 2.1. IF ANY MAN SIN, WE HAVE AN ADVOCATE

My Sin! my Sin, My God, these Cursed Dregs,
    Green, Yellow, Blew streakt Poyson hellish, ranck,
Bubs[1] hatcht in natures nest on Serpents Eggs,
    Yelp, Cherp and Cry; they set my Soule a Cramp.
    I frown, Chide, strik and fight them, mourn and Cry   5
    To Conquour them, but cannot them destroy.

verbs

I cannot kill nor Coop them up: my Curb
    'S less than a Snaffle in their mouth: my Rains
They as a twine thrid, snap: by hell they're spurd:
    And load my Soule with swagging loads of pains.   10
    Black Imps, young Divells, snap, bite, drag to bring
    And pick mee headlong hells dread Whirle Poole in.

Lord, hold thy hand: for handle mee thou may'st
    In Wrath: but, oh, a twinckling Ray of hope

1. Pustules.

All in the mind

Methinks I spie thou graciously display'st.   15
    There is an Advocate: a doore is ope.
    Sin's poyson swell my heart would till it burst,
    Did not a hope hence creep in't thus, and nurse't.

Joy, joy, Gods Son's the Sinners Advocate   *legal languag*
    Doth plead the Sinner guiltless, and a Saint.   20
But yet Atturnies pleas spring from the State
    The Case is in: if bad its bad in plaint.
    My Papers do contain no pleas that do
    Secure mee from, but knock me down to, woe.

I have no plea mine Advocate to give: 25
    What now? He'l anvill Arguments greate Store
Out of his Flesh and Blood to make thee live.
    O Deare bought Arguments: Good pleas therefore.
    Nails made of heavenly Steel, more Choice than gold
    Drove home, Well Clencht, eternally will hold.   30

Oh! Dear bought Plea, Deare Lord, what buy't so deare?
    What with thy blood purchase thy plea for me?
Take Argument out of thy Grave t'appeare
    And plead my Case with, me from Guilt to free.
    These maule both Sins, and Divells, and amaze   35
    Both Saints, and Angells; Wreath their mouths
        with praise.

What shall I doe, my Lord? what do, that I
    May have thee plead my Case? I fee thee will
With Faith, Repentance, and obediently
    Thy Service gainst Satanick Sins fulfill.   40
    I'l fight thy fields while Live I do, although
    I should be hackt in pieces by thy foe.

Make me thy Friend, Lord, be my Surety: I
    Will be thy Client, be my Advocate:
My Sins make thine, thy Pleas make mine hereby.   45

Thou wilt mee save, I will thee Celebrate.
Thou'lt kill my Sins that cut my heart within:
And my rough Feet shall thy smooth praises sing.

(1690; 1954)

From *Preparatory Meditations, Second Series*

4. MEDITATION. GAL. 4.24. WHICH THINGS ARE AN ALLEGORIE

My Gracious Lord, I would thee glory doe:
    But finde my Garden over grown with weeds:
My Soile is sandy; brambles o're it grow;
      My Stock is stunted; branch no good Fruits breeds.
      My Garden weed: Fatten my Soile, and prune   5
      My Stock, and make it with thy glory bloome.

O Glorious One, the gloriou'st thought I thincke
    Of thee falls black as Inck upon thy Glory.
The brightest Saints that rose, do Star like, pinck.
      Nay, Abrams Shine to thee's an Allegory,   10
      Or fleeting Sparke in th'Smoke, to typify
      Thee, and thy Glorious Selfe in mystery.

Should all the Sparks in heaven, the Stars there dance
    A Galliard, Round about the Sun, and stay
His Servants (while on Easter morn his prance   15
      Is o're, which old wives prate of) O brave Play.
      Thy glorious Saints thus boss thee round, which stand
      Holding thy glorious Types[1] out in their hand.

1. Old Testament prefigurements of Christ. Taylor, like most Puritans, read the Bible allegorically, applying New Testament insights to Old Testament episodes.

But can I thinck this Glory greate, its head
    Thrust in a pitchy cloude, should strangled ly   20
Or tucking up its beams should go to bed
    Within the Grave, darke me to glorify?
    This Mighty thought my hearts too streight for, though
    I hold it by the hand, and let not goe.

Then, my Blesst Lord, let not the Bondmaids type[2]   25
    Take place in mee. But thy blesst Promisd Seed.[3]
Distill thy Spirit through thy royall Pipe
    Into my Soule, and so my Spirits feed,
    Then them, and me still into praises right
    Into thy Cup where I to swim delight.   30

Though I desire so much, I can't o're doe.
    All that my Can contains, to nothing comes
When summed up, it onely Cyphers grows
    Unless thou set thy Figures to my Sums.
    Lord set thy Figure 'fore them, greate, or small.   35
    To make them something, and I'l give thee all.

    (1693; 1954)

2. Ishmael, Abraham's son by his slave Hagar.
3. Isaac, Abraham's son by Sarah.

7. MEDITATION. PS. 105.17. HE SENT A MAN BEFORE THEM, EVEN JOSEPH, WHO WAS SOLD ETC.

All Dull, my Lord, my Spirits flat, and dead
    All water sockt and sapless to the skin.
Oh! Screw mee up and make my Spirits bed
    Thy quickening vertue For my inke is dim,
    My pensill blunt. Doth Joseph type out thee?   5
    Haraulds of Angells sing out, Bow the Knee.

Is Josephs glorious shine a Type of thee?
    How bright art thou? He Envi'de was as well.
And so was thou. He's stript, and pick't, poore hee,
    Into the pit. And so was thou. They shell   10

Thee of thy Kirnell. He by Judah's sold
For twenty Bits, thirty for thee he'd told.

Joseph was tempted by his Mistress vile.
 Thou by the Divell, but both shame the foe.
Joseph was cast into the jayle awhile.   15
  And so was thou. Sweet apples mellow so.
  Joseph did from his jayle to glory run.
  Thou from Death's pallot rose like morning sun.

Joseph layes in against the Famine, and
 Thou dost prepare the Bread of Life for thine. 20
He bought with Corn for Pharaoh th'men and Land.
  Thou with thy Bread mak'st such themselves Consign
  Over to thee, that eate it. Joseph makes
  His brethren bow before him. Thine too quake.

Joseph constrains his Brethren till their sins   25
 Do gall their Souls. Repentance babbles fresh.
Thou treatest sinners till Repentance springs
  Then with him sendst a Benjamin like messe.[1]
  Joseph doth Cheare his humble brethren. Thou
  Dost stud with Joy the mourning Saints that bow. 30

Josephs bright shine th'Eleven Tribes must preach.
 And thine Apostles now Eleven, thine.
They beare his presents to his Friends: thine reach
  Thine unto thine, thus now behold a shine.
  How hast thou pensild out, my Lord, most bright 35
  Thy glorious Image here, on Josephs Light.

This I bewaile in me under this shine
 To see so dull a Colour in my Skin.
Lord, lay thy brightsome Colours on me thine.
  Scoure thou my pipes then play thy tunes therein. 40
  I will not hang my Harp in Willows by.
  While thy sweet praise, my Tunes doth glorify.

(1694; 1939)

1. When Joseph feasted his brothers, he gave his favorite, Benjamin, by far
the largest share (Gen. 43:34).

14. MEDITATION. COL. 2.3. IN WHOM ARE HID ALL THE TREASURES OF WISDOM, AND KNOWLEDGE

Halfe Dead: and rotten at the Coare: my Lord!
   I am Consumptive: and my Wasted lungs
Scarce draw a Breath of aire: my Silver Coard[1]
     Is loose. My buckles almost have no tongues.
     My Heart is Fistulate:[2] I am a Shell.   5
     In Guilt and Filth I wallow, Sent and Smell.

Shall not that Wisdom horded up in thee
   (One key whereof is Sacerdotall Types)
Provide a Cure for all this griefe in mee
     And in the Court of Justice save from Stripes,   10
     And purge away all Filth and Guilt, and bring
     A Cure to my Consumption as a King?

Shall not that Wisdom horded in thee (which
   Prophetick Types enucleate) forth shine
With Light enough a Saving Light to fix   15
     On my Poore Taper? And a Flame Divine?
     Making my Soule thy Candle and its Flame
     Thy Light to guide mee, till I Glory gain?

Shall not that Wisdom horded in thee up
   (Which Kingly Types do shine upon in thee)   20
Mee with its Chrystall Cupping Glasses cup
     And draine ill Humours wholy out of mee?
     Ore come my Sin? And mee adorn with Grace
     And fit me for thy Service, and thy Face?

How do these Pointers type thee out most right   25
   As Graces Officine[3] of Wisdom pure

1. Eccles. 12:6.
2. Laced with abnormal tubes connecting abscesses.
3. Laboratory.

The fingers Salves and Medicines so right
    That never faile, when usd, to worke a Cure?
    Oh! that it would my Wasted lungs recrute.
    And make my feeble Spirits upward shute.   30

How Glorious art thou, Lord? Cloathd with the Glory
    Of Prophets, Priests, and Kings? Nay all Types come
To lay their Glory on thee. (Brightsome Story).
    Their Rayes attend thee, as Sun Beams the Sun.
    And shall my Ulcer'd Soule have such reliefe?   35
    Such glorious Cure? Lord strengthen my beliefe.

Why dost not love, my Soule? or Love grow strong?
    These glorious Beams of Wisdom on thee shine.
Will not this Sunshine make thy branch green long,
    And flowrish as it doth to heaven climbe?   40
    Oh! chide thyselfe out of thy Lethargie,
    And unto Christ on Angells wings up fly.

Draw out thy Wisdom, Lord, and make mee just.
    Draw out thy Wisdom. Wisdoms Crown give mee.
With shining Holiness Candy my Crust: 45
    And make mee to thy Scepter bow the knee.
    Let thy rich Grace mee save from Sin, and Death:
    And I will tune thy Praise with holy Breath.

    (1695; 1954)

MEDITATION 44. JOH. 1.14. THE WORD WAS MADE FLESH

The Orator from Rhetorick gardens picks
    His Spangled Flowers of sweet-breathd Eloquence
Wherewith his Oratory brisk he tricks
    Whose Spicy Charms Eare jewells do commence.
    Shall bits of Brains be candid thus for eares?   5
    My Theme claims Sugar Candid far more cleare.

Things styld Transcendent, do transcende the Stile
　　Of Reason, reason's stares neere reach so high.
But Jacob's golden Ladder rounds do foile
　　All reasons Strides, wrought of THEANTHROPIE.[1]　　　10
　　Two Natures distance-standing, infinite,
　　Are Onifide, in person, and Unite.

In Essence two, in Properties each are
　　Unlike, as unlike can be. One All-Might
A Mite the other; One Immortall fair.　　　15
　　One mortall, this all Glory, that all night.
　　One Infinite, One finite. So for ever:
　　Yet ONED are in Person, part'd never.

The Godhead personated in Gods Son
　　Assum'd the Manhood to its Person known,　　　20
When that the Manhoods essence first begun
　　That it did never Humane person own.
　　Each natures Essence e're abides the same.
　　In person joynd, one person each do claim.

Oh! Dignifide Humanity indeed:　　　25
　　Divinely person'd: almost Deifide.
Nameing one Godhead person, in our Creed,
　　The Word-made-Flesh. Here's Grace's 'maizing stride.
　　The vilst design, that villany e're hatcht
　　Hath tap't such Grace in God, that can't be matcht.　　　30

Our Nature spoild: under all Curses groans
　　Is purg'd, tooke, grac'd with grace, united to
A Godhead person, Godhead-person owns
　　Its onely person. Angells, Lord its so.
　　This Union ever lasts, if not relate　　　35
　　Which Cov'nant claims Christs Manhood, separate.

You Holy Angells, Morning-Stars, bright Sparks,
　　Give place: and lower your top gallants. Shew

---

1. The union of divine and human natures in Christ.

Your top-saile Conjues[2] to our slender barkes:
 The highest honour to our nature's due.   40
 Its neerer Godhead by the Godhead made
 Than yours in you that never from God stray'd.

Here is good anchor hold: and argument
 To anchor here, Lord, make my Anchor stronge
And Cable, both of holy geer, out sent   45
 And in this anch'ring dropt and let at length.
 My bark shall safely ride then though there fall
 On't th'strongest tempests hell can raise of all.

Unite my Soule, Lord, to thyselfe, and stamp
 Thy holy print on my unholy heart.   50
I'st nimble be when thou destroyst my cramp
 And take thy paths when thou dost take my part.
 If thou wilt blow this Oaten Straw of mine,
 The sweetest piped praises shall be thine.

  (1701; 1960)

2. Congees; bows.

56. MEDITATION. JOH. 15.24. HAD I NOT DONE AMONGST THEM THE WORKS, THAT NONE OTHER MAN HATH DONE, ETC.

Should I with silver tooles delve through the Hill
 Of Cordilera for rich thoughts, that I
My Lord, might weave with an angelick skill
 A Damask Web of Velvet Verse thereby
 To deck thy Works up, all my Web would run   5
 To rags, and jags: so snicksnarld to the thrum.

Thine are so rich: Within, Without. Refin'd.
 No workes like thine. No Fruits so sweete that grow

On th'trees of righteousness, of Angell kinde
    And Saints, whose limbs reev'd with them bow
        down low.   10
    Should I search ore the Nutmeg Gardens shine
    Its fruits in flourish are but skegs to thine.

The Clove, when in its White'green'd blossoms shoots,
    Some Call the pleasentst sent the World doth show.
None Eye e're saw, nor nose e're smelt such Fruits   15
    My Lord, as thine, Thou Tree of Life in'ts blow.
    Thou Rose of Sharon, Vallies Lilly true
    Thy Fruits most sweet and Glorious ever grew.

Thou art a Tree of Perfect nature trim
    Whose golden lining is of perfect Grace   20
Perfum'de with Deity unto the brim,
    Whose fruits, of the perfection, grow, of Grace.
    Thy Buds, thy Blossoms, and thy fruits adorne
    Thyselfe, and Works, more shining than the morn.

Art, natures Ape, hath many brave things done[1]   25
    As th'Pyramids, the Lake of Meris vast
The Pensile Orchards built in Babylon,

1. In lines 25-36 Taylor reviews human artistic achievements by listing a variety of technical marvels indicative of man's ingenuity from ancient times to nearly contemporary experience. Lake Moeris, an artificial lake in Egypt, and the hanging gardens of Babylon show man's ability to rearrange nature to his advantage, while the Egyptian pyramids, Nero's golden palace, and the Colosseum built by Titus Vespasianus display architectural grandeur rivaling that of natural wonders.

Artistic arrangements of precious metals and jewels also show man's use of natural materials for his pleasure, as in the intricate tableware displayed at Dresden in Saxony. The military machines built by Archimedes to defend Syracuse against Rome and the clock designed by Conrad Dasypodius demonstrate the practical applications of man's technical skill, while the more fanciful or playful examples of mechanical ingenuity are seen in self-propelled artificial birds and insects. Even the infinitesimal metal lock and forty-three-link golden chain easily pulled by a real flea, which were designed by the Elizabethan blacksmith, Mark Scaliot, show the precise craftsmanship artists can achieve, even in useless endeavors. Taylor raises a note of caution, however, about man's imitations of a divine creativity by mentioning the talking head built by Albertus Magnus but destroyed by his pupil, Thomas Aquinas, as a diabolical contrivance.

Psammitich's Labyrinth. (arts Cramping task)
Archimedes his Engins made for war.
Romes Golden House. Titus his Theater.   30

The Clock at Strasburgh, Dresdens Table-Sight
    Regiamonts Fly of Steele about that flew.
Turrian's Wooden Sparrows in a flight.
        And th'Artificiall man Aquinas slew.
        Mark Scaliota's Lock, and Key and Chain   35
        Drawn by a Flea, in our Queen Betties reign.

Might but my pen in natures Inventory
    Its progress make, 't might make such things to jump
All which are but Inventions Vents or glory
        Wits Wantonings, and Fancies frollicks plump   40
        Within whose maws lies buried Times, and Treasures
        Embalmed up in thick dawbd sinfull pleasures.

Nature doth better work than Art: yet thine
    Out vie both works of nature and of Art.
Natures Perfection and the perfect shine   45
        Of Grace attend thy deed in ev'ry part.
        A Thought, a Word, and Worke of thine, will kill
        Sin, Satan, and the Curse: and Law fulfill.

Thou art the Tree of Life in Paradise,
    Whose lively branches are with Clusters hung   50
Of Lovely fruits, and Flowers more sweet than spice
        Bende down to us: and doe out shine the sun,
        Delightfull unto God, doe man rejoyce
        The pleasentst fruits in all Gods Paradise.

Lord feed mine eyes then with thy Doings rare,   55
    And fat my heart with these ripe fruites thou bearst.
Adorn my Life well with thy works, make faire
        My Person with apparrell thou prepar'st.
        My Boughs shall loaded bee with fruits that spring
        Up from thy Works, while to thy praise I sing.   60

    (1703; 1939)

77. MEDITATION. ZECH. 9.11. THE PIT
WHEREIN IS NO WATER

A State, a State, Oh! Dungeon State indeed.
    In which mee headlong, long agoe Sin pitcht:
As dark as Pitch, where Nastiness doth breed:
    And Filth defiles: and I am with it ditcht.
    A Sinfull State: This Pit no Water's in't.   5
    A Bugbare State: as black as any inke.

I once sat singing on the Summit high
    'Mong the Celestiall Coire in Musick Sweet
On highest bough of Paradisall joy,
    Glory and Innocence did in mee meet.   10
    I, as a Gold-Fincht Nighting Gale, tun'd ore
    Melodious Songs 'fore Glorie's Palace Doore.

But on this bough I tuning Pearcht not long:
    Th'Infernall Foe shot out a Shaft from Hell,
A Fiery Dart pilde with Sins poison strong: 15
    That struck my heart, and down I headlong fell.
    And from the Highest Pinicle of Light
    Into this Lowest pit more darke than night.

A Pit indeed of Sin: No water's here:
    Whose bottom's furthest off from Heaven bright,   20
And is next doore to Hell Gate, to it neer:
    And here I dwell in sad and solemn night,
    My Gold-Fincht Angell Feathers dapled in
    Hells Scarlet Dy fat, blood red grown with Sin.

I in this Pit all Destitute of Light   25
    Cram'd full of Horrid Darkness, here do Crawle
Up over head, and Eares, in Nauseous plight:
    And Swinelike Wallow in this mire, and Gall:

No Heavenly Dews nor Holy Waters drill:
Nor Sweet Aire Brieze, nor Comfort here distill.   30

Here for Companions, are Fears, Heart-Achs, Grief
    Frogs, Toads, Newts, Bats, Horrid Hob-Goblins, Ghosts:
Ill Spirits haunt this Pit: and no reliefe:
    Nor Coard can fetch me hence in Creatures Coasts.
    I who once lodgd at Heavens Palace Gate   35
    With full Fledgd Angells, now possess this fate.

But yet, my Lord, thy golden Chain of Grace
    Thou canst let down, and draw mee up into
Thy Holy Aire, and Glory's Happy Place.
    Out from these Hellish damps and pit so low.   40
    And if thy Grace shall do't, My Harp I'le raise,
    Whose Strings toucht by this Grace, Will twang thy
        praise.

    (1707; 1939)

95. MEDITATION. JOH. 14.2. I GO TO PREPARE A PLACE FOR YOU

What shall a Mote up to a Monarch rise?
    An Emmet[1] match an Emperor in might?
If Princes make their personall Exercise
    Betriming mouse holes, painting with delight!
    Or hanging Hornets nests with rich attire   5
    All that pretende to Wisdome would admire.

The Highest Office and Highst Officer
    Expende on lowest intrest in the world
The greatest Cost and wealthiest treasure far
    Twould shew mans wisdom's up in folly furld.   10

    1. Ant.

That Humane Wisdom's hatcht within the nest
Of addle brains which wisdom ne'er possesst.

But blush, poor Soule, at th'thought of such a thought
   Touching my Lord, the King of Kings most bright
As acting thus, for us all over nought,   15
      Worse than poor Ants, or Spider catchers mite
      Who goes away t'prepare's a place most cleare
      Whose Shine o're shines the shining Sunshine here.

Ye Heavens wonder, shall your maker come
   To Crumbs of Clay, bing'd all and drencht in Sin   20
To stop the gap with Graces boughs, defray
      The Cost the Law transgresst, doth on us bring?
      Thy head layst down under the axe on th'block
      That for our Sins did off the same there lop:

But that's not all. Thou now didst sweep Death's Cave   25
   Clean with thy hand: and leavest not a dust
Of Flesh, or Bone that there th'Elect dropt have,
      But bringst out all, new buildst the Fabrick just,
      (Having the Scrowle of Gods Displeasure clear'd)
      Bringst back the Soule putst in its tent new rear'd.   30

But thats not all: Now from Deaths realm, erect,
   Thou gloriously gost to thy Fathers Hall:
And pleadst their Case preparst them place well dect
      All with thy Merits hung. Blesst Mansions all.
      Dost ope the Doore lockt fast 'gainst Sins that so   35
      These Holy Rooms admit them may thereto.

But thats not all. Leaving these dolefull roomes
   Thou com'st and takst them by the hands, Most High,
Dost them translate out from their Death bed toombs,
      To th'rooms prepar'd filld with Eternall joy.   40
      Them Crownst and thronst there, there their lips
         be shall
      Pearld with Eternall Praises that's but all.

Lord Let me bee one of these Crumbs of thine.
 And though Im dust adorn me with thy graces
That though all flect with Sin, thy Grace may shine   45
  As thou Conductst me to these furnisht places.
  Make mee, thy Golden trumpet, sounded bee,
  By thy Good Spirits melody to thee.

  (1710; 1957)

142. MEDITATION. CAN. 6.9. MY DOVE IS ONE THE ONELY ONE OF HER MOTHER THE CHOICE ONE OF HER THAT BARE HER ETC.

What shall I say, my Deare Deare Lord? most Deare
 Of thee! My choisest words when spoke are then
Articulated Breath, soon disappeare.
  If wrote are but the Drivle of my pen
  Beblackt with my inke, soon torn worn out unless 5
  Thy Holy Spirit be their inward Dress.

What, what a Say is this. Thy Spouse doth rise.
 Thy Dove all Undefiled doth excell
All though but one the onely in thine Eyes
  All Queen and Concubines that bear the bell. 10
  Her excellence all excellency far
  Transcends as doth the Sun a pinking Star.

She is the Onely one her mother bore
 Jerusalem ever above esteems
Her for her Darling her choice one therefore   15
  Thou holdst her for the best that ere was seen.
  The Sweetest Flower in all thy Paradise
  And she that bore her Made her hers most Choice.

That power of thine that made the Heavens bow,
 And blush with shining glory ever cleare   20

Hath taken her within his glorious brow
    And made her Madam of his Love most Deare
    Hath Circled her within his glorious arms
    Of Love most rich, her shielding from all harms.

She is thy Dove, thy Undefiled, she shines   25
    In thy rich Righteousness all Lovely, White
The onely Choice one of her Mother, thine
    Most beautifull beloved, thy Delight.
    The Daughters saw and blessed her, the Queens
    And Concubines her praisd and her esteem.   30

Thy Love that fills the Heavens brimfull throughout
    Coms tumbling on her with transcendent bliss
Even as it were in golden pipes that spout
    In Streams from heaven, Oh! what love like this?
    This comes upon her, hugs her in its Arms   35
    And warms her Spirits. Oh! Celestiall Charms.

Make me a member of this Spouse of thine
    I humbly beg deck thus, as Tenis Ball
I shall struck hard on th'ground back bounce with Shine
    Of Praise up to the Chamber floor thy Hall,   40
    Possesses. And at that bright Doore I'l sing
    Thy sweetest praise untill thou'st take me in.

    (1718; 1960)

THREE

Timothy Dwight
(1752-1817)

SEVERAL GENERATIONS after Edward Taylor, Connecticut
Valley Calvinism found another poetic spokesman in Timothy
Dwight, better known for his success as president of Yale but
remembered as well for his literary achievements as one of the
Connecticut Wits, a loosely associated group of young poets
writing around the time of the Revolution. Dwight's verse reflects
a far more complex social experience than Taylor's frontier min-
istry, an emerging nationalism, and the influence of eighteenth-
century theories of reason and social order. But it reveals as well
a continuing emphasis on religious values and a powerful desire
to maintain the New England traditions built up by such settlers
as Bradstreet and Taylor.

By background, training, and vocation, Dwight personified the
tradition his writings defended. His grandfather, Jonathan Edwards
(grandson and successor of Solomon Stoddard), had led the Great
Awakening of the 1740s from his Northampton, Massachusetts,
pulpit, and young Dwight grew up in a Northampton still strongly
influenced by Edwards himself and by the division of rationalistic
Old Light and evangelical New Light Calvinism the Awakening
had precipitated. Timothy's parents encouraged his intellectual
precocity, and family legend recalls how the four-year-old boy
taught neighboring Indian children to read the catechism. The
story, however true, finds the essence of the man within the child:
purposeful, intelligent, conscientious, and inherently a teacher.
All these qualities would manifest themselves later in his writing.

Educated at Yale from 1765-1769, Dwight studied the classical languages, scripture, and mathematics while responding to the incipiently revolutionary fervor which led his classmates to wear Connecticut homespun for their commencement as a symbol of their support for American manufactures. Although the curriculum included no literary study as such and certainly no British literature, Dwight apparently read contemporary English poetry in the college library and shared his pleasure with John Trumbull. Excessive study and an insane dietary regimen brought temporary sickness and a lifelong eye problem, but Dwight graduated from Yale with a reputation for intellectual and moral excellence which led to his appointment, two years later, as a college tutor and master's degree candidate. Returning to Yale, he and Trumbull continued their discovery of eighteenth-century poetry, introduced literary study to the curriculum, and encouraged the poetic aspirations of their undergraduate friends Joel Barlow and David Humphreys, who would eventually be grouped with them as the Connecticut Wits. Dwight's master's *Dissertation on the History, Eloquence, and Poetry of the Bible* (1772) showed his combination of literary and religious interests, as did *The Conquest of Canäan*, which he began early in the 1770s. Married to Mary Woolsey in 1777 and ordained a minister the same year, he was well launched in his career when he left Yale to serve as a military chaplain in Washington's army.

Called back to Northampton in 1778 after his father's death, Dwight supported his mother, wife, twelve brothers and sisters, and his own children by running two farms, serving in the legislature, preaching, and running a private academy. Later, as minister to the prosperous town of Greenfield, Connecticut, he ran another innovative coeducational academy but found more time and stimulus for literary work. He published *The Conquest of Canäan* in 1785, *The Triumph of Infidelity* in 1788, and *Greenfield Hill* in 1794. When he became president of Yale in 1795 on the death of Taylor's grandson, Ezra Stiles, he restricted his literary effort to revision and completion of Barlow's edition of Watts's *Psalms* in 1797 and promulgated his ideas thereafter by teaching, curricular innovations, preaching, articles, letters, and two posthumously published prose works: *Theology* and *Travels in New England and New York*. Intensely active as a champion of New England Calvinism and federalism, he left a greater reputation as an educator and citizen than as a poet at his death in 1817.

A few prevailing beliefs characterized Dwight's writing, in verse as well as prose. The first was his pride in New England and, by extension, the United States insofar as the country reflected the traditions of his home region. He was one of the first to celebrate the northeastern landscape, the White Mountains of New Hampshire and sand dunes of Provincetown, as well as the cultivated fields of the Connecticut Valley. He hailed the Yankee people whose diligence had fructified the rugged land, and he attributed their prosperity (both actual and anticipated) to the beneficent effect of New England institutions: public schools, representative government, equal division of inherited property, and Congregational churches. To these institutions he credited the general level of competence among American citizens and the relatively classless society they had achieved. In his poetry Dwight honored these social forces and the qualities of character they fostered; his verses were meant both to inform outsiders of the golden mean he saw in Connecticut and to caution his American readers to maintain those institutions on which their happiness rested. His vision, while optimistic about America's future, grew steadily more conservative.

Frequently Dwight's concern for New England traditions encouraged a fierce parochialism, a strident defensiveness against countervailing influences, especially those from Europe. He attacked the bad influence of English fashions, on which he blamed tendencies among Americans toward social frippery, ostentatious manners, and immorality. Even more dangerous were the infidel theories emanating from such Englishmen as Hume and Shaftesbury and yet more threatening French thinkers, notably Voltaire. These philosophers, known to him more by reputation than by study, impressed him as threats to Christianity and to social order. The French Revolution, he thought, demonstrated the inevitable tendency of such ideas.[1] He reacted violently against the infidels and their theories and responded almost as angrily to what he found demeaning, patronizing, or false in European writings about

1. Esther E. Brown examines Dwight's response to French experience and compares it with the observations of Jefferson, Adams, Freneau, and Noah Webster in *The French Revolution and the American Man of Letters* (Columbia: The Curators of the University of Missouri, 1951).

America. He tried to defend his country against the menace of foreign ideas while representing its merits to any interested Europeans.

At all times, Timothy Dwight spoke as the champion of New England Congregationalism: the Calvinist faith he had inherited from his Puritan forebears and the high standards of Christian morality based on that faith. His writing, like Taylor's, served as an extension of his ministry, though Dwight's interest was in public affirmation of faith rather than private testing of grace. American Calvinism had changed, gradually but decisively, since Taylor's day, and the Great Awakening had profoundly altered the churches.[2] Dwight's Calvinism, New Light in the Edwardsean tradition, retained many familiar beliefs. Despite Enlightenment theories of the natural goodness of man or of his materialistic moral neutrality, Dwight held to the traditional Puritan view of human depravity and, therefore, of each man's need for the new birth of grace. He continued to believe as well in the providential ordering of history from the creation to the millennium by which progress could be expected, but only through God's direct intervention in human affairs, as in the Incarnation. Like his Puritan forebears, Dwight understood history typologically, interpreting contemporary events and Old Testament episodes as shadows or projections of Christ's redemptive sacrifice, which alone gave meaning to human experience.[3]

In other respects, Dwight's Calvinism diverged from Bradstreet's and Taylor's while remaining orthodox according to the standards of his times. Although he cared deeply about the conversion experience and life of grace, he emphasized Christianity as a force for social improvement rather than personal salvation. His own religious experience, for instance, had no place in his poetry, and the agonizing spiritual introspection of the Puritans cannot be found in it. Interested, instead, in the value of Christian churches

2. Alan Heimert's study, *Religion and the American Mind from the Great Awakening to the Revolution* (Cambridge, Mass.: Harvard University Press, 1966), offers a detailed examination of Old and New Light Calvinism, the changes within each group, and the political implications of religious transition.

3. This aspect of the Puritan imagination is ably investigated in the essays collected by Sacvan Bercovitch in *Typology and Early American Literature* (Amherst: University of Massachusetts Press, 1972).

in promoting social order, he was active in church associations among Connecticut Congregationalists and related groups, worked to unify Congregational and Presbyterian churches, and supported missionary societies spreading Calvinism to the northern and western frontiers. Institutional, socially directed, and moral rather than pious, his was the new Calvinism of postrevolutionary New England.

Dwight's main interest for the modern reader may well be his paradoxical situation as a transitional figure who managed, fairly successfully, to express latently Puritan ideas in the language of the Age of Reason. Both Calvinist and neoclassicist, he represented a position which must have been common in eighteenth-century America but finds little expression in our national literature except for some prose observations of John Adams. His period's emphasis on reason as man's distinctive attribute penetrated Dwight's intellectual method, encouraging his passion for acquiring and publishing facts, his enthusiasm for statistics, his agricultural experiments, and his introduction of chemistry and medicine to the Yale curriculum. Reason also encouraged his preference for "experimental," proven knowledge, however slowly amassed, over theoretical discoveries, however exciting. Like other neoclassicists, Dwight perceived man as essentially a social being, molded by the institutions of his various communities. The pilgrimage of the individual Christian toward God gave way in his writing to the evolution of the Christian community. And his moral emphasis linked him to Addison, Pope, and Johnson, who, like Jonathan Edwards, probed "the nature of true virtue" and the possibility of human happiness through benevolent living.

Influences on Dwight's literary practice show the same Calvinist-neoclassical fusion. His strongest literary influence was, of course, the Bible, followed by Milton. But at Yale he and Trumbull had discovered eighteenth-century English poetry, and his verse alludes to, parodies, and otherwise acknowledges Pope, Goldsmith, Gray, Crabbe, Thomson, Beattie, and many others. His literary friends, the other Connecticut Wits, shared his admiration and helped shape his neoclassical literary habits. The very name "Wits" reflects a concept of poetry considerably at variance with Milton's.

His choice of literary modes further illustrated Dwight's contemporary tastes. He wrote no confessional verse nor personal lyric in the style of Bradstreet and Taylor, nor did he write prayers except for a graduation hymn and his revision of Watts's *Psalms*. Rather, he attempted to compose in the grandest neoclassical style, starting with an epic, *The Conquest of Canäan,* and then settling for the more manageable mock-epic in *The Triumph of Infidelity.* *Greenfield Hill* showed his familiarity with the conventions of topographical poetry in eighteenth-century England, and he experimented in "America" (1771) and in parts of *The Conquest* and *Greenfield Hill* with the popular New World genre, "the-rising-glory-of-America" prophetic poem. His forms, though varied, tended toward heroic couplets, octosyllabic couplets, and blank verse.

A distinctively neoclassical quality of Dwight's verse was his sense of audience. His rhetoric always directed itself to his readers: not self, friend, or God as with the Puritan poets, but a generalized group of reasonable Christians linked to the author by a presumed sympathy in tastes and values. Such an audience could share his indignation in the satires and his sentiments in the more reflective poems. These readers could be expected to appreciate the simple dignity of Joshua's manners and the rude wisdom of a Yankee farmer.

Dwight's major poems clearly illustrate his concepts of poetry and his relationship to his craft. With characteristic ambition, he began his career with *The Conquest of Canäan,* a biblical epic in the Miltonic manner, though written in heroic couplets. The metric pattern, chosen to provide dignity and to charm the reader's ear, failed to achieve his purposes; it burdened his presentation with a jog-trot meter and forced him to link his verses with repetitious and generally unimaginative rhymes. His art suffered also from the mechanical psychological and rhetorical theories he borrowed from Lord Kames. To gain an effect of sublimity, he depended on imagery of mountains and storms; to sustain the reader's interest, he developed his narrative through a succession of particular scenes, with little overview of the total design. There were personal complications as well, particularly the love story of Irad and Selima, which he introduced in reference to his own recent courtship although it had no biblical precedent or literary justification. Writing and revising the epic over a period of almost fifteen years, he violated the original unity of his plan by including references to the American Revolution. Although Dwight rejected his critics' assumption that Joshua's conquest allegorized the War for Independence, he certainly emphasized the parallels within the poem and in his dedication of the work to General Washington. Imbued as he was with New England traditions, he must have seen the Israelites as types of Americans, and he certainly expected God's plan for salvation history to culminate in the New World. His epic, though flawed in many respects, demonstrated a variety of strengths: descriptive power, skill in characterization, and craftsmanship in developing small narrative units. Parts still show narrative ability, though the total effect of the epic is profoundly boring. Dwight probably should have avoided epic writing as unsuited to his talents, his audience, and his beliefs. A heroic military poem proved uncongenial to one with his intense antipathy to war.

The shorter compass and satiric tone of *The Triumph of Infidelity* allowed Dwight to make better use of his talents, though the mock-epic also betrayed a problem of design. The basic intention was to attack Old Light Calvinist heresies in America, specifically Charles Chauncy's theory of universal salvation, by introducing Satan as the narrator of a "progress" poem surveying the history of infidelity from paganism, through medieval Catholicism, to European Rationalism as promulgated by Hume and Voltaire (to whom the poem was sarcastically dedicated), and finally to America itself—hitherto protected by its orthodoxy from Satan's machinations. When the friends of immorality finally gathered in America, Satan observed the sinners encouraged in vice by the theoretical absence of Hell but ended the poem in dismay when Chauncy's theories captivated "not one friend of virtue." Dwight encountered problems trying to control his anger, trying to sustain Satan's point of view (would the Devil, for instance, be likely to salute Jonathan Edwards as "That moral Newton, and that second Paul"?), and trying to ignore the disproportion between Chauncy's theory and the grander infidelities of Europe. The modern reader finds difficulty as well in coping with the dated, provincial materials, better suited to pamphlet controversy than poetry.

Nevertheless, *The Triumph* has many merits. Dwight's satiric

portraits of American sinners remain amusing, particularly his
assaults on those arch-enemies of evangelical Calvinism the hypo-
crite and the smooth divine. His powerful ironic sense of the
divergence of appearance from reality, the ideal from the actual,
evoked memorable satiric passages, like this survey of Hume's
philosophy:

> All things roll on, by fix'd eternal laws;
> Yet no effect depends upon a cause:
> Hence every law was made by Chance divine,
> Parent most fit of order, and design!
> Earth was not made, but happen'd: Yet, on earth,
> All beings happen, by most stated birth;
> Each thing miraculous; yet strange to tell,
> Not God himself can shew a miracle.[4]

The same ironic perception helped him play off the four units
of his heroic couplets in clever, startling ways. Commenting on
the too-tolerant rationalist, for example, that "With him all *natural*
desires are good; / His thirst for stews; the Mohawk's thirst for
blood," he let the first three units proceed harmoniously before
shocking the reader into sense when the apparent balance and
actual incongruity of the fourth deflected attention to the ironic
meaning of "natural" in the basic premise and the dual implication
of "stews." So too, Dwight used the couplet in typical neoclassical
style for purposes of succinct, memorable definition when saluting
"Man, that illustrious brute of noblest shape, / A swine unbristled,
and an untail'd ape" to show that a purely materialistic philosophy
could distinguish man from the animals only by his physical
limitations. Man's sensual destiny as "The oyster's church-yard,
and the capon's tomb" then redirected attention to the escha-
tological concerns of orthodox religion.

No such problems of design and tone flawed his most successful
extended poem, *Greenfield Hill.* Although this topographical work
celebrating his home parish in Connecticut was originally planned
to imitate a different English poet in each of its seven sections,

4. "The Triumph of Infidelity," *The Major Poems of Timothy Dwight,* ed.
William J. McTaggart and William K. Bottorff (Gainesville, Fla.: Scholars' Facsim-
iles & Reprints, 1969), p. 343.

Dwight broke free from the restraints of exact imitation and simply wrote each part in an appropriate style reminiscent of British verse. "The Prospect" surveys the landscape in the style of Thomson's *Seasons;* "The Flourishing Village" then offers the Connecticut town as an answer to the socioeconomic problems presented in Goldsmith's "Deserted Village" (1770); the octosyllabic couplets of the third part condemn the British burning of neighboring Fairfield in the Revolution; Spenserian stanzas relate the historic tragedy of "The Destruction of the Pequods"; the minister and farmer advise the villagers in the differently cadenced octosyllabic couplets of parts five and six; and the poem ends with a prophecy of future glory, offered in appropriately noble heroic couplets.

Variety of form in *Greenfield Hill* suited the variety of topics and reflected as well Dwight's shifting sense of audience. Sometimes he addressed British readers likely to underestimate New England; at other times he addressed his Yankee neighbors, prone to betray its traditions or fail its promises. He praised America's beauty, its social opportunities, its supportive institutions, but he attacked savagely its moral failures, most notably slavery—that "spot of hell, deep smirch'd on human kind, / The uncur'd gangrene of the reasoning mind." Sin marred even the early history of Connecticut, and Dwight's reflection on the Pequod War showed him torn between pride in the courage of Puritans like Mason and Stoughton and sympathy for the Indian society obliterated by war. Significantly, he voiced the praise of the Puritan soldiers through the persona of the grandmother, whose childhood recollections would allow for less moral ambivalence than might his own narration.

As president of Yale, Dwight pretty much stopped writing poetry (except for a long work completed on his deathbed but since lost), so his work may be seen more as apprenticeship than mature performance. Probably he gave up literature mainly because he cared more about what he had to say than how to say it and because his ideas could reach an audience more directly in the classroom, pulpit, or periodical press. His ironic vision and his insight into character, two distinctive merits of his verse, could carry over effectively into prose; only his metrical facility went without further application.

Dwight's abandonment of poetry, like that of most other Connecticut Wits (Barlow excepted), reflects the limitations of American culture in his time as well as his own changing interests. A growing country, faced with the crises of independence, called on its citizens to exert their practical rather than their creative talents—in fact made no distinction between them. When John Adams wrote that American constitutions were contrived, not by divine inspiration, but by the same "use of reason and the senses" to which he attributed other American achievements, he specifically linked Dwight's and Barlow's poetry with Godfrey's quadrant, Franklin's electrical experiments, and Boylston's inoculation as products simply of reason and hard work.[5] With opportunities for public service and economic advancement, young men ignored the arts, and Dwight observed once that he knew no American willing to live in a garret for the sake of poetry. There were few native models of artistic achievement and inadequate teaching and criticism. A mechanical theory of composition by which poems could supposedly be written in conformity to specific rhetorical rules encouraged aspiring authors to venture beyond their abilities and court disaster.[6] The problem of audience also loomed large in a period when poetry was viewed as a public persuasive art, allied to oratory, rather than as personal imaginative expression. Americans read poetry, much of it newspaper satire, but took little interest in national epics or other serious writing beyond the satisfaction of knowing that such things could be written in the United States and, in fact, had been.

For Dwight, there were additional problems. The eye ailment that began in his undergraduate days forced him to compose verses in his head, memorize long chunks of a poem for eventual dictation, and forego close editorial revision. His ambition also created difficulties; having aspired too soon to the heights of epic poetry, he was humiliated by the lukewarm response to his efforts. He might have overcome these obstacles had he possessed creative

5. "Defense of the American Constitutions," *The Political Writings of John Adams: Representative Selections* (New York: The Liberal Arts Press, 1954), p. 117.

6. George Bigelow explores the effect of rhetorical theory on eighteenth-century American poetic practice in *Rhetoric and American Poetry of the Early National Period*, University of Florida Monographs, Humanities no. 4 (Gainesville: University of Florida Press, 1960).

imagination in proportion to his ambition; instead he had talent, a message, and a boundless capacity for hard work—better qualities in a teacher than an artist. But as a forceful writer with frequently impressive insights, as a transitional figure in the change from a Calvinistic to a scientific world order, and as an example of the artist searching out a place in the new American republic, he deserves the attention of modern readers and retains a significant, if minor, place in our literary heritage.

BIBLIOGRAPHIC NOTE

No complete edition of Dwight's poetry is now in print, but several books offer access to the major works. *The Major Poems of Timothy Dwight*, ed. William J. McTaggart and William K. Bottorff (Gainesville, Fla.: Scholars' Facsimiles & Reprints, 1969), includes "America," *The Conquest of Canäan, The Triumph of Infidelity, Greenfield Hill*, and his *Dissertation on the History, Eloquence, and Poetry of the Bible*. Vernon L. Parrington's anthology, *The Connecticut Wits* (New York: Thomas Y. Crowell Co., 1925), reprinted in 1969 with a foreword by Kenneth Silverman, includes Book VIII of *The Conquest of Canäan*, parts of *Greenfield Hill*, and complete texts of *The Triumph of Infidelity* and several shorter poems. There is also a facsimile of the 1788 edition of *The Conquest of Canäan* (Westport, Conn.: Greenwood Press, 1970).

The only extended biography is Charles E. Cunningham's study, *Timothy Dwight 1752-1817: A Biography* (New York: The Macmillan Co., 1942). Further information about Dwight and critical perspective on his work may be found in Kenneth Silverman's *Timothy Dwight*, Twayne's United States Authors Series (New York: Twayne Publishers, 1969), and in the introduction to Barbara Miller Solomon's edition of Dwight's *Travels in New England and New York*, The John Harvard Library, vol. 1, pp. ix-xlvii (Cambridge, Mass.: Belknap Press of Harvard University Press, 1969).

The best examination of Dwight's literary circle is still Leon Howard's book, *The Connecticut Wits* (Chicago: University of Chicago Press, 1943). Other works providing useful insight into the poet's literary environment include Kenneth Silverman's survey, *A Cultural History of the American Revolution* (New York: Thomas Y. Crowell Co., 1976), and Lewis P. Simpson's anthology,

The Federalist Literary Mind: Selections from the Monthly Anthology and Boston Review, 1803-1811 (Baton Rouge: Louisiana State University Press, 1962).

THE TEXT

Dwight's poems are arranged chronologically in this edition, according to dates of publication. His habit of holding work for years and occasionally revising it before publishing, however, prevents accurate dating by composition. *The Conquest of Canä-an,* for instance, was started in 1771 but did not appear until 1785. I have based the text of this anthology on the facsimile reproduction of *The Major Poems of Timothy Dwight,* ed. William J. McTaggart and William K. Bottorff (Gainesville, Fla.: Scholars' Facsimiles & Reprints, 1969), modifying the original edition only to add closing quotation marks where they have been omitted. Archaic and sometimes inconsistent spellings have been retained, along with the confusing punctuation of the facsimile because it is impossible to distinguish accurately between the poet's intentions and his printers' errors. As Dwight's limited eyesight forced him to memorize and dictate his poems, there is no reason to suppose that he proofread manuscripts or even books attentively. Luckily, the questions which arise about Dwight's style, particularly about the relationship between syntax and punctuation, seldom obscure his meaning; and confusion can generally be resolved by reading disputed passages aloud—following the sense with the ear rather than the eye.

From *The Conquest of Canäan* (Book VI)[1]

    In scenes of distant death bold Hezron stands,
Dies his blue arms, and pains his aged hands;
Full many a chief his veteran falchion crowns,

1. This excerpt presents part of the Battle of Ai, transposed by Dwight to precede the Battle of Gibeon for dramatic effect. It illustrates his tendency to present fighting in terms of particularized man-to-man combats in the style of

Thick flit the shades, and blood the verdure drowns.
Impetuous Carmi springs the chief to meet,   425
Conscious of youth, and light with nimble feet;
His arm all active strews the sanguine ground,
Wakes the deep groan, and deals the frequent wound:
Full on his angry sword the warriors rush,
Impel th' upright, the falling heedless crush: 430
No chief the fury of his arm withstands,
And ruin widens o'er bold Hezron's bands.
Amaz'd, the hero saw the deluge spread,
And wide, and wider rise the piles of dead,
Flight first commence in hosts that own his sway,   435
And proud Ai hail a second conquering day:
From his sad bosom heav'd a heavy groan;
Round the whole war he miss'd his favourite son:
Untaught to droop, he hopes congenial fire
May yet ward shame, and yet the troops inspire.—   440
Where now, he cries, are fled the boasts of morn?
The towering stalk? the brow of lifted scorn?
Then Judah's warriors promis'd deeds of fame,
Hiss'd impious flight, and spurn'd the dastard's shame.
Far other scenes now rend these hapless eyes;   445
The foe advances, and the boaster flies;
Broke but by fear, ye wing inglorious flight,
Giants in words, and maidens in the fight;
Oh had kind Heaven dispens'd a speedier doom,
And this frail form in Bashan[2] found a tomb!   450
Then had these palsied limbs, in peace repos'd;
Unpain'd with shame, these eyes in triumph clos'd;

Homer, his emphasis on nobility of character (or lack thereof) in both Israelite
and Canaanite characters, and his sensitivity to the horrors of war. Dwight's
preference for parallel narrative structure and his habit of linking American with
biblical history are also apparent.

In this scene, the romantic hero, Irad, first attempts armed combat, despite
the hesitation of his generous but protective father, Hezron. Joshua's forces are
hard-pressed by their enemies.

2. Kingdom conquered by Moses and seen by him as a promise of Joshua's
conquests in his passage to Canaan (Deut. 3).

134 Timothy Dwight

Pleas'd to the last, survey'd my favourite race,
View'd no base flight, and bled for no disgrace.—
Hence, hence, ye timorous souls, to Joshua fly,   455
And tell the Chief, ye saw your leader die.
    The hero spoke; and urg'd by passion's force,
On furious Carmi bent his aged course;
Awful in gleam of arms, the chiefs appear,
Here the bold youth, the white-hair'd hero there: 460
But ere his sword great Hezron could extend,
Or circling bands their ancient chief defend,
A long, bright lance his wary foe beheld,
And snatch'd it glittering on the bloody field;
Swift through the hero's side he forc'd the steel;   465
Pierc'd to the heart, the aged warrior fell;
There lay, a corse, bespread with purple stains,
The form, that triumph'd on a hundred plains.
    On Ridgefield's[3] hills, to shame to virtue dead,
Thus dastard bands the foe inglorious fled;   470
When Wooster[4] singly brav'd the deathful ground,
Fir'd hosts in vain, and met the fatal wound.
In dangers born, to arms in childhood train'd,
From Gallia's heroes many a palm he gain'd;
With freedom's sacred flame serenely glow'd   475
For justice arm'd, and sought the field for GOD;
With steady zeal his nation's interest lov'd;
(No terror touch'd him, and no injury mov'd)
Far in the front, with dauntless bosom bled,
And crown'd the honours of his hoary head.   480
    Bent o'er his foe, the lovely Carmi stood,
And view'd, with tears of grief, his bursting blood;
And thus—Unhappy sire, he sadly cried—
Perhaps thy monarch's joy, thy nation's pride.—
How like my father's bends thy hoary brow?   485

3. Ridgefield, Connecticut, scene of revolutionary battle, April 27, 1777, after
the Battle of Danbury.
4. David Wooster, a Yale graduate and Continental Army officer, killed at
the Battle of Danbury.

His limbs, his countenance, and his locks of snow,
All in thy venerable face I see—
Perhaps the parent of a son like me—
    He spoke; and fiercely wheel'd his bloody sword,
Sprang to the fight, and many a hero gor'd;   490
His voice, his eyes the joyful host inspire,
And through the sweetness flames a dreadful fire.
Active as light, o'er trembling ranks he hung;
Shouts shook the plains, the frighted forests rung:
Unnumber'd sullen groans were heard around;   495
Unnumber'd corses cloath'd the purple ground:
From post to post retir'd pale Judah's train,
And chief on chief increas'd the piles of slain.
Dark as an evening cloud, bold Ai was driven,
Gloom'd all the fields, and cast a shade on heaven;   500
Wide roll'd the storm; wide drove the dust along,
And ruin hover'd o'er the flying throng.
    Meantime, brave Irad turn'd his sparkling eyes,
And saw in distant fields the clouds arise;
Sad flight and terror fill'd the backward plain,   505
And the foe shouted o'er his kindred slain.
As, when autumnal clouds the skies deform,
Bursts the wild whirlwind from the gloomy storm;
Hoarse crash the pines; oaks stiffly stubborn fall,
And sudden thunders listening swains appall: 510
So, wing'd by Heaven, impetuous Irad flew;
As swift their darling chief the youths pursue;
Whelm'd in their path, the falling bands expire,
And crowds of warriors from their steps retire.
    Now, where brave Carmi swept the purple ground,   515
Terrific Irad shook his buckler's round;
Alike in years they seem'd, alike in arms,
Of equal stature, and of rival charms:
Nor this, nor that, the dangerous fight can yield;
But each demands the empire of the field.   520
From the fierce chiefs the wondering bands retreat;
Blows following blows their sounding shields repeat;

Uncleft, each faithful orb the stroke rebounds,
Blunts the keen blade, and intercepts the wounds:
'Till Irad's nimble arm, with sudden wheel,   525
Through Carmi's side impels the fatal steel,
Pure streams of crimson stain the subject ground,
And the freed soul pervades the gaping wound.
   Not that fair pride, that soul-supporting flame,
That lights the splendors of th' immortal name;   530
Not all the bravery nature can impart,
Nor the fond wishes of a virgin's heart,
Nor parents' vows, nor nations' prayers could save
The young, bright hero from an early grave.
He fell, with beauty's fairest beams adorn'd,   535
While foes admir'd him, and while Irad mourn'd.
Ah youth, too soon allotted to the tomb,
Oh had kind Heaven dispens'd a softer doom,
On thy fair deeds a sweet reward bestow'd,
And op'd the mansions of the bless'd abode!   540
   Thus, where sad Charlestown[5] lifts her hills on high,
Where once gay structures charm'd the morning sky,
Ere Howe's[6] barbarian hand in savage fire
Wrapp'd the tall dome, and whelm'd the sacred spire,
In life's fair prime, and new to war's alarms,   545
Brave Warren[7] sunk, in all the pride of arms.
With me, each generous mind the hour recall,
When pale Columbia mourn'd her favourite's fall;
Mourn'd the bright statesman, hero, patriot, fled,
The friend extinguish'd, and the genius dead;   550
While he, the darling of the wise, and good,
Seal'd his firm truth, and built his name in blood.

     (1771–1785; 1785)

5. Charlestown, Massachusetts, scene of the Battle of Bunker Hill, June 17, 1775.
  6. Sir William Howe, commander of the king's forces in Boston, 1775-1776.
  7. Dr. Joseph Warren, Massachusetts patriot, killed at Bunker Hill.

Couplets

From *The Triumph of Infidelity*[1]

Milton

THE GATHERING

And now the morn arose; when o'er the plain
Gather'd, from every side, a numerous train;
To quell those fears, that rankled still within,
And gain new strength, and confidence, to sin.
There the half putrid Epicure was seen,   5
His cheeks of port, and lips with turtle green,
Who hop'd a long eternity was given,
To spread good tables, in some eating heaven.
The leacher there his lurid visage shew'd,
The imp of darkness, and the foe of good;   10
Who fled his lovely wife's most pure embrace,
To sate on hags, and breed a mongrel race;
A high-fed horse, for others wives who neigh'd;
A cur, who prowl'd around each quiet bed;
A snake, far spreading his impoison'd breath,   15
And charming innocence to guilt, and death.
Here stood Hypocrisy, in sober brown,
His sabbath face all sorrow'd with a frown.
A dismal tale he told of dismal times,
And this sad world brimful of saddest crimes,   20
Furrow'd his cheeks with tears for others sin,
But clos'd his eyelids on the hell within.
There smil'd the smooth Divine, unus'd to wound
The sinners heart, with hell's alarming sound.
No terrors on his gentle tongue attend;   25
No grating truths the nicest ear offend.
That strange new-birth, that methodistic grace,

emphasis on marriage and fidelity

1. This excerpt introduces the climactic scene when Satan gathers and surveys
those followers won to him by the hope of universal salvation. He attracts a
flock of sensualists, rationalists, and lax Christians, but not one "friend of virtue"
is deceived.

anti-methodism

Nor in his heart, nor sermons, found a place.
Plato's fine tales he clumsily retold,
Trite, fireside, moral seasaws, dull as old;   30
His Christ, and bible, plac'd at good remove,
Guilt hell-deserving, and forgiving love.
'Twas best, he said, mankind should cease to sin;
Good fame requir'd it; so did peace within:
Their honours, well he knew, would ne'er be driven;   35
But hop'd they still would please to go to heaven.
Each week, he paid his visitation dues;
Coax'd, jested, laugh'd; rehears'd the private news;
Smoak'd with each goody, thought her cheese excell'd;
Her pipe he lighted, and her baby held.   40
Or plac'd in some great town, with lacquer'd shoes,
Trim wig, and trimmer gown, and glistening hose,   *hierarchy*
He bow'd, talk'd politics, learn'd manners mild;
Most meekly questioned, and most smoothly smil'd;
At rich mens jests laugh'd loud their stories prais'd;   45
Their wives new patterns gaz'd, and gaz'd, and gaz'd;
Most daintily on pamper'd turkies din'd;
Nor shrunk with fasting, nor with study pin'd:
Yet from their churches saw his brethren driven,
Who thunder'd truth, and spoke the voice of heaven,   50
Chill'd trembling guilt, in Satan's headlong path,
Charm'd the feet back, and rous'd the ear of death.
"Let fools," he cried, "starve on, while prudent I
Snug in my nest shall live, and snug shall die."
    There stood the infidel of modern breed,   55
Blest vegetation of infernal seed,
Alike no Deist, and no Christian, he;   *Religion of*
But from all principle, all virtue, free.   *nature*
To him all things the same, as good or evil;
Jehovah, Jove, the Lama, or the Devil;   60
Mohammed's braying, or Isaiah's lays;
The Indian's powaws, or the Christian's praise.
With him all *natural* desires are good;
His thirst for stews; the Mohawk's thirst for blood:
Made, not to know, or love, the all beauteous mind;   65

Or wing thro' heaven his path to bliss refin'd:
But his dear self, choice Dagon!² to adore;
To dress, to game, to swear, to drink, to whore;
To race his steeds; or cheat, when others run;
Pit tortur'd cocks, and swear 'tis glorious fun: 70
His soul not cloath'd with attributes divine;
But a nice watch-spring to that grand machine,
That work more nice than Rittenhouse³ can plan,
The body; man's chief part; himself, the man;
Man, that illustrious brute of noblest shape,   75
A swine unbristled, and an untail'd ape:
To couple, eat, and die—his glorious doom—
The oyster's church-yard, and the capon's tomb.

      (1788?; 1788)

2. Philistine god.
3. David Rittenhouse, American astronomer and mathematician, especially
noted for his planetarium.

Blank Verse

From *Greenfield Hill*

PART I: THE PROSPECT

FROM southern isles, on winds of gentlest wing,
Sprinkled with morning dew, and rob'd in green,
Life in her eye, and music in her voice,
Lo Spring returns, and wakes the world to joy!
Forth creep the smiling herbs; expand the flowers;   5
New-loos'd, and bursting from their icy bonds,
The streams fresh-warble, and through every mead
Convey reviving verdure; every bough,
Full-blown and lovely, teems with sweets and songs;
And hills, and plains, and pastures feel the prime.   10

    As round me here I gaze, what prospects rise?

Search for American Dream

England

Etherial! matchless! such as Albion's sons,
Could Albion's isle an equal prospect boast,
In all the harmony of numerous song,
Had tun'd to rapture, and o'er Cooper's hill,[1]
And Windsor's beauteous forest,[2] high uprais'd,   15
And sent on fame's light wing to every clime.
Far inland, blended groves, and azure hills,
Skirting the broad horizon, lift their pride.
Beyond, a little chasm to view unfolds
Cerulean mountains, verging high on Heaven,   20
In misty grandeur. Stretch'd in nearer view,
Unnumber'd farms salute the cheerful eye;
Contracted there to little gardens; here outspread
Spacious, with pastures, fields, and meadows rich;   25
Where the young wheat it's glowing green displays,
Or the dark soil bespeaks the recent plough,
Or flocks and herds along the lawn disport.

    Fair is the landscape; but a fairer still
Shall soon inchant the soul—when harvest full   30
Waves wide its bending wealth. Delightful task!
To trace along the rich, enamell'd ground,
The sweetly varied hues; from India's corn,
Whose black'ning verdure bodes a bounteous crop,
Through lighter grass, and lighter still the flax,   35
The paler oats, the yellowish barley, wheat
In golden glow, and rye in brighter gold.
These soon the sight shall bless. Now other scenes
The heart dilate, where round, in rural pride
The village spreads its tidy, snug retreats,   40
That speak the industry of every hand.

    How bless'd the sight of such a numerous train
In such small limits, tasting every good
Of competence, of independence, peace,
And liberty unmingled; every house   45

1. Subject of a topographical poem by Sir John Denham.
2. Reference to "Windsor Forest," a topographical poem by Alexander Pope.

On its own ground, and every happy swain
Beholding no superior, but the laws,
And such as virtue, knowledge, useful life,
And zeal, exerted for the public good,
Have rais'd above the throng. For here, in truth,   50
Not in pretence, man is esteem'd as man.
Not here how rich, of what peculiar blood,
Or office high; but of what genuine worth,
What talents bright and useful, what good deeds,
What piety to God, what love to man,   55
The question is. To this an answer fair
The general heart secures. Full many a rich,
Vile knave, full many a blockhead, proud
Of ancient blood, these eyes have seen float down
Life's dirty kennel, trampled in the mud,   60
Stepp'd o'er unheeded, or push'd rudely on;
While Merit, rising from her humble skiff
To barks of nobler, and still nobler size,
Sail'd down the expanding stream, in triumph gay,
By every ship saluted.   65

                    Hail, O hail
My much-lov'd native land! New Albion hail!
The happiest realm, that, round his circling course,
The all-searching sun beholds. What though the breath
Of Zembla's winter shuts thy lucid streams,   70
And hardens into brass thy generous soil;
Though, with one white, and cheerless robe, thy hills,
Invested, rise a long and joyless waste;
Leafless the grove, and dumb the lonely spray,
And every pasture mute: What though with clear   75
And fervid blaze, thy summer rolls his car,
And drives the languid herd, and fainting flock
To seek the shrouding umbrage of the dale;
While Man, relax'd and feeble, anxious waits
The dewy eve, to slake his thirsty frame: 80
What though thy surface, rocky, rough, and rude,
Scoop'd into vales, or heav'd in lofty hills,

Or cloud-embosom'd mountains, dares the plough,
And threatens toil intense to every swain:
What though foul Calumny, with voice malign,   85
Thy generous sons, with every virtue grac'd,
Accus'd of every crime, and still rolls down
The kennell'd stream of impudent abuse:
Yet to high HEAVEN my ardent praises rise,
That in thy lightsome vales he gave me birth,   90
All-gracious, and allows me still to live.

    Cold is thy clime, but every western blast
Brings health, and life, and vigour on his wings;
Innerves the steely frame, and firms the soul
With strength and hardihood; wakes each bold   95
And manly purpose; bears above the ills,
That stretch, upon the rack, the languid heart
Of summer's maiden sons, in pleasure's lap,
Dandled to dull respose. Exertion strong
Marks their whole life. Mountains before them sink   100
To mole-hills; oceans bar their course in vain.
Thro' the keen wintry wind they breast their way,
Or summer's fiercest flame. Dread dangers rouse
Their hearts to pleasing conflict; toils and woes,
Quicken their ardour: while, in milder climes,   105
Their peers effeminate they see, with scorn
On lazy plains, dissolv'd in putrid sloth,
And struggling hard for being. Thy rough soil
Tempts hardy labour, with his sturdy team,
To turn, with sinewy hand, the stony glebe,   110
And call forth every comfort from the mould,
Unpromising, but kind. Thy houses, barns,
Thy granaries, and thy cellars, hence are stor'd
With all the sweets of life: while, thro' thy realm,
A native beggar rarely pains the sight.   115

    Thy summer glows with heat; but choicest fruits
Hence purple in the sun; hence sparkling flowers
Gem the rich landschape; double harvests hence

Load the full fields: pale Famine scowls aloof,
And Plenty wantons round thy varied year.   120

    Rough is thy surface; but each landschape bright,
With all of beauty, all of grandeur dress'd,
Of mountains, hills, and sweetly winding vales,
Of forests, groves, and lawns, and meadows green,
And waters, varied by the plastic hand,   125
Through all their fairy splendour, ceaseless charms,
Poetic eyes. Springs bubbling round the year,
Gay-wand'ring brooks, wells at the surface full,
Yield life, and health, and joy, to every house,
And every vivid field. Rivers, with foamy course,   130
Pour o'er the ragged cliff the white cascade,
And roll unnumber'd mills; or, like the Nile,
Fatten the beauteous interval; or bear
The sails of commerce through the laughing groves.

    With wisdom, virtue, and the generous love   135
Of learning, fraught, and freedom's living flame,
Electric, unextinguishable, fir'd,
Our Sires established, in thy cheerful bounds,
The noblest institutions, man has seen,
Since time his reign began. In little farms   140
They measur'd all thy realms, to every child
In equal shares descending; no entail
The first-born lifting into bloated pomp,
Tainting with lust, and sloth, and pride, and rage,
The world around him: all the race beside,   145
Like brood of ostrich, left for chance to rear,
And every foot to trample. Reason's sway
Elective, founded on the rock of truth,
Wisdom their guide, and equal good their end,
They built with strength, that mocks the battering storm,   150
And spurns the mining flood; and every right
Dispens'd alike to all. Beneath their eye,
And forming hand, in every hamlet, rose
The nurturing school; in every village, smil'd

The heav'n-inviting church, and every town   155
A world within itself, with order, peace,
And harmony, adjusted all its weal.

    Hence every swain, free, happy, his own lord,
With useful knowledge fraught, of business, laws,
Morals, religion, life, unaw'd by man,   160
And doing all, but ill, his heart can wish,
Looks round, and finds strange happiness his own;
And sees that happiness on laws depend.
On this heav'n-laid foundation rests thy sway;
On knowledge to discern, and sense to feel,   165
That free-born rule is life's perennial spring
Of real good. On this alone it rests.
For, could thy sons a full conviction feel,
That government was noxious, without arms,
Without intrigues, without a civil broil,   170
As torrents sweep the sand-built structure down,
A vote would wipe it's very trace away.
Hence too each breast is steel'd for bold defence;
For each has much to lose. Chosen by all,
The messenger of peace, by all belov'd,   175
Spreads, hence, the truth and virtue, he commands.
Hence manners mild, and sweet, their peaceful sway
Widely extend. Refinement of the heart
Illumes the general mass. Even those rude hills,
Those deep embow'ring woods, in other lands   180
Prowl'd round by savages, the same soft scenes,
Mild manners, order, virtue, peace, disclose;
The howling forest polish'd as the plain.

    From earliest years, the same enlightened soul
Founded bright schools of science. Here the mind   185
Learn'd to expand it's wing, and stretch it's flight
Through truth's broad fields. Divines, and lawyers, hence,
Physicians, statesmen, all with wisdom fraught,
And learning, suited to the use of life,
And minds, by business, sharpen'd into sense,   190

Sagacious of the duty, and the weal,
Of man, spring numberless; and knowledge hence
Pours it's salubrious streams, through all the spheres
Of human life. Its bounds, and generous scope,
Hence Education opens, spreading far   195
Through the bold yeomanry, that fill thy climes,
Views more expanded, generous, just, refin'd,
Than other nations know. In other lands,
The mass of man, scarce rais'd above the brutes,
Drags dull the horsemill round of sluggish life: 200
Nought known, beyond their daily toil; all else
By ignorance' dark curtain hid from sight.
Here, glorious contrast! every mind, inspir'd
With active inquisition, restless wings
Its flight to every flower, and, settling, drinks   205
Largely the sweets of knowledge.

                        Candour, say,
Is this a state of life, thy honest tongue
Could blacken? These a race of men, thy page
Could hand to infamy? The shameful task   210
Thy foes at first began, and still thy foes,
Laborious, weave the web of lies. 'Tis hence
The generous traveller round him looks, amaz'd,
And wonders at our unexpected bliss.

    But chief, Connecticut! on thy fair breast   215
These splendours glow. A rich improvement smiles
Around thy lovely borders; in thy fields
And all that in thy fields delighted dwell.
Here that pure, golden mean, so oft of yore
By sages wish'd, and prais'd, by Agur's[3] voice   220
Implor'd, while God th' approving sanction gave
Of wisdom infinite; that golden mean,
Shines unalloy'd; and here the extended good,
That mean alone secures, is ceaseless found.

    3. Biblical prophet, who prayed for a condition neither of vanity nor riches
but of simple sufficiency (Prov. 30:7-9).

Oh, would some faithful, wise, laborious mind,   225
Develope all thy springs of bliss to man;
Soon would politic visions fleet away,
Before awakening truth! Utopias then,
Ancient and new, high fraught with fairy good,
Would catch no more the heart. Philosophy   230
Would bow to common-sense; and man, from facts,
And real life, politic wisdom learn.

Ah then, thou favour'd land, thyself revere!
Look not to Europe, for examples just
Of order, manners, customs, doctrines, laws,   235
Of happiness, or virtue. Cast around
The eye of searching reason, and declare
What Europe proffers, but a patchwork sway;
The garment Gothic, worn to fritter'd shreds,
And eked from every loom of following times.   240
Such as his sway, the system shows entire,
Of silly pomp, and meanness train'd t' adore;
Of wealth enormous, and enormous want;
Of lazy sinecures, and suffering toil;
Of grey-beard systems, and meteorous dreams;   245
Of lordly churches, and dissention fierce,
Rites farsical, and phrenzied unbelief.
See thick and fell her lowering gibbets stand,
And gibbets still employ'd! while, through thy realms,
The rare-seen felon startles every mind   250
And fills each mouth with news. Behold her jails
Countless, and stow'd with wretches of all kinds!
Her brothels, circling, with their tainted walls,
Unnumber'd female outcasts, shorne from life,
Peace, penitence, and hope; and down, down plung'd   255
In vice' unbottom'd gulph! Ye demons, rise,
Rise, and look upward, from your dread abode;
And, if you've tears to shed, distil them here!
See too, in countless herds, the mistress vile,
Even to the teeth of matron sanctity,   260
Lift up her shameless bronze, and elbow out

The pure, the chaste, the lovely angel-form
Of female excellence! while leachers rank, and
Bloated, call aloud on vengeance' worms,
To seize their prey, on this side of the grave.   265
See the foul theatre, with Upaz[4] steams,
Impoisoning half mankind! See every heart
And head from dunghills up to thrones, moon'd high
With fashion, frippery, falling humbly down
To a new head-dress; barbers, milliners,   270
Taylors, and mantua-makers, forming gods,
Their fellow-millions worship! See the world
All set to sale; truth, friendship, public trust,
A nation's weal, religion, scripture, oaths,
Struck off by inch of candle! Mark the mien,   275
Out-changing the Cameleon; pleasing all,
And all deceiving! Mark the snaky tongue,
Now lightly vibrating, now hissing death!
See war, from year to year, from age to age,
Unceasing, open on mankind the gates   280
Of devastation; earth wet-deep with blood,
And pav'd with corpses; cities whelm'd in flames;
And fathers, brothers, husbands, sons, and friends,
In millions hurried to th' untimely tomb;
To gain a wigwam, built on Nootka Sound,   285
Or Falkland's fruitful isles; or to secure
That rare soap-bubble, blown by children wise,
Bloated in air, and ting'd with colours fine,
Pursu'd by thousands, and with rapture nam'd
National honour. But what powers suffice   290
To tell the sands, that form the endless beach,
Or drops, that fill the immeasurable deep.

　　Say then, ah say, would'st thou for these exchange
Thy sacred institutions? thy mild laws?
Thy pure religion? morals uncorrupt?   295
Thy plain and honest manners? order, peace,

4. Wealthy city, known in the Bible as a source of gold for heathen luxuries
(Jer. 10:9).

And general weal? Think whence this weal arose.
From the same springs it still shall ceaseless rise.
Preserve the fountains sweet, and sweetest streams
Shall still flow from them. Change, but change alone,   300
By wise improvement of thy blessings rare;
And copy not from others. Shun the lures
Of Europe. Cherish still, watch, hold,
And hold through every trial, every snare,
All that is thine. Amend, refine, complete;   305
But still the glorious stamina retain.
Still, as of yore, in church, and state, elect
The virtuous, and the wise; men tried, and prov'd,
Of steady virtue, all thy weal to guide;
And HEAVEN shall bless thee, with a parent's hand.   310

When round I turn my raptur'd eyes, with joy
O'erflowing, and thy wonderous bliss survey,
I love to think of those, by whom that bliss
Was purchas'd; those firm councils, that brave band,
Who nobly jeoparded their lives, their all,   315
And cross'd temptation's whirlpool, to secure,
For us, and ours, this rich estate of good.
Ye souls illustrious, who, in danger's field,
Instinct with patriot fire, each terror brav'd;
And fix'd as these firm hills, the shock withstood   320
Of war's convulsing earthquake, unappall'd,
Whilst on your labours gaz'd, with reverent eyes,
The pleas'd and wondering world; let every good,
Life knows, let peace, esteem, domestic bliss,
Approving conscience, and a grateful land,   325
Glory through every age, and Heaven at last,
To crown the splendid scene, your toils reward.

Heavens, what a matchless group of beauties rare
Southward expands! where, crown'd with yon tall oak,
Round-hill the circling land and sea o'erlooks;   330
Or, smoothly sloping, Grover's beauteous rise,
Spreads it's green sides, and lifts its single tree,

Glad mark for seamen; or, with ruder face,
Orchards, and fields, and groves, and houses rare,
And scatter'd cedars, Mill-hill meets the eye;   335
Or where, beyond, with every beauty clad,
More distant heights in vernal pride ascend.
On either side, a long, continued range,
In all the charms of rural nature dress'd,
Slopes gently to the main. Ere Tryon[5] sunk   340
To infamy unfathom'd, thro' yon groves
Once glister'd Norwalk's white-ascending spires,
And soon, if HEAVEN permit, shall shine again.
Here, sky-encircled, Stratford's churches beam;
And Stratfield's turrets greet the roving eye.   345
In clear, full view, with every varied charm,
That forms the finish'd landschape, blending soft
In matchless union, Fairfield and Green's Farms
Give lustre to the day. Here, crown'd with pines
And skirting groves, with creeks and havens fair   350
Embellish'd, fed with many a beauteous stream,
Prince of the waves, and ocean's favorite child,
Far westward fading in confusion blue,
And eastward stretch'd beyond the human ken,
And mingled with the sky, there Longa's Sound[6]   355
Glorious expands. All hail! of waters first
In beauties of all kinds; in prospects rich
Of bays, and arms, and groves, and little streams,
Inchanting capes and isles, and rivers broad,
That yield eternal tribute to thy wave!   360
In use supreme: fish of all kinds, all tastes,
Scaly or shell'd, with floating nations fill
Thy spacious realms; while, o'er thy lucid waves,
Unceasing Commerce wings her countless sails.
Safe in thy arms, the treasure moves along,   365
While, beat by Longa's coast, old ocean roars
Distant, but roars in vain. O'er all thy bounds,

5. William Tryon, royal governor of New York. In 1777 he led a loyalist invasion
of Connecticut, destroying Danbury, Fairfield, and Norwalk.
6. Long Island Sound.

What varied beauties, changing with the sun,
Or night's more lovely queen, here splendid glow.
Oft, on thy eastern wave, the orb of light   370
Refulgent rising, kindles wide a field
Of mimic day, slow sailing to the west,
And fading with the eve; and oft, through clouds,
Painting their dark skirts on the glassy plain,
The strong, pervading lustre marks th' expanse,   375
With streaks of glowing silver, or with spots
Of burnish'd gold; while clouds, of every hue,
Their purple shed, their amber, yellow, grey,
Along the faithful mirror. Oft, at eve,
Thron'd in the eastern sky, th' ascending moon,   380
Distain'd with blood, sits awful o'er the wave,
And, from the dim dark waters, troubled calls
Her dreary image, trembling on the deep,
And boding every horror. Round yon isles,
Where every Triton, every Nereid, borne   385
From eastern climes, would find perpetual home,
Were Grecian fables true, what charms intrance
The fascinated eye! where, half withdrawn
Behind yon vivid slope, like blushing maids,
They leave the raptur'd gaze. And O how fair   390
Bright Longa spreads her terminating shore,
Commix'd with whit'ning cliffs, with groves obscure,
Farms shrunk to garden-beds, and forests fallen
To little orchards, slow-ascending hills,
And dusky vales, and plains! These the pleas'd eye   395
Relieve, engage, delight; with one unchang'd,
Unbounded ocean, wearied, and displeas'd.

     Yet scarce six suns are pass'd, since these wide bounds,
So still so lovely now, were wanton'd o'er
By sails of British foes, with thunders dread   400
Announcing desolation to each field,
Each town, and hamlet; in the sheltering night
Wafting base throngs of plunderers to our coast,
The bed of peace invading; herds and flocks

Purloining from the swain; and oft the house   405
Of innocence and peace, in cruel flames
With fell revenge, encircling. Now, afar
With shame retir'd, his bands no more, no more
(And oh may HEAVEN the fond prediction seal)
Shall hostile bands, from earth's extended bounds,   410
Th' infernal talk resume. Henceforth, through time,
To peace devoted, 'till millenian suns
Call forth returning Eden, arts of peace
Shall triumph here. Speed, oh speed, ye days
Of bliss divine! when all-involving HEAVEN,   415
The mystery finish'd, come the second birth
Of this sin-ruin'd, this apostate world,
And clos'd the final scene of wild misrule,
All climes shall clothe again with life, and joy,
With peace, and purity; and deathless spring   420
Again commence her bright, etherial reign.
    O who can paint, like Nature? who can boast
Such scenes, as here inchant the lingering eye?
Still to thy hand, great parent of the year!
I turn obsequious; still to all thy works   425
Of beauty, grandeur, novelty, and power,
Of motion, light, and life, my beating heart
Plays unison; and, with harmonious thrill,
Inhales such joys, as Avarice never knew.

    Ah! knew he but his happiness, of men   430
Not the least happy he, who, free from broils,
And base ambition, vain and bust'ling pomp,
Amid a friendly cure, and competence,
Tastes the pure pleasures of parochial life.
What though no crowd of clients, at his gate,   435
To falshood, and injustice, bribe his tongue,
And flatter into guilt; what though no bright,
And gilded prospects lure ambition on
To legislative pride, or chair of state;
What though no golden dreams entice his mind   440
To burrow, with the mole, in dirt, and mire;

What though no splendid villa, Eden'd round
With gardens of enchantment, walks of state,
And all the grandeur of superfluous wealth,
Invite the passenger to stay his steed,   445
And ask the liveried foot-boy, "who dwells here?"
What though no swarms, around his sumptuous board,
Of soothing flatterers, humming in the shine
Of opulence, and honey, from its flowers,
Devouring, 'till their time arrives to sting,   450
Inflate his mind; his virtues, round the year,
Repeating, and his faults, with microscope
Inverted, lessen, till they steal from sight:
Yet, from the dire temptations, these present,
His state is free; temptations, few can stem;   455
Temptations, by whose sweeping torrent hurl'd
Down the dire steep of guilt, unceasing fall,
Sad victims, thousands of the brightest minds,
That time's dark reign adorn; minds, to whose grasp
Heaven seems most freely offer'd; to man's eye,   460
Most hopeful candidates for angels' joys.

   His lot, that wealth, and power, and pride forbids,
Forbids him to become the tool of fraud,
Injustice, misery, ruin; saves his soul
From all the needless labours, griefs, and cares,   465
That avarice, and ambition, agonize;
From those cold nerves of wealth, that, palsied, feel
No anguish, but its own; and ceaseless lead
To thousand meannesses, as gain allures.

   Though oft compell'd to meet the gross attack   470
Of shameless ridicule, and towering pride,
Sufficient good is his; good, real, pure,
With guilt unmingled. Rarely forc'd from home,
Around his board, his wife and children smile;
Communion sweetest, nature here can give,   475
Each fond endearment, office of delight,

With love and duty blending. Such the joy,
My bosom oft has known. His, too, the task,
To rear the infant plants, that bud around;
To ope their little minds to truth's pure light;   480
To take them by the hand, and lead them on,
In that straight, narrow road, where virtue walks;
To guard them from a vain, deceiving world;
And point their course to realms of promis'd life.

His too th' esteem of those, who weekly hear   485
His words of truth divine; unnumber'd acts
Of real love attesting, to his eye,
Their filial tenderness. Where'er he walks,
The friendly welcome and inviting smile
Wait on his steps, and breathe a kindred joy.   490

Oft too in friendliest Association join'd,
He greets his brethren, with a flowing heart,
Flowing with virtue; all rejoic'd to meet,
And all reluctant parting; every aim,
Benevolent, aiding with purpose kind;   495
While, season'd with unblemish'd cheerfulness,
Far distant from the tainted mirth of vice,
Their hearts disclose each contemplation sweet
Of things divine; and blend in friendship pure,
Friendship sublim'd by piety and love.   500

All virtue's friends are his: the good, the just,
The pious, to his house their visits pay,
And converse high hold of the true, the fair,
The wonderful, the moral, the divine:
Of saints, and prophets, patterns bright of truth,   505
Lent to a world of sin, to teach mankind,
How virtue, in that world, can live, and shine;
Of learning's varied realms; of Nature's works;
And that bless'd book, which gilds man's darksome way,
With light from heaven; of bless'd Messiah's throne   510

And kingdom; prohesies divine fulfill'd,
And prophesies more glorious, yet to come,
In renovated days; of that bright world,
And all the happy trains, which that bright world
Inhabit, whither virtue's sons are gone: 515
While GOD the whole inspires, adorns, exalts,
The source, the end, the substance, and the soul.

This too the task, the bless'd, the useful task,
To invigour order, justice, law, and rule;
Peace to extend, and bid contention cease;   520
To teach the words of life; to lead mankind
Back from the wild of guilt, and brink of woe,
To virtue's house and family; faith hope,
And joy, t' inspire; to warm the soul,
With love to GOD, and man; to cheer the sad,   525
To fix the doubting, rouse the languid heart;
The wandering to restore; to spread with down,
The thorny bed of death; console the poor,
Departing mind, and aid its lingering wing.

To him, her choicest pages Truth expands,   530
Unceasing, where the soul-intrancing scenes,
Poetic fiction boasts, are real all:
Where beauty, novelty, and grandeur, wear
Superior charms, and moral worlds unfold
Sublimities, transporting and divine.   535

Not all the scenes, Philosophy can boast,
Tho' them with nobler truths he ceaseless blends,
Compare with these. They, as they found the mind,
Still leave it; more inform'd, but not more wise.
These wiser, nobler, better, make the man.   540

Thus every happy mean of solid good
His life, his studies, and profession yield.
With motives hourly new, each rolling day,
Allures, through wisdom's path, and truth's fair field,
His feet to yonder skies. Before him heaven   545

Shines bright, the scope sublime of all his prayers,
The meed of every sorrow, pain, and toil.

 Then, O ye happy few! whom GOD allows
To stand his messengers, in this bad world,
And call mankind to virtue, weep no more,   550
Though pains and toils betide you: for what life,
On earth, from pains and toils was ever free?
When Wealth and Pride around you gaily spread
Their vain and transient splendour, envy not.
How oft (let virtue weep!) is this their all?   555
For you, in sunny prospect, daily spring
Joys, which nor Pride can Taste, nor Wealth can boast;
That, planted here, beyond the wintery grave
Revive and grow with ever vernal bloom.

 Hail these, oh hail! and be 't enough for you,   560
To 'scape a world unclean; a life to lead
Of usefulness, and truth; a Prince to serve,
Who suffers no sincere and humble toil
To miss a rich reward; in Death's dark vale,
To meet unbosom'd light; beyond the grave   565
To rise triumphant, freed from every stain,
And cloth'd with every beauty; in the sky
Stars to outshine; and, round th' eternal year,
With saints, with angels, and with CHRIST, to reign.

PART II: THE FLOURISHING VILLAGE[1]

FAIR Verna! loveliest village of the west;
Of every joy, and every charm, possess'd;
How pleas'd amid thy varied walks I rove,
Sweet, cheerful walks of innocence, and love,
And o'er thy smiling prospects cast my eyes,   5

1. Comparing the Connecticut village with his impressions of England, Dwight
emphasizes the satisfactions with which diligence, cooperation, and decent habits
may be rewarded. His portrait of the slave, however, interrupts the happy scene
with the reminder that man's full and proper development depends upon liberty.

And see the seats of peace, and pleasure, rise,
And hear the voice of Industry resound,
And mark the smile of Competence, around!
Hail, happy village! O'er thy cheerful lawns,
With earliest beauty, spring delighted dawns;   10
The northward sun begins his vernal smile;
The spring-bird carols o'er the cressy rill:
The shower, that patters in the ruffled stream,
The ploughboy's voice, that chides the lingering team,   15
The bee, industrious, with his busy song,
The woodman's axe, the distant groves among,
The waggon, rattling down the rugged steep,
The light wind, lulling every care to sleep,
All these, with mingled music, from below,   20
Deceive intruding sorrow, as I go.

    How pleas'd, fond Recollection, with a smile,
Surveys the varied round of wintery toil!
How pleas'd, amid the flowers, that scent the plain,
Recalls the vanish'd frost, and sleeted rain;
The chilling damp, the ice-endangering street,   25
And treacherous earth that slump'd beneath the feet.

    Yet even stern winter's glooms could joy inspire:
Then social circles grac'd the nutwood fire;
The axe resounded, at the sunny door;
The swain, industrious, trimm'd his flaxen store;   30
Or thresh'd, with vigorous flail, the bounding wheat,
His poultry round him pilfering for their meat;
Or slid his firewood on the creaking snow;
Or bore his produce to the main below;
Or o'er his rich returns exulting laugh'd;   35
Or pledg'd the healthful orchard's sparkling draught:
While, on his board, for friends and neighbours spread,
The turkey smoak'd, his busy housewife fed;
And Hospitality look'd smiling round,
And Leisure told his tale, with gleeful sound.   40

Then too, the rough road hid beneath the sleigh,
The distant friend despis'd a length of way,
And join'd the warm embrace, and mingling smile,
And told of all his bliss, and all his toil;
And, many a month elaps'd, was pleas'd to view   45
How well the houshold far'd, the children grew;
While tales of sympathy deceiv'd the hour,
And Sleep, amus'd, resign'd his wonted power.

    Yes! let the proud despise, the rich deride,
These humble joys, to Competence allied: 50
To me, they bloom, all fragrant to my heart,
Nor ask the pomp of wealth, nor gloss of art.
And as a bird, in prison long confin'd,
Springs from his open'd cage, and mounts the wind,
Thro' fields of flowers, and fragrance, gaily flies,   55
Or re-assumes his birth-right, in the skies:
Unprison'd thus from artificial joys,
Where pomp fatigues, and fussful fashion cloys,
The soul, reviving, loves to wander free
Thro' native scenes of sweet simplicity;   60
Thro' Peace' low vale, where Pleasure lingers long,
And every songster tunes his sweetest song,
And Zephyr hastes, to breathe his first perfume,
And Autumn stays, to drop his latest bloom:
'Till grown mature, and gathering strength to roam,   65
She lifts her lengthen'd wings, and seeks her home.

    But now the wintery glooms are vanish'd all;
The lingering drift behind the shady wall;
The dark-brown spots, that patch'd the snowy field;
The surly frost, that every bud conceal'd;   70
The russet veil, the way with slime o'erspread,
And all the saddening scenes of March are fled.

    Sweet-smiling village! loveliest of the hills!
How green thy groves! How pure thy glassy rills!

With what new joy, I walk thy verdant streets!   75
How often pause, to breathe thy gale of sweets;
To mark thy well-built walls! thy budding fields!
And every charm, that rural nature yields;
And every joy, to Competence allied,
And every good, that Virtue gains from Pride!   80

    No griping landlord here alarms the door,
To halve, for rent, the poor man's little store.
No haughty owner drives the humble swain
To some far refuge from his dread domain;
Nor wastes, upon his robe of useless pride,   85
The wealth, which shivering thousands want beside;
Nor in one palace sinks a hundred cots;
Nor in one manor drowns a thousand lots;
Nor, on one table, spread for death and pain,
Devours what would a village well sustain.   90

    O Competence, thou bless'd by Heaven's decree,
How well exchang'd is empty pride for thee!
Oft to thy cot my feet delighted turn,
To meet thy chearful smile, at peep of morn;
To join thy toils, that bid the earth look gay;   95
To mark thy sports, that hail the eve of May;
To see thy ruddy children, at thy board,
And share thy temperate meal, and frugal hoard;
And every joy, by winning prattlers giv'n,
And every earnest of a future Heaven.   100

    There the poor wanderer finds a table spread,
The fireside welcome, and the peaceful bed.
The needy neighbour, oft by wealth denied,
There finds the little aids of life supplied;
The horse, that bears to mill the hard-earn'd grain;   105
The day's work given, to reap the ripen'd plain;
The useful team, to house the precious food,
And all the offices of real good.

There too, divine Religion is a guest,
And all the Virtues join the daily feast.   110
Kind Hospitality attends the door,
To welcome in the stranger and the poor;
Sweet Chastity, still blushing as she goes;
And Patience smiling at her train of woes;
And meek-eyed Innocence, and Truth refin'd,   115
And Fortitude, of bold, but gentle mind.

Thou pay'st the tax, the rich man will not pay;
Thou feed'st the poor, the rich man drives away.
Thy sons, for freedom, hazard limbs, and life,
While pride applauds, but shuns the manly strife: 120
Thou prop'st religion's cause, the world around,
And shew'st thy faith in works, and not in sound.

Say, child of passion! while, with idiot stare,
Thou seest proud grandeur wheel her sunny car;
While kings, and nobles, roll bespangled by,   125
And the tall palace lessens in the sky;
Say, while with pomp thy giddy brain runs round,
What joys, like these, in splendour can be found?
Ah, yonder turn thy wealth-inchanted eyes,
Where that poor, friendless wretch expiring lies!   130
Hear his sad partner shriek, beside his bed,
And call down curses on her landlord's head,
Who drove, from yon small cot, her houshold sweet,
To pine with want, and perish in the street.
See the pale tradesman toil, the livelong day,   135
To deck imperious lords, who never pay!
Who waste, at dice, their boundless breadth of soil,
But grudge the scanty meed of honest toil.
See hounds and horses riot on the store,
By HEAVEN created for the hapless poor!   140
See half a realm one tyrant scarce sustain,
While meagre thousands round him glean the plain!
See, for his mistress' robe, a village sold,

Whose matrons shrink from nakedness and cold!
See too the Farmer prowl around the shed,   145
To rob the starving houshold of their bread;
And seize, with cruel fangs, the helpless swain,
While wives, and daughters, plead, and weep, in vain;
Or yield to infamy themselves, to save
Their sire from prison, famine, and the grave.   150

    There too foul luxury taints the putrid mind,
And slavery there imbrutes the reasoning kind:
There humble worth, in damps of deep despair,
Is bound by poverty's eternal bar:
No motives bright the etherial aim impart,   155
Nor one fair ray of hope allures the heart.

    But, O sweet Competence! how chang'd the scene,
Where thy soft footsteps lightly print the green!
Where Freedom walks erect, with manly port,
And all the blessings to his side resort,   160
In every hamlet, Learning builds her schools,
And beggars, children gain her arts, and rules;
And mild Simplicity o'er manners reigns,
And blameless morals Purity sustains.

    From thee the rich enjoyments round me spring,   165
Where every farmer reigns a little king;
Where all to comfort, none to danger, rise;
Where pride finds few, but nature all supplies;
Where peace and sweet civility are seen,
And meek good-neighbourhood endears the green.   170
Here every class (if classes those we call,
Where one extended class embraces all,
All mingling, as the rainbow's beauty blends,
Unknown where every hue begins or ends)
Each following, each, with uninvidious strife,   175
Wears every feature of improving life.
Each gains from other comeliness of dress,
And learns, with gentle mein to win and bless,

With welcome mild the stranger to receive,
And with plain, pleasing decency to live.   180
Refinement hence even humblest life improves;
Not the loose fair, that form and frippery loves;
But she, whose mansion is the gentle mind,
In thought, and action, virtuously refin'd.
Hence, wives and husbands act a lovelier part,   185
More just the conduct, and more kind the heart;
Hence brother, sister, parent, child, and friend,
The harmony of life more sweetly blend;
Hence labour brightens every rural scene;
Hence cheerful plenty lives along the green;   190
Still Prudence eyes her hoard, with watchful care,
And robes of thrift and neatness, all things wear.

freedom

But hark! what voice so gaily fills the wind?
Of care oblivious, whose that laughing mind?
'Tis yon poor black, who ceases now his song,   195
And whistling, drives the cumbrous wain along.
He never, dragg'd, with groans, the galling chain;
Nor hung, suspended, on th' infernal crane;
No dim, white spots deform his face, or hand,
Memorials hellish of the marking brand!   200
No seams of pincers, scars of scalding oil;
No waste of famine, and no wear of toil.
But kindly fed, and clad, and treated, he
Slides on, thro' life, with more than common glee.
For here mild manners good to all impart,   205
And stamp with infamy th' unfeeling heart;
Here law, from vengeful rage, the slave defends,
And here the gospel peace on earth extends.

He toils, 'tis true; but shares his master's toil;
With him, he feeds the herd, and trims the soil;   210
Helps to sustain the house, with clothes, and food,
And takes his portion of the common good:
Lost liberty his sole, peculiar ill,
And fix'd submission to another's will.

Realistic ?

Ill, ah, how great! without that cheering sun,   215
The world is chang'd to one wide, frigid zone;
The mind, a chill'd exotic, cannot grow,
Nor leaf with vigour, nor with promise blow;
Pale, sickly, shrunk, it strives in vain to rise,
Scarce lives, while living, and untimely dies.   220

      See fresh to life the Afric infant spring,
And plume its powers, and spread its little wing!
Firm is it's frame, and vigorous is its mind,
Too young to think, and yet to misery blind.
But soon he sees himself to slavery born;   225
Soon meets the voice of power, the eye of scorn;
Sighs for the blessings of his peers, in vain;
Condition'd as a brute, tho' form'd a man.
Around he casts his fond, instinctive eyes,
And sees no good, to fill his wishes, rise: 230
(No motive warms, with animating beam,
Nor praise, nor property, nor kind esteem,
Bless'd independence, on his native ground,
Nor sweet equality with those around;)
Himself, and his, another's shrinks to find,   235
Levell'd below the lot of human kind.
Thus, shut from honour's paths, he turns to shame,
And filches the small good, he cannot claim.
To sour, and stupid, sinks his active mind;
Find joys in drink, he cannot elsewhere find;   240
Rule disobeys; of half his labour cheats;
In some safe cot, the pilfer'd turkey eats;
Rides hard, by night, the steed, his art purloins;
Serene from conscience' bar himself essoins;[2]
Sees from himself his sole redress must flow,   245
And makes revenge the balsam of his woe.

      Thus slavery's blast bids sense and virtue die;
Thus lower'd to dust the sons of Afric lie.
Hence sages grave, to lunar systems given,

      2. Offers an excuse for absence from trial.

Shall ask, why two-legg'd brutes were made by HEAVEN;   250
HOME³ seek, what pair first peopled Afric's vales,
And nice MONBODDO⁴ calculate their tails.

   O thou chief curse, since curses here began;
First guilt, first woe, first infamy of man;
Thou spot of hell, deep smirch'd on human kind,   255
The uncur'd gangrene of the reasoning mind;
Alike in church, in state, and houshold all,
Supreme memorial of the world's dread fall;
O slavery! laurel of the Infernal mind,
Proud Satan's triumph over lost mankind!   260

   See the fell Spirit mount his sooty car!
While Hell's black trump proclaims the finish'd war;
Her choicest fiends his wheels exulting draw,
And scream the fall of GOD's most holy law.
In dread procession see the pomp begin,   265
Sad pomp of woe, of madness, and of sin!
Grav'd on the chariot, all earth's ages roll,
And all her climes, and realms, to either pole.
Fierce in the flash of arms, see Europe spread!
Her jails, and gibbets, fleets, and hosts, display'd!   270
Awe-struck, see silken Asia silent bow!
And feeble Afric writhe in blood below!
Before, peace, freedom, virtue, bliss, move on,
The spoils, the treasures, of a world undone;
Behind, earth's bedlam millions clank the chain,   275
Hymn their disgrace, and celebrate their pain;
Kings, nobles, priests, dread senate! lead the van,
And shout "Te-Deum!" o'er defeated man.

   Oft, wing'd by thought, I seek those Indian isles,
Where endless spring, with endless summer smiles,   280

3. Henry Home, Lord Kames, Scottish jurist and philosopher known for his writings on criticism, law, and the history of man.
4. James Burnett, Lord Monboddo, Scottish judge and philosopher, who speculated on man's relationship to the orangutan and other animals.

Where fruits of gold untir'd Vertumnus[5] pours,
And Flora dances o'er undying flowers.
There, as I walk thro' fields as Eden gay,
And breathe the incense of immortal May,
Ceaseless I hear the smacking whip resound;   285
Hark! that shrill scream! that groan of death-bed sound!
See those throng'd wretches pant along the plain,
Tug the hard hoe, and sigh in hopeless pain!
Yon mother, loaded with her sucking child,
Her rags with frequent spots of blood defil'd,   290
Drags slowly fainting on; the fiend is nigh;
Rings the shrill cowskin; roars the tyger-cry;
In pangs, th' unfriended suppliant crawls along,
And shrieks the prayer of agonizing wrong.

    Why glows yon oven with a sevenfold fire?   295
Crisp'd in the flames, behold a man expire!
Lo! by that vampyre's hand, yon infant dies,
It's brains dash'd out, beneath it's father's eyes.
Why shrinks yon slave, with horror, from his meat?
Heavens! 'tis his flesh, the wretch is whipp'd to eat.   300
Why streams the life-blood from that female's throat?
She sprinkled gravy on a guest's new coat!

   .   .   .   .   .   .
    .   .   .   .   .   .[6]

    Why croud those quivering blacks yon dock around?   305
Those screams announce; that cowskin's shrilling sound.
See, that poor victim hanging from the crane,
While loaded weights his limbs to torture strain;
At each keen stroke, far spouts the bursting gore,
And shrieks, and dying groans, fill all the shore.   310
Around, in throngs, his brother-victims wait,
And feel, in every stroke, their coming fate;
While each, with palsied hands, and shuddering fears,
The cause, the rule, and price, of torment bears.

    5. Roman god of changing seasons, thought to preside over the transition from
blossom to fruit.
    6. The two lines of ellipses appear in the original edition and presumably reflect
Dwight's intention for the poem.

Hark, hark, from morn to night, the realm around,   315
The cracking whip, keen taunt, and shriek, resound!
O'ercast are all the splendors of the spring;
Sweets court in vain; in vain the warblers sing;
Illusions all! 'tis Tartarus[7] round me spreads
His dismal screams, and melancholy shades.   320
The damned, sure, here clank th' eternal chain,
And waste with grief, or agonize with pain.
A Tartarus new! inversion strange of hell!
Guilt wreaks the vengeance, and the guiltless feel.
The heart, not form'd of flint, here all things rend;   325
Each fair a fury, and each man a fiend;
From childhood, train'd to every baleful ill,
And their first sport, to torture, and to kill.

   ⟶   Ask not, why earthquakes rock that fateful land;[8]
Fires waste the city; ocean whelms the strand;   330
Why the fierce whirlwind, with electric sway,
Springs from the storm, and fastens on his prey,
Shakes heaven, rends earth, upheaves the cumbrous wave,
And with destruction's besom fills the grave:
Why dark disease roams swift her nightly round,   335
Knocks at each door, and wakes the gasping sound.

    Ask, shuddering ask, why, earth-embosom'd sleep
The unbroken fountains of the angry deep:
Why, bound, and furnac'd, by the globe's strong frame,
In sullen quiet, waits the final flame: 340
Why surge not, o'er yon isles it's spouting fires,
'Till all their living world in dust expires.
Crimes sound their ruin's moral cause aloud,
And all heaven, sighing, rings with cries of brother's blood.

    Beside yon church, that beams a modest ray,   345
With tidy neatness reputably gay,

---

7. Hell, in classical mythology.
8. Dwight still indicates a belief in special providences by which God punishes
sinful societies with natural disasters.

When, mild and fair, as Eden's seventh-day light,
In silver silence, shines the Sabbath bright,
In neat attire, the village housholds come,
And learn the path-way to the eternal home.   350
Hail solemn ordinance! worthy of the SKIES;
Whence thousand richest blessings daily rise;
Peace, order, cleanliness, and manners sweet,
A sober mind, to rule submission meet,
Enlarging knowledge, life from guilt refin'd,   355
And love to God, and friendship to mankind.
In the clear splendour of thy vernal morn,
New-quicken'd man to light, and life, is born;
The desert of the mind with virtue blooms;
It's flowers unfold, it's fruits exhale perfumes;   360
Proud guilt dissolves, beneath the searching ray,
And low debasement, trembling, creeps away;
Vice bites the dust; foul Error seeks her den;
And God, descending, dwells anew with men.
Where yonder humbler spire salutes the eye,   365
It's vane slow turning in the liquid sky,
Where, in light gambols, healthy striplings sport,
Ambitious learning builds her outer court;
A grave preceptor, there, her usher stands,
And rules, without a rod, her little bands.   370
Some half-grown sprigs of learning grac'd his brow:
Little he knew, though much he wish'd to know,
Inchanted hung o'er Virgil's honey'd lay,
And smil'd, to see desipient[9] Horace play;
Glean'd scraps of Greek; and, curious, trac'd afar,   375
Through Pope's clear glass, the bright Mæonian star.[10]
Yet oft his students at his wisdom star'd,
For many a student to his side repair'd,
Surpriz'd, they heard him Dilworth's knots[11] untie,
And tell, what lands beyond the Atlantic lie.   380

9. Enjoying light, trivial pleasures.
10. Homer.
11. Mathematical problems in Thomas Dilworth's popular textbook, *The Schoolmaster's Assistant.*

Many his faults; his virtues small, and few;
Some little good he did, or strove to do;
Laborious still, he taught the early mind,
And urg'd to manners meek, and thoughts refin'd;
Truth he impress'd, and every virtue prais'd;   385
While infant eyes, in wondering silence, gaz'd;
The worth of time would, day by day, unfold,
And tell them, every hour was made of gold.
Brown Industry he lov'd; and oft declar'd
How hardy Sloth, in life's sad evening, far'd;   390
Through grave examples, with sage meaning, ran,
Whist[12] was each form, and thus the tale began.

"Beside yon lonely tree, whose branches bare
Rise white, and murmur to the passing air,
There, where the twining briars the yard enclose,   395
The house of Sloth stands hush'd in long repose."

"In a late round of solitary care,
My feet instinct to rove, they knew not where,
I thither came. With yellow blossoms gay,
The tall rank weed begirt the tangled way: 400
Curious to view, I forc'd a path between,
And climb'd the broken stile, and gaz'd the scene."

"O'er an old well, the curb half-fallen spread,
Whose boards, end-loose, a mournful creaking made;
Poiz'd on a leaning post, and ill-sustain'd,   405
In ruin sad, a mouldering swepe remain'd;
Useless, the crooked pole still dangling hung,
And, tied with thrumbs, a broken bucket swung."

"A half-made wall around the garden lay,
Mended, in gaps, with brushwood in decay.   410
No culture through the woven briars was seen,
Save a few sickly plants of faded green:

12. Hushed.

The starv'd potatoe hung it's blasted seeds,
And fennel struggled to o'ertop the weeds.
There gaz'd a ragged sheep, with wild surprise,   415
And too lean geese upturn'd their slanting eyes."

"The cottage gap'd, with many a dismal yawn,
Where, rent to burn, the covering boards were gone;
Or, by one nail, where others endwise hung,
The sky look'd thro', and winds portentous rung.   420
In waves, the yielding roof appear'd to run,
And half the chimney-top was fallen down."
"The ancient cellar-door, of structure rude,
With tatter'd garments calk'd, half open stood.
There, as I peep'd, I saw the ruin'd bin;   425
The sills were broke; the wall had crumbled in;
A few, long-emptied casks lay mouldering round,
And wasted ashes sprinkled o'er the ground;
While, a sad sharer in the houshold ill,
A half-starved rat crawl'd out, and bade farewell."   430

"One window dim, a loop-hole to the sight,
Shed round the room a pale, penurious light;
Here rags gay-colour'd eked the broken glass;
There panes of wood supplied the vacant space."

"As, pondering deep, I gaz'd, with gritty roar,   435
The hinges creak'd, and open stood the door.
Two little boys, half-naked from the waist,
With staring wonder, ey'd me, as I pass'd.
The smile of Pity blended with her tear—
Ah me! how rarely Comfort visit here!"   440

"On a lean hammoc, once with feathers fill'd,
His limbs by dirty tatters ill conceal'd,
Tho' now the sun had rounded half the day,
Stretch'd at full length, the lounger snoring lay:
While his sad wife, beside her dresser stood,   445
And wash'd her hungry houshold's meagre food,

His aged sire, whose beard, and flowing hair,
Wav'd silvery, o'er his antiquated chair,
Rose from his seat; and, as he watch'd my eye,
Deep from his bosom heav'd a mournful sigh—   450
"Stranger, he cried, once better days I knew;"
And, trembling, shed the venerable dew.
I wish'd a kind reply; but wish'd in vain;
No words came timely to relieve my pain:
To the poor parent, and her infants dear,   455
Two mites I gave, besprinkled with a tear;
And, fix'd again to see the wretched shed,
Withdrew in silence, clos'd the door, and fled."

    "Yet this so lazy man I've often seen
Hurrying, and bustling, round the busy green;   460
The loudest prater, in a blacksmith's shop;
The wisest statesman, o'er a drunken cup;
(His sharp-bon'd horse, the street that nightly fed,
Tied, many an hour, in yonder tavern-shed)
In every gambling, racing match, abroad: 465
But a rare hearer, in the house of God."

    "Such, such, my children, is the dismal cot,
Where drowsy Sloth receives her wretched lot:
But O how different is the charming cell,
Where Industry and Virtue love to dwell!"   470

    "Beyond that hillock, topp'd with scatter'd trees,
That meet, with freshest green, the hastening breeze,
There, where the glassy brook reflects the day,
Nor weeds, nor sedges, choke its crystal way,
Where budding willows feel the earliest spring,   475
And wonted red-breasts safely nest, and sing,
A female Worthy lives; and all the poor
Can point the way to her sequester'd door."

    "She, unseduc'd by dress and idle shew,
The forms, and rules, of fashion never knew;   480

Nor glittering in the ball, her form display'd;
Nor yet can tell a diamond, from a spade.
Far other objects claim'd her steady care;
The morning chapter, and the nightly prayer;
The frequent visit to the poor man's shed;   485
The wakeful nursing, at the sick man's bed;
Each day, to rise, before the early sun;
Each day, to see her daily duty done;
To cheer the partner of her houshold cares,
And mould her children, from their earliest years."   490

"Small is her house; but fill'd with stores of good;
Good, earn'd with toil, and with delight bestow'd.
In the clean cellar, rang'd in order neat,
Gay-smiling Plenty boasts her casks of meat,
Points, to small eyes, the bins where apples glow,   495
And marks her cyder-butts, in stately row.
Her granary, fill'd with harvest's various pride,
Still sees the poor man's bushel laid aside;
Here swells the flaxen, there the fleecy store,
And the long wood-pile mocks the winter's power: 500
White are the swine; the poultry plump and large;
For every creature thrives, beneath her charge."

"Plenteous, and plain, the furniture is seen;
All form'd for use, and all as silver clean.
On the clean dresser, pewter shines arow;   505
The clean-scower'd bowls are trimly set below;
While the wash'd coverlet, and linen white,
Assure the traveller a refreshing night."

"Oft have I seen, and oft still hope to see,
This friend, this parent to the poor and me,   510
Tho' bent with years, and toil, and care, and woe,
Age lightly silver'd on her furrow'd brow,
Her frame still useful, and her mind still young,
Her judgment vigorous, and her memory strong,
Serene her spirits, and her temper sweet,   515

And pleas'd the youthful circle still to meet,
Cheerful, the long-accustom'd task pursue,
Prevent the rust of age, and life renew;
To church, still pleas'd, and able still, to come,
And shame the lounging youth, who sleep at home."   520

   "Such as her toils, has been the bright reward;
For Heaven will always toils like these regard.
Safe, on her love, her truth and wisdom tried,
Her husband's heart, thro' lengthened life, relied;
From little, daily saw his wealth increase,   525
His neighbours love him, and his houshold bless;
In peace and plenty liv'd, and died resign'd,
And, dying, left six thousand pounds behind.
Her children, train'd to usefulness alone,
Still love the hand, which led them kindly on,   530
With pious duty, own her wise behest,
And, every day, rise up, and call her bless'd."

   "More would ye know, of each poor hind enquire,
Who sees no sun go down upon his hire;
A cheerful witness, bid each neighbour come;   535
Ask each sad wanderer, where he finds a home;
His tribute even the vilest wretch will give,
And praise the useful life, he will not live."

   "Oft have the prattlers, GOD to me has giv'n,
The flock, I hope, and strive, to train for Heaven,   540
With little footsteps, sought her mansion dear,
To meet the welcome, given with heart sincere;
And cheer'd with all, that early minds can move,
The smiles of gentleness, and acts of love,
At home, in lisping tales, her worth display'd,   545
And pour'd their infant blessings on her head."

   "Ye kings, of pomp, ye nobles proud of blood,
Heroes of arms, of science sages proud!
Read, blush, and weep, to see, with all your store,

Fame, genius, knowledge, bravery, wealth, and power,　　550
Crown'd, laurell'd, worshipp'd, gods beneath the sun,
Far less of real good enjoy'd, or done."

　　Such lessons, pleas'd, he taught. The precepts new
Oft the young train to early wisdom drew;
And, when his influence willing minds confess'd,　　555
The children lov'd him, and the parents bless'd;
But, when by soft indulgence led astray,
His pupil's hearts had learn'd the idle way,
Tho' constant, kind, and hard, his toils had been,
For all those toils, small thanks had he, I ween.　　560

　　Behold yon humbler mansion lift its head!
Where infant minds to science door are led.
As now, by kind indulgence looss'd to play,
From place to place, from sport to sport, they stray,
How light their gambols frolic o'er the green!　　565
How their shrill voices cheer the rural scene!
Sweet harmless elves! in Freedom's houshold born,
Enjoy the raptures of your transient morn;
And let no hour of anxious manhood see
Your minds less innocent, or bless'd, or free!　　570

　　See too, in every hamlet, round me rise
A central school-house, dress'd in modest guise!
Where every child for useful life prepares,
To business moulded, ere he knows its cares;
In worth matures, to independence grows,　　575
And twines the civic garland o'er his brows.

　　Mark, how invited by the vernal sky,
Yon cheerful group of females passes by!
Whose hearts, attun'd to social joy, prepare
A friendly visit to some neighbouring fair.　　580
How neatness glistens from the lovely train!
Bright charm! which pomp to rival tries in vain.

Ye Muses! dames of dignified renown,
Rever'd alike in country, and in town,
Your bard the mysteries of a visit show;   585
For sure your Ladyships those mysteries know:
What is it then, obliging Sisters! say,
The debt of social visiting to pay?

'Tis not to toil before the idol pier;
To shine the first in fashion's lunar sphere;   590
By sad engagements forc'd, abroad to roam,
And dread to find the expecting fair, at home!
To stop at thirty doors, in half a day,
Drop the gilt card, and proudly roll away;
To alight, and yield the hand, with nice parade;   595
Up stairs to rustle in the stiff brocade;
Swim thro' the drawing room, with studied air;
Catch the pink'd beau, and shade the rival fair;
To sit, to curb, to toss, with bridled mien,
Mince the scant speech, and lose a glance between;   600
Unfurl the fan, display the snowy arm,
And ope, with each new motion, some new charm;
Or sit, in silent solitude, to spy
Each little failing, with malignant eye;
Or chatter, with incessancy of tongue,   605
Careless, if kind, or cruel, right, or wrong;
To trill of us, and ours, of mine, and me,
Our house, our coach, our friends, our family,
While all th' excluded circle sit in pain,
And glance their cool contempt, or keen disdain: 610
T' inhale, from proud Nanking, a sip of tea,
And wave a curtsey trim, and flirt away:
Or waste, at cards, peace, temper, health and life,
Begin with sullenness, and end in strife,
Lose the rich feast, by friendly converse given,   615
And backward turn from happiness, and heaven.

It is, in decent habit, plain and neat,

To spend a few choice hours, in converse sweet;
Careless of forms, to act th' unstudied part,
To mix in friendship, and to blend the heart;   620
To choose those happy themes, which all must feel,
The moral duties, and the houshold weal,
The tale of sympathy, the kind design,
Where rich affections soften, and refine;
T' amuse, to be amus'd, to bless, be bless'd,   625
And tune to harmony the common breast;
To cheer, with mild good-humour's sprightly ray,
And smooth life's passage, o'er its thorny way;
To circle round the hospitable board,
And taste each good, our generous climes afford;   630
To court a quick return, with accents kind,
And leave, at parting, some regret behind.

    Such, here, the social intercourse is found;
So slides the year, in smooth enjoyment, round.

    Thrice bless'd the life, in this glad region spent,   635
In peace, in competence, and still content;
Where bright, and brighter, all things daily smile,
And rare and scanty, flow the streams of ill;
Where undecaying youth sits blooming round,
And Spring looks lovely on the happy ground;   640
Improvement glows, along life's cheerful way,
And with soft lustre makes the passage gay.
Thus oft, on yonder Sound, when evening gales
Breath'd o'er th' expanse, and gently fill'd the sails,
The world was still, the heavens were dress'd in smiles,   645
And the clear moon-beam tipp'd the distant isles,
On the blue plain a lucid image gave,
And capp'd, with silver light, each little wave;
The silent splendour, floating at our side,
Mov'd as we mov'd, and wanton'd on the tide;   650
While shadowy points, and havens, met the eye,
And the faint-glimmering landmark told us home was nigh.

Ah, dire reverse! in yonder eastern clime,
Where heavy drags the sluggish car of time;
The world unalter'd by the change of years,   655
Age after age, the same dull aspect wears;
On the bold mind the weight of system spread,
Resistless lies, a cumbrous load of lead;
One beaten course, the wheels politic keep,
And slaves of custom, lose their woes in sleep;   660
Stagnant is social life; no bright design,
Quickens the sloth, or checks the sad decline.
The friend of man casts round a wishful eye,
And hopes, in vain, improving scenes to spy;
Slow o'er his head, the dragging moments roll,   665
And damp each cheerful purpose of the soul.

Thus the bewilder'd traveller, forc'd to roam
Through a lone forest, leaves his friends, and home;
Dun evenings hangs the sky; the woods around
Join their dun umbrage o'er the russet ground;   670
At every step, new gloom inshrouds the skies;
His path grows doubtful, and his fears arise:
No woodland songstress soothes his mournful way;
No taper gilds the gloom with cheering ray;
On the cold earth he laps his head forlorn,   675
And watching, looks, and looks, to spy the lingering morn.

And when new regions prompt their feet to roam,
And fix, in untrod fields, another home,
No dreary realms our happy race explore,
Nor mourn their exile from their native shore.   680
For there no endless frosts the glebe deform,
Nor blows, with icy breath, perpetual storm:
No wrathful suns, with sickly splendour glare,
Nor moors, impoison'd, taint the balmy air,
But medial climates change the healthful year;   685
Pure streamlets wind, and gales of Eden cheer;
In misty pomp the sky-topp'd mountains stand,

And with green bosom humbler hills expand:
With flowery brilliance smiles the woodland glade;
Full teems the soil, and fragrant twines the shade.   690
There cheaper fields the numerous houshold charm,
And the glad sire gives every son a farm;
In falling forests, Labour's axe resounds;
Opes the new field; and wind the fence's bounds;
The green wheat sparkles; nods the towering corn;   695
And meads, and pastures, lessening wastes adorn.
Where howl'd the forest, herds unnumber'd low;
The fleecy wanderers fear no prowling foe;
The village springs; the humble school aspires;
And the church brightens in the morning fires!   700
Young Freedom wantons; Art exalts her head;
And infant Science prattles through the shade.
There changing neighbours learn their manners mild;
And toil and prudence dress th' improving wild:
The savage shrinks, nor dares the bliss annoy;   705
And the glad traveller wonders at the joy.

      All hail, thou western world! by heaven design'd
Th' example bright, to renovate mankind.
Soon shall thy sons across the mainland roam;
And claim, on far Pacific shores, their home;   710
Their rule, religion, manners, arts, convey,
And spread their freedom to the Asian sea.
Where erst six thousand suns have roll'd the year
O'er plains of slaughter, and o'er wilds of fear,
Towns, cities, fanes, shall lift their towery pride;   715
The village bloom, on every streamlets side;
Proud Commerce, mole[13] the western surges lave;
The long, white spire lie imag'd on the wave;
O'er morn's pellucid main expand their sails,
And the starr'd ensign court Korean gales.   720
Then nobler thoughts shall savage trains inform;
Then barbarous passions cease the heart to storm:
No more the captive circling flames devour;

13. Pier; dock.

Through the war path the Indian creep no more;
No midnight scout the slumbering village fire;   725
Nor the scalp'd infant stain his gasping sire:
But peace, and truth, illume the twilight mind,
The gospel's sunshine, and the purpose kind.
Where marshes teem'd with death, shall meads unfold;
Untrodden cliffs resign their stores of gold;   730
The dance refin'd on Albion's margin move,
And her lone bowers rehearse the tale of love.
Where slept perennial night, shall science rise,
And new-born Oxfords cheer the evening skies;
Miltonic strains the Mexic hills prolong,   735
And Louis murmurs to Sicilian song.

    Then to new climes the bliss shall trace its way,[14]
And Tartar desarts hail the rising day;
From the long torpor startled China wake;
Her chains of misery rous'd Peruvia break;   740
Man link to man; with bosom bosom twine;
And one great bond the house of Adam join;
The sacred promise full completion know,
And peace, and piety, the world o'erflow.

14. In these lines Dwight integrates hopes for America's westward expansion
and growing world influence with his expectation of the Christian millennium.

PART IV: THE DESTRUCTION OF THE PEQUODS[1]

AH me! while up the long, long vale of time,
Reflection wanders towards th' eternal vast,
How starts the eye, at many a change sublime,
Unbosom'd dimly by the ages pass'd!
What Mausoleums crowd the mournful waste!   5
The tombs of empires fallen! and nations gone!

1. Here Dwight explores the romantic associations of Indian antiquities while
presenting one of the most violent and destructive episodes in early New England
history: the vengeful elimination of the Pequod Indians by English settlers and
their Mohegan allies in 1637.

Each, once inscrib'd, in gold, with "AYE TO LAST"
Sate as a queen; proclaim'd the world her own,
And proudly cried, "By me no sorrows shall be known."

Soon fleets the sunbright Form, by man ador'd.   10
Soon fell the Head of gold, to Time a prey;
The Arms, the Trunk, his cankering tooth devour'd;
And whirlwinds blew the Iron dust away.
Where dwelt imperial Timur? [2]—far astray,
Some lonely-musing pilgrim now enquires: 15
And, rack'd by storms, and hastening to decay,
Mohammed's Mosque foresees it's final fires;
And Rome's more lordly Temple day by day expires.

As o'er proud Asian realms the traveller winds,
His manly spirit, hush'd by terror, falls;   20
When some deceased town's lost site he finds,
Where ruin wild his pondering eye appals;
Where silence swims along the moulder'd walls,
And broods upon departed Grandeur's tomb.
Through the lone, hollow aisles sad Echo calls,   25
At each slow step; deep sighs the breathing gloom,
And weeping fields, around, bewail their Empress' doom.

Where o'er an hundred realms, the throne uprose,
The screech-owl nests, the panther builds his home;
Sleep the dull newts, the lazy adders doze,   30
Where pomp and luxury danc'd the golden room.
Low lies in dust the sky-resembled dome;
Tall grass around the broken column waves;
And brambles climb, and lonely thistles bloom:
The moulder'd arch the weedy streamlet laves,   35
And low resound, beneath, unnumber'd sunken graves.
Soon fleets the sun-bright Form, by man ador'd;
And soon man's dæmon chiefs from memory fade.
In musty volume, now must be explor'd,

2. Tamerlane, fourteenth-century Mongol conqueror, famous for his cruelty
as well as his military achievements.

Where dwelt imperial nations, long decay'd.   40
The brightest meteors angry clouds invade;
And where the wonders glitter'd, none explain.
Where Carthage, with proud hand, the trident sway'd,
Now mud-wall'd cots sit sullen on the plain,
And wandering, fierce, and wild, sequester'd Arabs reign.   45

In thee, O Albion! queen of nations, live
Whatever splendours earth's wide realms have known;
In thee proud Persia sees her pomp revive;
And Greece her arts; and Rome her lordly throne:
By every wind, thy Tyrian fleets are blown;   50
Supreme, on Fame's dread roll, thy heroes stand;
All ocean's realms thy naval scepter own;
Of bards, of sages, how august thy band!
And one rich Eden blooms around thy garden'd land.

But O how vast thy crimes! Through heaven's great year,   55
When few centurial suns have trac'd their way;
When southern Europe, worn by feuds severe;
Weak, doating, fallen, has bow'd to Russian sway;
And setting Glory beam'd her farewell ray;
To wastes, perchance, thy brilliant fields shall turn;   60
In dust, thy temples, towers, and towns decay;
The forest howl, where London's turrets burn;
And all thy garlands deck thy sad, funereal urn.

Some land, scarce glimmering in the light of fame,
Scepter'd with arts, and arms (if I divine)   65
Some unknown wild, some shore without a name,
In all thy pomp, shall then majestic shine.
As silver-headed Time's slow years decline,
Not ruins only meet th' enquiring eye:
Where round yon mouldering oak vain brambles twine,   60
The filial stem, already towering high,
Erelong shall stretch his arms, and nod in yonder sky.

Where late resounded the wild, woodland roar,

Now heaves the palace, now the temple smiles;
Where frown'd the nude rock, and the desert shore,   75
Now pleasure sports, and business want beguiles,
And Commerce wings her flight to thousand isles;
Culture walks forth; gay laugh the loaded fields;
And jocund Labour plays his harmless wiles;
Glad Science brightens; Art her mansion builds;   80
And Peace uplifts her wand, and HEAVEN his blessing
    yields.

O'er these sweet fields, so lovely now, and gay,
Where modest Nature finds each want supplied,
Where home-born Happiness delights to play,
And counts her little flock, with houshold pride,   85
Long frown'd, from age to age, a forest wide:
Here hung the slumbering bat; the serpent dire
Nested his brood, and drank th' impoison'd tide;
Wolves peal'd, the dark, drear night, in hideous choir;
Nor shrunk th' unmeasur'd howl from Sol's terrific fire.   90

No charming cot imbank'd the pebbly stream;
No mansion tower'd, nor garden teem'd with good;
No lawn expanded to the April beam;
Nor mellow harvest hung it's bending load;
Nor science dawn'd; nor life with beauty glow'd;   95
Nor temple whiten'd, in th' enchanting dell;
In clusters wild, the sluggish wigwam stood;
And, borne in snaky paths, the Indian fell
Now aim'd the death unseen, now scream'd the tyger-yell.
Even now, perhaps, on human dust I tread,   100
Pondering, with solemn pause, the wrecks of time;
Here sleeps, perchance, among the vulgar dead,
Some Chief, the lofty theme of Indian rhyme,
Who lov'd Ambition's cloudy steep to climb,
And smil'd, deaths, dangers, rivals, to engage;   105
Who rous'd his followers' souls to deeds sublime,
Kindling to furnace heat vindictive rage,
And soar'd Cæsarean heights, the Phœnix of his age.

In yon small field, that dimly steals from sight,
(From yon small field these meditations grow)   110
Turning the sluggish soil, from morn to night,
The plodding hind, laborious, drives his plough,
Nor dreams, a nation sleeps, his foot below.
There, undisturbed by the roaring wave,
Releas'd from war, and far from deadly foe,   115
Lies down, in endless rest, a nation brave,
And trains, in tempests born, there find a quiet grave.

Oft have I heard the tale, when matron sere
Sung to my infant ear the song of woe;
Of maiden meek, consum'd with pining care,   120
Around whose tomb the wild-rose lov'd to blow;
Or told, with swimming eyes, how, long ago,
Remorseless Indians, all in midnight dire,
The little, sleeping village, did o'erthrow,
Bidding the cruel flames to heaven aspire,   125
And scalp'd the hoary head, and burn'd the babe with fire.

Then, fancy-fir'd, her memory wing'd it's flight,
To long-forgotten wars, and dread alarms,
To chiefs obscure, but terrible in fight,
Who mock'd each foe, and laugh'd at deadliest harms,   130
Sydneys in zeal, and Washingtons in arms.
By instinct tender to the woes of man,
My heart bewildering with sweet pity's charms,
Thro' solemn scenes, with Nature's step, she ran,
And hush'd her audience small, and thus the tale began.   135

"Thro' verdant banks where Thames's [3] branches glide,
Long held the Pequods an extensive sway;
Bold, savage, fierce, of arms the glorious pride,
And bidding all the circling realms obey.
Jealous, they saw the tribes, beyond the sea,   140
Plant in their climes; and towns, and cities, rise;
Ascending castles foreign flags display;

3. Connecticut river.

Mysterious art new scenes of life devise;
And steeds insult the plains, and cannon rend the skies."

"They saw, and soon the strangers' fate decreed,   145
And soon of war disclos'd the crimson sign;
First, hapless Stone! [4] they bade thy bosom bleed,
A guiltless offering at th' infernal shrine:
Then, gallant Norton! [5] the hard fate was thine,
By ruffians butcher'd, and denied a grave: 150
Thee, generous Oldham! [6] next the doom malign
Arrested; nor could all thy courage save;
Forsaken, plunder'd, cleft, and buried in the wave."

"Soon the sad tidings reach'd the general ear;
And prudence, pity, vengeance, all inspire: 155
Invasive war their gallant friends prepare;
And soon a noble band, with purpose dire,
And threatening arms, the murderous fiends require:
Small was the band, but never taught to yield;
Breasts fac'd with steel, and souls instinct with fire: 160
Such souls, from Sparta, Persia's world repell'd,
When nations pav'd the ground. and Xerxes flew the field."
"The rising clouds the Savage Chief descried,
And, round the forest, bade his heroes arm;
To arms the painted warriors proudly hied,   165
And through surrounding nations rung the alarm.
The nations heard; but smil'd, to see the storm,
With ruin fraught, o'er Pequod mountains driven;
And felt infernal joy the bosom warm,

4. Captain John Stone of Virginia, whose murder by a splinter group of Pequods
while on a trading expedition along the Connecticut River was a major cause
of English military action against the Indians.
5. Captain Norton, a member of Stone's party and another victim of the same
ambush.
6. John Oldham, English trader, murdered by Pequods on an expedition to
Block Island. His death was the immediate cause of the war, although according
to colonial documents and William Bradford's *History of Plymouth Plantation*
he seems to have been (like Stone) an opportunist and scoundrel.

To see their light hang o'er the skirts of even,   170
And other suns arise, to gild a kinder heaven."

"Swift to the Pequod fortress Mason[7] sped,
Far in the wildering wood's impervious gloom;
A lonely castle, brown with twilight dread;
Where oft th' embowel'd captive met his doom,   175
And frequent heav'd, around the hollow tomb;
Scalps hung in rows, and whitening bones were strew'd;
Where, round the broiling babe, fresh from the womb,
With howls the Powaw fill'd the dark abode,   180
And screams, and midnight prayers, invok'd the Evil god."

"There too, with awful rites, the hoary priest,
Without, beside the moss-grown altar, stood,
His sable form in magic cincture dress'd,
And heap'd the mingled offering to his god,
What time, with golden light, calm evening glow'd.   185
The mystic dust, the flower of silver bloom,
And spicy herb, his hand in order strew'd;
Bright rose the curling flame; and rich perfume
On smoky wings upflew, or settled round the tomb."

"Then, o'er the circus, danc'd the maddening throng,   190
As erst the Thyas[8] roam'd dread Nysa[9] round,
And struck, to forest notes, th' ecstatic song,
While slow, beneath them, heav'd the wavy ground.
With a low, lingering groan, of dying sound,
The woodland rumbled; murmur'd deep each stream;   195
Shrill sung the leaves; all ether sigh'd profound;
Pale tufts of purple topp'd the silver flame,
And many-colour'd Forms on evening breezes came."

"Thin, twilight Forms; attir'd in changing sheen
Of plumes, high-tinctur'd in the western ray;   200

7. John Mason, leader of the English and Mohegan expedition against the Pequods.
8. Bacchanalian maidens.
9. Legendary home of Bacchus, classical god of wine and revelry.

Bending, they peep'd the fleecy folds between,
Their wings light-rustling in the breath of May.
Soft-hovering round the fire, in mystic play,
They snuff'd the incense, wav'd in clouds afar,
Then, silent, floated toward the setting day: 205
Eve redden'd each fine form, each misty car;
And through them faintly gleam'd, at times, the
        Western star."

"Then (so tradition sings), the train behind,
In plumy zones of rainbow'd beauty dress'd,
Rode the Great Spirit, in th' obedient wind,   210
In yellow clouds slow-sailing from the west.
With dawning smiles, the God his votaries bless'd,
And taught where deer retir'd to ivy dell;
What chosen chief with proud command to invest;
Where crept th' approaching foe, with purpose fell,   215
And where to wind the scout, and war's dark storm dispel."

"There, on her lover's tomb, in silence laid,
While still, and sorrowing, shower'd the moon's pale beam,
At times, expectant, slept the widow'd maid,
Her soul far-wandering on the sylph-wing'd dream.   220
Wafted from evening skies, on sunny stream,
Her darling Youth with silver pinions shone;
With voice of music, tun'd to sweetest theme,
He told of shell-bright bowers, beyond the sun,
Where years of endless joy o'er Indian lovers run."   225
"But now no awful rites, nor potent spell,
To silence charm'd the peals of coming war;
Or told the dread recesses of the dell,
Where glowing Mason led his bands from far:
No spirit, buoyant on his airy car,   230
Controul'd the whirlwind of invading fight:
Deep died in blood, dun evening's falling star
Sent sad, o'er western hills, it's parting light,
And no returning morn dispers'd the long, dark night."

"On the drear walls a sudden splendour glow'd,   235
There Mason shone, and there his veterans pour'd.
Anew the Hero claim'd the fiends of blood,
While answering storms of arrows round him shower'd,
And the war-scream the ear with anguish gor'd.
Alone, he burst the gate: the forest round   240
Re-echoed death; the peal of onset roar'd;
In rush'd the squadrons; earth in blood was drown'd;
And gloomy spirits fled, and corses hid the ground."

"Not long in dubious fight the host had striven,
When, kindled by the musket's potent flame,   245
In clouds, and fire, the castle rose to heaven,
And gloom'd the world, with melancholy beam.
Then hoarser groans, with deeper anguish, came;
And fiercer fight the keen assault repell'd:
Nor even these ills the savage breast could tame;   250
Like hell's deep caves, the hideous region yell'd,
'Till death, and sweeping fire, laid waste the hostile field."

"Soon the sad tale their friends surviving heard;
And Mason, Mason, rung in every wind;
Quick from their rugged wilds they disappear'd,   255
Howl'd down the hills, and left the blast behind.
Their fastening foes, by generous Stoughton[10] join'd,
Hung o'er the rear, and every brake explor'd;
But such dire terror seiz'd the savage mind,
So swift and black a storm behind them lowr'd,   260
On wings of raging fear, thro' spacious realms they scowr'd."

(O thou, to earth the second blessing given,
Of heart divine, of aspect angel-sweet,
O meek Religion! second-born of Heaven,
Cloth'd with the sun, the world beneath thy feet!   265
Softer than lambs on yonder hillocks bleat,
Thy music charms to kindness savage man,

10. Israel Stoughton, another leader of the Connecticut forces.

Since first, from Calvary's height, with love replete,
Thy wondrous course, in sunny sheen, began,
And, o'er the death-struck globe, thro' startled nations ran.   270

When pride and wrath awake the world to arms,
How heaves thy snowy breast with fainting throe!
While lust and rapine trumpet death's alarms,
And men 'gainst men with fiery vengeance glow.
In Europe oft, that land of war, and woe,   275
As her sad steps the lingering mourner draws,
How slowly did thy feet entangled go,
Chain'd by vile tests, and prison'd round by laws;
While bigotry and rage in blood insteep'd thy cause!

When o'er th' Atlantic wild, by Angels borne,   280
Thy pilgrim barque explor'd it's western way,
With spring and beauty bloom'd the waste forlorn,
And night and chaos shrunk from new-born day.
Dumb was the savage howl; th' instinctive lay
Wav'd, with strange warblings, thro' the woodland's bound;   285
The village smil'd; the temple's golden ray
Shot high to heaven; fair culture clothed the ground;
Art blossom'd; cities sprang; and sails the ocean crown'd.

As on heaven's sacred hill, of hills the queen,
At thy command, contention foul shall cease,   290
Thy solar aspect, every storm serene,
And smooth the rugged wild of man to peace;
So here thy voice (fair earnest of the bliss!)
Transform'd the savage to the meekly child.
Hell saw, with pangs, her hideous realm decrease;   295
Wolves play'd with lambs; the tyger's heart grew mild;
And on his own bright work the GODHEAD, look'd and
      smil'd.

Hail Elliot! Mayhew hail! [11] by HEAVEN inform'd

11. John Eliot and Thomas Mayhew, seventeenth-century Puritan ministers
famous for their missionary work among the Massachusetts Indians.

With that pure love, which clasps the human kind;
To virtue's path even Indian feet you charm'd,   300
And lit, with wisdom's beam, the dusky mind:
From torture, blood, and treachery, refin'd,
The new-born convert lisp'd MESSIAH's name.
Mid Choirs complacent, in pure rapture join'd,
Your praise resounds, on yonder starry frame,   305
While souls, redeem'd from death, their earthly saviours
    claim.

Oh had the same bright spirit ever reign'd;
Nor trader villains foul'd the Savage mind;
Nor Avarice pin'd for boundless breadth of land;
Nor, with slow death, the wretches been consign'd   310
To India's curse, that poisons half mankind!
Then, O divine Religion! torture's blaze
Less frequent round thy tender heart had twin'd;
On the wild wigwam peace had cast it's rays,
And the tremendous whoop had chang'd to hymns of
    praise.   315

Fierce, dark, and jealous, is the exotic soul,
That, cell'd in secret, rules the savage breast.
There treacherous thoughts of gloomy vengeance roll,
And deadly deeds of malice unconfess'd;
The viper's poison rankling in it's nest.   320
Behind his tree, each Indian aims unseen:
No sweet oblivion soothes the hate impress'd:
Years fleet in vain: in vain realms intervene:
The victim's blood alone can quench the flames within.

Their knives the tawny tribes in slaughter steep,   325
When men, mistrustless, think them distant far;
And, when blank midnight shrouds the world in sleep,
The murderous yell announces first the war.
In vain sweet smiles compel the fiends to spare;
Th' unpitied victim screams, in tortures dire;   330
The life-blood stains the virgin's bosom bare;

Cherubic infants, limb by limb expire;
And silver'd Age sinks down in slowly-curling fire.

Yet savages are men. With glowing heat,
Fix'd as their hatred, friendship fills their mind;   335
By acts with justice, and with truth, replete,
Their iron breasts to softness are inclin'd.
But when could War of converts boast refin'd?
Or when Revenge to peace and sweetness move?
His heart, man yields alone to actions kind;   340
His faith, to creeds, whose soundness virtues prove,
Thawn in the April sun, and opening still to love.

Senate august! that sway'st Columbian climes,
Form'd of the wise, the noble, and humane,
Cast back the glance through long-ascending times,   345
And think what nations fill'd the western plain.
Where are they now? What thoughts the bosom pain,
From mild Religion's eye how streams the tear,
To see so far outspread the waste of man,
And ask "How fell the myriads, HEAVEN plac'd here!"   350
Reflect, be just, and feel for Indian woes severe.

But cease, foul Calumny! with sooty tongue,
No more the glory of our sires belie.
They felt, and they redress'd, each nation's wrong;
Even Pequod foes they view'd with generous eye,   355
And, pierc'd with injuries keen, that Virtue try,
The savage faith, and friendship, strove to gain:
And, had no base Canadian fiends[12] been nigh,
Even now soft Peace had smil'd on every plain,
And tawny nations liv'd, and own'd MESSIAH's reign.)   360

"Amid a circling marsh, expanded wide,
To a lone hill the Pequods wound their way;
And none, but Heaven, the mansion had descried,
Close-tangled, wild, impervious to the day;

12. Like many New Englanders, Dwight blamed French Canadians for the
hostility of local Indian tribes.

But one poor wanderer, loitering long astray.   365
Wilder'd in labyrinths of pathless wood,
In a tall tree embower'd, obscurely lay:
Strait summon'd down, the trembling suppliant show'd
Where lurk'd his vanish'd friends, within their drear abode."

"To death, the murderers were anew requir'd,   370
A pardon proffer'd, and a peace assur'd;
And, though with vengeful heat their foes were fir'd,
Their lives, their freedom, and their lands, secur'd.
Some yielding heard. In fastness strong immur'd,
The rest the terms refus'd, with brave disdain,   375
Near, and more near, the peaceful Herald lur'd;
Then bade a shower of arrows round him rain,
And wing'd him swift, from danger, to the distant plain."

"Through the sole, narrow way, to vengeance led,
To final fight our generous heroes drew;   380
And Stoughton now had pass'd the moor's black shade,
When hell's terrific region scream'd anew.
Undaunted, on their foes they fiercely flew;
As fierce, the dusky warriors crowd the fight;
Despair inspires; to combat's face they glue;   385
With groans, and shouts, they rage, unknowing flight,
And close their sullen eyes, in shades of endless night."

Indulge, my native land! indulge the tear,
That steals, impassion'd, o'er a nation's doom:
To me each twig, from Adam's stock, is near,   390
And sorrows fall upon an Indian's tomb.
And, O ye Chiefs! in yonder starry home,
Accept the humble tribute of this rhyme.
Your gallant deeds, in Greece, or haughty Rome,
By Maro[13] sung, or Homer's harp sublime,   395
Had charm'd the world's wide round, and triumph'd over
    time.

    (1787–1794; 1794)

13. Virgil.

FOUR

Philip Freneau
(1752-1832)

BORN THE same year as Timothy Dwight and, like him, a revolutionary patriot, Philip Freneau was nonetheless a distinctly different poet—different in values, voice, and literary style. He represented a newer strain in American thought: more liberal, more secular, and more attuned to change than the wit from Connecticut, a place where, Freneau once wrote, rhymes "Come rattling down on Greenfield's reverend son" and where the climate somehow encouraged large families, huge pumpkins, and lengthy poems.[1] By his attempts to establish himself as a professional writer in a republic with no established literary class and to use his art to instruct his readers in democratic, humanitarian attitudes, Freneau illustrated more dramatically than Dwight the problems of the imaginative man in a materialistic society. The general failure of his career deserves sympathetic attention, just as a few of his poems, superbly crafted and beautifully evocative of universal human feelings, offer lasting pleasure.

Freneau was born in New York and raised in New Jersey, the son of a Huguenot merchant. Spending his childhood on a farm in Monmouth, New Jersey, he developed a lifelong affection for rural life and for the ocean, visible from his family home. Although his father's business failure and death in 1767 troubled the poet's childhood, his family somehow managed to send him to Princeton to be educated for the Presbyterian clergy. In some respects Freneau's college years resembled Dwight's. They encountered the same restricted curriculum, the same concern with religious

1. Lewis Leary, "Philip Freneau," *Major Writers of Early American Literature,* ed. Everett Emerson (Madison: University of Wisconsin Press, 1972), p. 267.

formation of the students, the same levity among the young men, and the same patriotic distractions as the colonies moved toward revolution. When Freneau graduated in 1771, he took with him a fine classical education and a poetic reputation based on the class poem, "On the Rising Glory of America," which he wrote in collaboration with Hugh Henry Brackenridge, but he had discarded his ministerial ambitions. After a disastrous experiment at teaching in a rural school, he studied law and divinity before settling his ambitions on a literary career—in those days, necessarily journalistic. He published patriotic satires in various newspapers and wrote more ambitious, imaginative verses for private publication.

Unsettled in his plans, Freneau withdrew from political tensions by sailing to the Virgin Islands in 1776, where he remained for two years as a guest of friends in Santa Cruz. While in the Caribbean, Freneau participated in several privateering adventures, and his ship was captured by the British on his return to New York in 1778. When released, he joined the New Jersey militia. The decisive experience of the war years for Freneau came in 1780 when he was captured by an English vessel while a passenger on the American *Aurora* and was imprisoned, first on the *Scorpion* and then on the *Hunter*, a hospital ship. The atrocities he witnessed and the injustice he felt fired the rhetoric of "The British Prison Ship" (1781) and inspired even harsher political satires than he had written earlier. His war poems— satiric, celebratory, and elegiac—won him a permanent reputation as "the Poet of the American Revolution."

After the war Freneau's career followed a pattern of activity and withdrawal anticipatory of Whitman's. He repeatedly ventured out into the public arena as a political journalist, only to withdraw to his New Jersey farm or put out to sea as master of a coastal vessel. All three activities contributed to his poetry, and his literary productivity is the one steady element in his career.

He won his greatest fame, or notoriety, as a political journalist, associated first with revolutionary causes and then with Jefferson's Republicanism and the French Revolution. As publisher of the *National Gazette* in Philadelphia from 1791 to 1793, Freneau entered fiercely into political controversies, to the extent that Jefferson once claimed that the paper "has saved our Constitution, which was galloping fast into monarchy," but he incurred the anger of Federalist leaders—Hamilton, Adams, and even Washington—who derisively labeled him "that rascal Freneau." Hamilton, in particular, assaulted Freneau through a rival newspaper and called attention to the apparent conflict of interest in antigovernmental journalism from a man holding an appointment as translator with Jefferson's State Department. The combined pressures of political opposition, Philadelphia's yellow fever epidemic, the Genêt Affair in which Freneau exhibited excessive zeal for the new French Republic, and nonpaying subscribers forced Freneau to give up his effort. Retiring to New Jersey, he edited an almanac and brought out a short-lived paper, the *Jersey Chronicle.* In 1797 he returned to New York to help edit *The Time-Piece,* which was intended as a purely literary journal but rapidly grew political. Less than a year later Freneau withdrew permanently from journalism except for occasional scattered contributions.

In 1790 Freneau had married Eleanor Forman, and the responsibility of supporting his mother, wife, and four daughters forced him to work periodically as master of coastal trading vessels. He seems not to have particularly enjoyed the nautical life itself but liked the opportunity to travel, meet people, and try the effect of various environments. He always returned to New Jersey, however, and retired there in 1807. There were continuing financial troubles and a disastrous fire which destroyed his home and manuscripts in 1818, forcing a move to a neighboring farmhouse. He spent his last years preparing revised editions of his older poems and occasionally publishing new ones. In 1832 he froze to death in a field near his home, having been lost in a snowstorm when returning at night from town.

Most of Freneau's poems appeared first in newspapers; some, like *The American Village* (1772), *American Liberty* (1775), and *A Voyage to Boston* (1775), were published separately. Successive collected editions appeared whenever Freneau could find a large enough prospective audience and a willing publisher. *Poems* was published in 1786 and his *Miscellaneous Works* in 1788. There were other editions in 1795 and 1809 and a volume of later work in 1815. His last poems were printed in New York and New Jersey magazines. Unlike Bradstreet, Taylor, or Dwight, Freneau defined himself principally as a poet and aspired to a more successful literary career than he achieved.

Each of the three intertwining threads of Freneau's career affected his writing, and each edition of the poems exhibits the continuing variety of his interests. Journalistic concerns, however, tended for a long period to dominate his writing, largely because editorial duties required regular production of topical verses. Freneau's public reputation rested largely on his satires, most of which reacted too directly to immediate controversies to be of interest to the modern reader; they are simply editorials. Typical of Freneau's political rhetoric, but more accessible today, is "George the Third's Soliloquy" (1779). Written in the neoclassical mock-epic tradition, it presents the king agonizing privately over his military humiliations. A burlesque quality of degradation counterpoints the mock-heroism, as the royal troops turn out to be British felons wishing themselves safe home in jail. There are amusing lines in the satire, and the basic situation suggests promise, but the overall effect is one of strained shrillness. The rhetoric might encourage the patriots to whom it was directed but could hardly persuade a Loyalist; the irony, unlike that of Franklin's revolutionary prose satires, provides no illuminating insights. The same tendencies mar most of Freneau's political satires; they are seldom amusing or informative. Some, such as his attacks on Loyalists, can be painful in their hostility and lack of compassion. Freneau expressed his anger more effectively in the personal denunciations of "The British Prison Ship," an autobiographical record of abuse more than a satire.

His public spirit and journalistic involvement led Freneau to write other kinds of poetry, including the memorably controlled elegy, "To the Memory of the Brave Americans" (1781). As editor of the *National Gazette*, Freneau asserted himself as a public figure and often composed verses for political banquets and celebrations. His popular "Ode" (1793) represents these effectively in its libertarian theme, exultant tone, and obvious suitability for public performance, preferably in song. "A Picture of the Times" (1782) shows the poet teaching democratic principles in a nonsatiric verse essay, and his 1809 tribute to Jefferson demonstrates that Freneau's governmental concerns long outlived his editorial duties.

Freneau's nautical experiences and travels contributed quite different elements to his poetry. In "The Beauties of Santa Cruz" (1779), for instance, he demonstrated a remarkable imagistic power in his descriptions of the exotic landscape. His travels encouraged him to write gracious though ephemeral light verse, offering a balance to the impassioned earnestness of his political writings. The people he met in his wanderings entered into the poems, and Freneau often wrote through fictive personae representing various regions and occupations: Captain Sinbat, a sailor; Hezekiah Salem, a Yankee deacon; Robert Slender, a Philadelphia weaver; Tomo-Cheeki, an Indian sage. The same characters narrated many of his prose sketches as well; although not fully rounded characters nor adequately differentiated from one another, they represented a new direction for American poetry.

Alternations of activity and rest, public life and privacy, in Freneau's career are reflected in his poetry's shifting emphasis between reason, or public instruction, and fancy, or private imagination, and the importance of fanciful verse throughout his lifetime corresponded to the poet's recurring need to withdraw to his farm for reflection and renewal. His first poems emphasized this need, especially "The Power of Fancy" (1770) with its exploration of the varied sensations imagination might evoke. He seldom yielded so completely to fancy as in "The House of Night" (1779), an early, gothic poem on the death of Death with its recurrent motif, "Fancy, I own thy power," but his work shows an emphasis on imaginative experience and sense impressions far beyond that of any previous American poet, an exploration of fancy which at times anticipates Poe. Some of his strongest poems involve a tension between reason and fancy; in "The Indian Burying Ground" (1787) rational theories of death dissolve, at least temporarily, before the force of Indian mythology, so that "Reason's self shall bow the knee / To shadows and delusions here."

All these currents of Freneau's interests appear in "The Beauties of Santa Cruz" and give a subtle tension to the poem, not always perceptible on the first reading. Superficially, this is a topographical poem, distinguished from *Greenfield Hill* by its exotic subject matter more than literary method. Freneau clearly revels in the opportunity to draw beautiful pictures and to evoke the senses of touch and taste to enhance his visual impressions. But the poem is more than a travelogue. Consider, for instance, the question of tone. The speaker, a visitor from the north, addresses himself to a "shepherd" still in the mainland colonies, already at war with England. He realizes, then, that inviting the shepherd to Santa Cruz involves an abdication of patriotic responsibility, and he is clearly uncomfortable in his knowledge and in the questions it raises for his own future. The poet hopes to return to Santa Cruz, if duty now calls him home, and to retire there if possible, but he sees it as a permanent home only for those drugged by sugarcane. His awareness of tyranny at home awakens him to related problems in his island paradise. He worries about the effect of the tropical climate on health and that of the sensual life on character. He recalls that Santa Cruz is governed by Denmark, another foreign monarchy. He is appalled by slavery and by the greed which allows one man to buy, use, and sell another. When he describes the island's devastating hurricanes, he seems to link natural destruction with moral judgment, in the manner of the Puritans. There is an attractiveness to the beauty of Santa Cruz but also a destructiveness. Despite the surface charm of the poetic landscape, a steady subversive force of imagery expresses fear, danger, and warning. The Animal plant Freneau describes may serve as an emblem for the island itself: beautiful, until touched; enticing, if not closely examined; destroyed by any human contact or even a poet's shadow.

Despite tonal contradictions in his poems, Freneau's basic values come across clearly in all his writings. Always, he was a patriot—proud of his country for what it was going to be rather than for what it had been or actually was. Unlike Dwight, Freneau ascribed little value to the achievements of the colonists. When he examined American history, he went way back in "The Pictures of Columbus" (1774) to the original dream and its frustration by greed and ambition. For the most part, Freneau preferred to look toward a future when dreams of freedom and equality would be accomplished. He stressed the importance of freedom, not just independence from England, but freedom of thought and expression in the new republic.

Freneau's concern for democracy expressed itself in frequent denunciations of aristocracy. He attacked the king during the

Revolution, and he assailed the Loyalists he suspected of aristo-
cratic ambitions; later he denounced any discoverable tendency
to exalt officeholders in the style of European nobility. Birthday
odes for public leaders, pretentious manners, even President
Washington's stately coach met with scorn, and one may sympa-
thize with Freneau's egalitarian ideals despite the limited poetic
merit in such topical attacks. He presented his views more posi-
tively in his tribute to Jefferson and more generally in "A Picture
of the Times" (1782). Concern for freedom and equality showed
itself also in Freneau's contempt for social, political, and religious
institutions which tended to enshrine the past or slow the nation's
progress toward an egalitarian future. The institutions Dwight
saw as safeguards of American values impressed Freneau as de-
structive.

His democratic commitment encouraged Freneau to write as
a spokesman for the oppressed, and his poetry reflected his com-
passion for America's defeated or forgotten people: slaves, Indians,
old veterans, and the poor. He was interested in exploring man's
nature, without the Puritan bias toward theories of depravity,
and he discovered that man was neither good nor bad by nature
but capable of being either. People, he found, could almost always
be corrupted by greed and were disposed to tragic violence, but
they were also capable of benevolence. One result of his travels
was a tendency to consider the effect of landscape and climate
on character, and his political writings show concern for the
brutalizing moral effect of aristocratic institutions.

Freneau's most haunting and most characteristic theme was that
of transiency. He reflected continually on the passage of time
and the ephemeral quality of beauty. "The Wild Honey Suckle"
(1786), his best-known and most nearly perfect poem, evokes
melancholy awareness of nature's mutability, "the frail duration
of a flower." "The Deserted Farm-House" (1785) presents the
erasure of man from his works, a theme and symbol like that
of Robert Frost's "Directive" (1946). In "The Vanity of Existence"
(1781), Freneau considers how starlit dreams subside to mundane
reality: "A bank of mud around me lay, / And sea-weed on the
river's bed." The theme of transiency recurs charmingly in a late
poem, "To a Caty-Did" (1815), and in "A Fragment of Bion,"

which Freneau first translated in 1789 and published, in his final version, in 1822. It was his most characteristic, most consistent, and most persuasively articulated theme.

For strength to deal with his melancholy, Freneau turned repeatedly to classical literature and its counsel of stoic fortitude.[2] As his translation of Bion acknowledged, the wise man would accept mortality without self-pity and live life as fully as possible in the face of death. Chance and uncertainty could be met with calmness.

Underlying Freneau's classical stoicism was his belief in Deism, an eighteenth-century philosophy which he shared with Jefferson, Franklin (at times), and many of the British and French authors he admired. Not an atheist, although some readers labeled him such, Freneau believed in God as the originating and ordering principle of the universe and trusted, as a result, that the world was fundamentally harmonious and good. Where he departed from his original Christianity, however, was in his denial that God acts personally in history, through special providences or the Incarnation. Man's relationship to the deity was one of rational respect rather than adoration; he had not offended God with sin, nor could he please God with worship. The best service he could offer would be to help his fellow man and to promote benevolent order within society. Man's greatest capacity was reason rather than faith, and all truths would eventually emerge from rational inquiry. These Deistic ideas are most clearly stated in late poems such as "On the Universality and Other Attributes of the God of Nature," "On the Uniformity and Perfection of Nature," and "On the Religion of Nature," all published in his 1815 *Poems on American Affairs;* but they are evident as well in poems throughout his career.

The striking differences between Freneau's poetry and that of his contemporary, Dwight, result in part from their differing philosophical and political convictions and in part from contrasting literary sources. Though both had studied classical literature,

2. Freneau's use of the classics for philosophical and literary purposes is most fully explored by Nelson F. Adkins in *Philip Freneau and the Cosmic Enigma: The Religious and Philosophical Speculations of an American Poet* (New York: New York University Press, 1949), pp. 57-79.

Freneau found more inspiration in Greek and Roman poetry, especially Horace. He translated classical poems, imitated them, alluded to them, and often introduced his poems with classical epigraphs. His verses also show familiarity with Shakespeare and Milton, as one would expect, and with the most popular neoclassical British writers: Dryden, Addison, Pope, Swift, and Churchill. Freneau responded as well to Gray and the Graveyard Poets, Young and Blair, with their interest in melancholy and concern for the effect of transiency and death on the poetic imagination. His devotion to fancy linked him also, of course, with his preromantic English contemporaries. And Freneau was the first American poet to reverse source studies by exerting a small but traceable influence on English literature, when Scott borrowed a line from "To the Memory of the Brave Americans" for his "Marmion" (1808).

In various ways Freneau's writing marks the transition from neoclassical to romantic writing in America, although neoclassicism remained the dominant force. In poetic modes he emphasized the typical eighteenth-century epics, mock-epics, satires, and verse essays, written in blank verse or couplets, mainly heroic couplets; but he experimented as well with the more flexible and musical form of the ode and with lyrics in various stanzaic patterns. Although much of his verse can only be considered doggerel, the best poems match the form to the idea with superb craftsmanship and flawless taste. The varied tones of his poetry also reveal its transitional quality. Sometimes he wrote as the reasonable neoclassical man talking to others equally urbane; sometimes he was the strident champion of freedom and sounded like many other minor satirists of his time. But when he spoke as a man of feeling and fancy, he introduced a new voice to American poetry. So, too, with language, which shifted from Miltonic eloquence, to studied neoclassical diction, to experiments with local dialects. His subject matter also moved outside neoclassical conventions to take in the honeysuckle and katydid.

His professional ambition as a literary man in the new republic exposed Freneau to a less agreeable transition. Unlike Dwight, Taylor, and Bradstreet, Freneau tried to make his living by poetry but found circumstances dismally unsupportive. European poetry, at that time, was still dominated by a leisure class, unconcerned with money, by gentlemen like Pope, who could find enough subscribers to guarantee the sale of his translations of Homer, and by authors fortunate enough to find aristocratic patrons. America had no such literary class nor patrons of the arts, and Freneau would have despised them had they existed. Unfortunately, the farmers, tradesmen, and ordinary people to whom he directed his work tended not to buy books regularly and often neglected to pay for their newspaper subscriptions. Publishers had no advertising or marketing systems to reach a thinly scattered literary market; so the poet had to make do by publishing his own newspaper or otherwise earning his living.

The problem of audience affected Freneau artistically as well as financially. His complaints in "To an Author" (1788) may have been overstated, as he certainly resented the modest successes of such "rival bards" as Dwight and Barlow and Irving's later international celebrity; but the lack of a critical audience, capable of discerning and valuing his best efforts, certainly hurt him. His most popular, most frequently reprinted poems were trifling examples of light verse like "The Dish of Tea" (1791); his better work was ignored. The need to please an unsophisticated audience probably encouraged Freneau in some of his worst traits: overwriting, bombastic rhetoric, repetition, overstrained humor, and formless doggerel. Most of his poems are simply bad—boring and even embarrassing to a sympathetic reader. They reflect poorly on his audience, of course, but also on the poet himself, whose critical judgment should have recognized their failure. But Freneau somehow managed to find his own voice at times and wrote a few beautiful poems which keep his memory alive. Although he is valued chiefly for his historical importance as Poet of the American Revolution and an early romantic voice in the young republic, Freneau wrote some of the finest, most timeless poems in American literature. He accomplished less than he had hoped but more than he ever realized.

BIBLIOGRAPHIC NOTE

Freneau's poems and many prose sketches associated with them are now available in facsimile editions, edited by Lewis Leary and published by Scholars' Facsimiles & Reprints, Delmar, New York. *The Poems (1786) and Miscellaneous Works (1788) of Philip Freneau* appeared in 1975, as did *The Writings in Prose and Verse of Hezekiah Salem. Poems Written between the Years 1768 & 1794, Poems Written and Published during the American Revolutionary War,* and *A Collection of Poems on American Affairs and a Variety of Other Subjects Chiefly Moral and Political (1815)* were published in 1976. Leary also edited Freneau's late work, printed in journals during the poet's lifetime but not included in any of his books, in *The Last Poems of Philip Freneau* (Westport, Conn.: Greenwood Press, 1945).

Readers can also find Freneau's poetry in Fred Lewis Pattee's complete but often inaccurate edition, *Poems of Philip Freneau,* 3 vols. (Princeton, N.J.: Princeton University Press, 1902-1907; reprinted, New York: Russell & Russell, 1963). For most purposes, the selection in Harry Hayden Clark's edition, *Poems of Freneau* (New York: Harcourt, Brace, 1929; reprinted, New York: Hafner, 1960), would be quite adequate.

The first major biography of the poet is Lewis Leary's book, *That Rascal Freneau: A Study in Literary Failure* (New Brunswick, N.J.: Rutgers University Press, 1941; reprinted, New York: Octagon Books, 1964, 1971). Also of interest is Jacob Axelrad's biography, *Philip Freneau: Champion of Democracy* (Austin: University of Texas Press, 1967).

Several critical studies offer useful introductions to Freneau's poetry: Mary Weatherspoon Bowden's book, *Philip Freneau,* Twayne's United States Authors Series (New York: Twayne Publishers, 1976), and Lewis Leary's chapter, "Philip Freneau," in *Major Writers of Early American Literature,* ed. Everett Emerson (Madison: University of Wisconsin Press, 1972), pp. 245-271. Nelson F. Adkins offers more philosophical than literary analysis in *Philip Freneau and the Cosmic Enigma: The Religious and Philosophical Speculations of an American Poet* (New York: New York University Press, 1949).

THE TEXT

I have arranged Freneau's poems chronologically by order of publication to demonstrate the progress of his career and the variety of his interests, but I have generally followed the 1809 edition, *Poems Written and Published during the American Revolutionary War* (Delmar, N.Y.: Scholars' Facsimiles & Reprints, 1976), which represents Freneau's final revision of most of his work. "Ode," not included in Freneau's later editions, follows the text of *Poems Written Between the Years 1768 & 1794* (Delmar, N.Y.: Scholars' Facsimiles & Reprints, 1976). "Lines Addressed to Mr. Jefferson," "On the Uniformity and Perfection of Nature," "On the Universality and Other Attributes of the God of Nature," "On the Religion of Nature," and "Stanzas to a Caty-Did" derive from *A Collection of Poems on American Affairs* (Delmar, N.Y.: Scholars' Facsimiles & Reprints, 1976). Lewis Leary's edition of *The Last Poems of Philip Freneau* (Westport, Conn.: Greenwood Press, 1945) provides the text for "A Fragment of Bion."

From *The Poems of Philip Freneau*

ODE TO FANCY[1]

Wakeful, vagrant, restless thing,
Ever wandering, on the wing,
Who thy wonderous source can find,
FANCY, regent of the mind;
A spark from Jove's resplendent throne,   5
But thy nature all unknown.
   This spark of bright, celestial flame,
From Jove's seraphic altar came,
And hence mankind in man may trace,
Resemblance to the immortal race   10
    Ah! what is all this mighty WHOLE,

[handwritten marginalia: Fancy as bird]

[handwritten marginalia: ruler]

[handwritten marginalia: Higher ruler]

[handwritten marginalia: is it all fabrication]

1. This poem is a much reduced version of "The Power of Fancy," written in 1770. Editing his work in 1795, Freneau broke the original poem into the "Ode to Fancy," saluting man's imagination as a variant on divine creativity, and "Fancy's Ramble," illustrating the poet's ability to roam at will through a wide variety of images transcending space and time.

[handwritten note at bottom: The Poet of the Revolution]

These suns and stars that round us roll!
What are they all, where'er they shine,
But *Fancies* of the Power Divine!
What is this *globe*, these *lands*, and *seas*,   15
And *heat*, and *cold*, and *flowers*, and *trees*,
And *life*, and *death*, and *beast*, and *man*,
And *time*—that with the *sun* began—
But thoughts on reason's scale combined,
Ideas of the Almighty mind!   20
    Fancy, thou the muse's pride,
In thy painted realms reside
Endless images of things,
Fluttering each on golden wings,
Ideal objects, such a store,   25
The universe can hold no more:
Fancy, to thy power we owe
Half our happiness below;
By thee Elysian groves[2] were made,
Thine were the notes that Orpheus[3] play'd;   30
By thee was Pluto charmed so well
While rapture seiz'd the crowds of hell—
Come, O come—perceived by none,
You and I will walk alone.

    (1770; 1786)

2. The home of the happy dead, in Greek mythology.
3. The mythical Greek hero, who charmed Pluto, the king of hell, by the power
of his music and won the opportunity to take his dead wife Eurydice back to
the land of the living.

THE VERNAL AGUE[1]

Where the pheasant roosts at night,
Lonely, drowsy, out of sight,
Where the evening breezes sigh
Solitary, there stray I.

Close along the shaded stream,   5

1. The title identifies a spring sickness, characterized by alternating attacks
of chills and fever.

Source of many a youthful dream,
Where branchy cedars dim the day   *reclaiming*
There I muse, and there I stray. .

Yet, what can please amid this bower,
That charmed the eye for many an hour!   10
The budding leaf is lost to me,
And dead the bloom on every tree.

The winding stream, that glides along,
The lark, that tunes her early song,
The mountain's brow, the sloping vale,   15
The murmuring of the western gale,

Have lost their charms!—the blooms are gone!
Trees put a darker aspect on,
The stream disgusts that wanders by,
And every zephyr brings a sigh.   20

Great guardian of our feeble kind!—
Restoring Nature, lend thine aid!
And o'er the features of the mind
Renew those colours, that must fade,
    When vernal suns forbear to roll,   25
    And endless winter chills the soul.

    (1775?; 1786)

THE VISION OF THE NIGHT[1]

[A FRAGMENT]

Let others draw from smiling skies their theme
And tell of climes, that boast unceasing light:

1. This is a fragment of "The House of Night," a long gothic poem on the death of Death which Freneau first published in 1779, then revised by expansion in the 1786 edition of his poems, and finally revised by contraction in this 1809 version. A facsimile of the original poem accompanies Lewis Leary's article, "The Dream Visions of Philip Freneau," *Early American Literature* 11, no. 2 (Fall 1976): 174-182.

I draw a darker scene replete with gloom,
I sing the horrors, and the shades of night.

Stranger, believe the truth experience tells,　　　　　5
Poetic dreams are of a livelier cast
Than those, which o'er the sober brain diffused,
Repeat the images of some action past.

Fancy, I own thy power! when sunk in sleep,
Thou playest thy wild delusive part so well,　　　　　10
You raise us into immortality,
Depict new heavens, or draw dark scenes of hell.

By some sad means, when reason holds no sway,
Lonely I roved at midnight o'er a plain
Where murmuring streams, and mingling rivers flow　　15
Far from their springs, and seek the sea again.

Sweet vernal *May*—tho' then thy woods, in bloom,
Flourished, yet nought of this could Fancy see:
No wild pinks blessed the meads, no green the fields,
And naked seemed to stand each lifeless tree.　　　　20

Dark was the sky, and not one friendly star
Shone from the zenith, or horizon clear;
Mist sate upon the plains, and darkness rode
In her dark chariot, with her ebon spear.

And from the wilds, the late resounding note　　　　25
Issued, of the loquacious whipperwill[2]
Hoarse, howling dogs, and nightly-roving wolves
Clamoured from far-off cliffs, invisible.

Rude, from the deep, vast foaming Chesapeke
I heard the winds the dashing waves assail:　　　　　30
And saw from far, by picturing fancy formed,
The black ship travelling thro' the adverse gale.

---

2. A bird peculiar to America; of a solitary nature, that never sings but in the night. Her note resembles the above name, given to her by the country people (Freneau's note).

At last, by chance, and guardian fancy, led,
I reached a noble dome, raised fair and high,
And saw the light from upper-windows glare, 35
Presage of mirth and hospitality.

And, by that light, around the dome appeared
A mournful garden of autumnal hue,
Its lately pleasing flowers, all drooping, stood
Amidst high weeds, that in rank plenty grew. 40

The primrose there, the violet darkly blue,
Daisies, and fair narcissus ceased to rise;
Gay spotted pinks their charming bloom withdrew,
And polyanthus quenched its thousand dyes.

No pleasant fruit, or blossom gaily smiled— 45
Nought but unhappy plants and trees were seen,
The yew, the myrtle, and the gloomy elm,
The cypress, with her melancholy green:

There cedars dark, the osier, and the pine,
Shorn tamarisks, and weeping willows grew; 50
The poplar tall, the lotos, and the lime,
And pyracantha, did her leaves renew:

The poppy, there, companion to repose,
Displayed her blossoms, that began to fall;
And there the purple amaranthus rose, 55
With mint, strong-scented, for the funeral.

And here and there, with laurel shrubs between,
A tombstone lay, inscribed with strains of woe;
And stanzas sad, throughout the dismal green,
Lamented for the dead, that slept below. 60

Among the graves a spiry building stood,
Whose tolling bell, resounding through the shade,
Sung doleful ditties to the adjacent wood;
And many a dismal, drowsy thing it said:

Grey "Elegy in
Country Churchyard"

"This fabric tall, with towers and chancels graced,   65
"Was raised by churchmen's hands, in ages fled;
"The roof they painted, and the beams they braced,
"And texts from *Moses* o'er the walls they spread:

"But wicked were their hearts, for they refused
"To aid the helpless orphan, when distrest;   70
"The shivering, naked stranger they mis-used,
"And banished from their doors the starving guest.

"By laws protected, cruel and prophane,
"The poor man's ox these monsters drove away;—
"And left distress to attend the infant train,   75
"No friend to comfort, and no bread to stay!

"But heaven looked on, with keen resentful eye,
"And doomed them to perdition and the grave;
"That, as they felt not for the wretch distrest,
"So heaven no pity on their souls would have.   80

"In pride they raised this building, tall and fair;
"Their hearts were on perpetual mischief bent:
"With pride they preached, and pride was in their prayer;
"With pride they were deceived——and so to hell they
    went."

(1779; 1786)

THE BEAUTIES OF SANTA CRUZ[1]

Sweet orange grove, the fairest of the isle,
    In thy soft shade luxuriously reclined,
Where, round my fragrant bed, the flowrets smile,
    In sweet delusions I deceive my mind.

---

1. Or St. Croix, a Danish island (in the American Archipelago), commonly,
tho' erroneously included in the cluster of the Virgin Islands; belonging to the
crown of Denmark (Freneau's note).

But *Melancholy's glooms assail my breast,*
　　For potent nature reigns despotic there;—
A nation ruined, and a world oppressed,
　　Might rob the boldest Stoic of a tear.

SICK of thy northern glooms, come, shepherd, seek
More equal climes, and a serener sky:
Why shouldst thou toil amid thy frozen ground,
Where half years' snows, a barren prospect, lie,

When thou mayst go where never frost was seen,
Or north-west winds with cutting fury blow,
Where never ice congealed the limpid stream,
Where never mountain tipt its head with snow?

Twice ten days prosperous gales thy barque shall bear
To isles that flourish in perpetual green,
Where richest herbage glads each fertile vale,
And ever verdant plants on every hill are seen.

Nor dread the dangers of the billowy deep,
Autumnal winds shall safely waft thee o'er;
Put off the timid heart, or, man unblest,
Ne'er shalt thou reach this gay enchanting shore.

Thus *Judah's* tribes beheld the promised land,
While *Jordan's* angry waters swelled between;
Thus, trembling on the brink, I see them stand,
Heaven's type in view, the Canaanitish green.

Thus, some mean souls, in spite of age and care,
Are held so firmly to this earth below,
They never wish to cross fate's dusky main
That parting them and happiness, doth flow.

Though Reason's voice might whisper to the soul
That nobler climes for man the heavens design—
Come, shepherd, haste—the northern breezes blow,
No more the slumbering winds thy barque confine.

Sweet orange grove! the fairest of the isle,
In thy soft shade luxuriously reclined,
Where, round my fragrant bed the flowerets smile,
In sweet delusions I deceive my mind.   40

But Melancholy's glooms assail my breast,
For potent nature reigns despotic there;—
A nation ruined, and a world oppressed,
Might rob the boldest Stoic of a tear.

From the vast caverns of old Ocean's bed   45
Fair Santa Cruz arising, laves her waist,
The threatening waters roar on every side,
For every side by ocean is embraced.

Sharp, craggy rocks repell the surging brine,
Whose caverned sides by restless billows wore,   50
Resemblance claim to that remoter isle
Where once the winds' proud lord the sceptre bore.

Betwixt old Cancer and the mid-way line,
In happiest climate, lies this envied isle:
Trees bloom throughout the year, soft breezes blow,   55
And fragrant Flora wears a lasting smile.

Cool, woodland streams from shaded cliffs descend,
The dripping rock no want of moisture knows,
Supplied by springs that on the skies depend,
That fountain feeding as the current flows.   60

Such were the isles which happy *Flaccus*[2] sung,
Where one tree blossoms while another bears,
Where spring forever gay, and ever young,
Walks her gay round through her unceasing years.

2. The Roman poet, Horace.

Such were the climes which youthful Eden saw   65
Ere crossing fates destroyed her golden reign—
Reflect upon thy loss, unhappy man,
And seek the vales of *Paradise* again.

No lowering skies are here—the neighbouring sun
Clear and unveiled, his brilliant journey goes,   70
Each morn emerging from the ambient main,
And sinking there, each evening, to repose.

In June's fair month the spangled traveller gains
The utmost limits of his northern way,
And blesses with his beams cold lands remote,   75
Sad Greenland's coast, and Hudson's frozen bay.

The shivering swains of these unhappy climes
Behold the side-way monarch through the trees,
Here glows his fiercer heat, his vertic beams,
Tempered with cooling gales and trade-wind breeze.   80

The native here, in golden plenty blest,
Bids from the soil the verdant harvests spring;
Feasts in the abundant dome, the joyous guest;
Time short,—life easy,—pleasure on the wing.

Here, fixt to-day in plenty's smiling vales,   85
Just as the year revolves, they laugh or groan;
September comes, seas swell with horrid gales,
And old Port-Royal's[3] fate is found their own!

And though so near heaven's blazing lamp doth run,
They court the beam that sheds the golden day,   90

3. Jamaican city destroyed by an earthquake in 1692. Freneau wrote a poem
about it, called "At Port Royal" (1786).

And hence are called the children of the sun,
Who, without fainting, bear his downward ray.

No threatening tides upon their island rise,
Gay Cynthia[4] scarce disturbs the ocean here,
No waves approach her orb, and, she, as kind,   95
Attracts no oceans to her silver sphere.

The happy waters boast, of various kinds,
Unnumbered myriads of the scaly race,
Sportive they glide above the deluged sand,
Gay as their clime, in ocean's ample vase.   100

Some streaked with burnished gold, resplendent, glare,
Some cleave the limpid deep, all silvered o'er,
Some, clad in living green, delight the eye,
Some red, some blue; of mingled colours more.

Here glides the spangled dolphin through the deep,   105
The giant carcased whales at distance stray,
The huge green turtles wallow through the wave,
Well pleased alike with land or water, they.

The *Rainbow* cuts the deep, of varied green,
The well-fed *Grouper* lurks remote, below,   110
The swift *Bonetta* coasts the watery scene,
The diamond-coated *Angels* kindle as they go,

Delicious to the taste, salubrious food,
Which might some temperate, studious sage allure
To curse the fare of his abstemious cell   115
And turn, for once, a cheerful epicure.

Unhurt mayest thou this luscious food enjoy,
To fulness feast upon the scaly kind,
These, well selected from a thousand more,
Delight the taste, and leave no bane behind.   120

4. The moon, in classical mythology.

Nor think *Hygeia*[5] is a stranger here—
To sensual souls the clime may fatal prove,
Anguish and death attend, and pain severe,
The midnight revel, and licentious love.

Full many a swain, in youth's serenest bloom   125
Is borne untimely to this alien clay,
Constrained to slumber in a foreign tomb,
Far from his friends, his country far away.

Yet if devoted to a sensual soul,
If fondly their own ruin they create,   130
These victims to the banquet and the bowl
Must blame their folly, only, not their fate.

But thou who first drew breath in northern air,
At early dawn ascend the sloping hills:
And oft, at noon, to lime-tree shades repair,   135
Where some soft stream from neighbouring groves distills,

And with it mix the liquid of the lime.
The old-aged essence of the generous cane,
And sweetest syrups of this liquorish clime,
And drink, to cool thy thirst, and drink again.   140

This happy beverage, joy-inspiring bowl,
Dispelling far the shades of mental night,
Beams bright ideas on the awakening soul,
And sorrow turns to pleasure and delight.

Sweet verdant isle! through thy dark woods I rove   145
And learn the nature of each native tree,
The *fustic* hard, the poisonous *manchineel*,
Which for its fragrant apple pleaseth thee;

Alluring to the smell, fair to the eye,
But deadliest poison in the taste is found—   150

5. The goddess of health, in the Grecian mythology (Freneau's note).

O shun the dangerous tree, nor touch, like *Eve,*
This interdicted fruit, in Eden's ground.

The lowly *mangrove* fond of watery soil,
The white-barked *gregory,* rising high in air,
The *mastic* in the woods you may descry,   155
Tamarind, and lofty bay-trees flourish there.

Sweet orange groves in lonely vallies rise
And drop their fruits, unnoticed and unknown,
The cooling acid limes in hedges grow,
The juicy lemons swell in shades their own.   160

Soft, spungy plums on trees wide spreading hang,
Bell-apples here, suspended, shade the ground,
Plump *grenadilloes,* and *güavas* grey,
With *melons,* in each plain and vale abound.

The conic-formed *cashew,* of juicy kind,   165
That bears at once an apple and a nut;
Whose poisonous coat, indignant to the lip,
Doth in its cell a wholesome kernel shut.

The prince of fruits, which some *jayama*[6] call,
Anana some, the happy flavoured *pine;*   170
In which unite the tastes and juices all
Of apple, quince, peach, grape, and nectarine,

Grows to perfection here, and spreads his crest,
His diadem towards the parent sun;
His diadem, in fiery blossoms drest,   175
Stands armed with swords, from potent Nature won.

Yon' cotton shrubs with bursting knobs behold,
Their snow white locks these humbler groves array;
On slender trees the blushing coffee hangs,
Like thy fair cherry, and would tempt thy stay.   180

6. Pineapple.

Safe from the winds, in deep retreats, they rise;
Their utmost summit may thine arm attain;
Taste the moist fruit, and from thy closing eyes
Sleep shall retire, with all his drowsy train.

The spicy berry, they *güava* call,   185
Swells in the mountains on a stripling tree;
These some admire, and value more than all,
My humble verse, besides, unfolds to thee.

The smooth white cedar, here, delights the eye,
The bay-tree, with its aromatic green,   190
The sea-side grapes, sweet natives of the sand,
And pulse, of various kinds, on trees are seen.

Here mingled vines, their downward shadows cast,
Here, clustered grapes from loaded boughs depend,
Their leaves no frosts, their fruits no cold winds blast, 195
But, reared by suns, to time alone they bend.

The plantane and banana flourish here,
Of hasty growth, and love to fix their root
Where some soft stream of ambling water flows,
To yield full moisture to their clustered fruit.   200

No other trees so vast a leaf can boast,
So broad, so long—through these, refreshed, we stray,
And though the noon-sun his fierce radiance shed,
These friendly leaves shall shade us all the way,

And tempt the cooling breeze to hasten there,   205
With its sweet odorous breath to charm the grove;
High shades and verdant seats, while underneath
A little stream by mossy banks doth rove,

Where once the Indian dames slept with their swains,
Or fondly kissed the moon-light eves away;—   210
The lovers fled, the tearful stream remains,
And only I console it with my lay!

Among the shades of yonder whispering grove
The green palmettoes mingle, tall and fair,
That ever murmur, and forever move,   215
Fanning with wavy bough the ambient air.

Pomegranates grace the wild, and sweet-sops there
Ready to fall, require the helping hand,
Nor yet neglect the papaw or mamee,
Whose slighted trees with fruits unheeded stand.   220

Those shaddocks juicy shall thy taste delight,
And yon' high fruits, the noblest of the wood,
That cling in clusters to the mother tree,
The cocoa-nut, rich, milky, healthful food.

O grant me, gods, if yet condemned to stray,   225
At least to spend life's sober evening here,
To plant a grove where winds yon' sheltered bay,
And pluck those fruits, that frost nor winter fear.

Cassada shrubs abound—transplanted here
From every clime, exotic blossoms blow;   230
Here Asia plants her flowers, here Europe trees,
And hyperborean herbs, unwintered, grow.

Here, a new herbage glads the generous steed,
Mules, goats, and sheep, enjoy these pastures fair,
And for thy hedges, Nature has decreed,   235
Guards of thy toils, the date and prickly pear.

But chief the glory of these Indian isles
Springs from the sweet, uncloying sugar cane:
Hence comes the planter's wealth, hence commerce sends
Such floating piles, to traverse half the main.   240

Whoe'er thou art that leavest thy native shore
And shalt to fair West-India climates come,

Taste not the enchanting plant—to taste forbear,
If ever thou wouldst reach thy much-loved home.

Ne'er through the isle permit thy feet to rove,   245
Or, if thou dost, let prudence lead the way,
Forbear to taste the virtues of the cane,
Forbear to taste what will complete your stay.

Whoever sips of this enchanting juice,
Delicious nectar, fit for Jove's own hall,   250
Returns no more from his loved Santa Cruz,
But quits his friends, his country, and his all.

And thinks no more of home—Ulysses so
Dragged off by force his sailors from that shore
Where *lotos* grew, and, had not strength prevailed,   255
They never would have sought their country more.

No annual toil inters this thrifty plant,
The stalk lopt off, refreshing showers prolong
To future years, unfading and secure,
The root so vigorous, and the juice so strong.   260

Unnumbered plants, beside, these climates yield,
And grass peculiar to the soil that bears:
Ten thousand various herbs array the field,
This glads thy palate, that thy health repairs.

Along the shore a wonderous *flower* is seen,   265
Where rocky ponds receive the surging wave,
Some drest in yellow, some attired in green,
Beneath the water, their gay branches lave.

This mystic plant, with its bewitching charms
Too surely springs from some enchanted bower,   270
Fearful it is, and dreads impending harms,
And ANIMAL, the natives call the flower.

From the smooth rock its little branches rise,
The object of thy view, and that alone,
Feast on its beauties with thy ravished eyes,   275
But aim to touch it, and—the flower is gone.

Nay, if thy shade but intercept the beam
That gilds the boughs beneath some briny lake,
Swift they retire, like a deluding dream,
And even a shadow for destruction take.   280

Warned by experience, hope not thou to gain
The magic plant, thy curious hand invades;
Returning to the light, it mocks thy pain,
Deceives all grasp, and seeks its native shades!

On yonder blue-browed hill, fresh harvests rise,   285
Where the dark tribe from Afric's sun burnt plain,
Oft o'er the ocean turn their wishful eyes
To isles remote, high looming o'er the main.

And view soft seats of ease and fancied rest,
Their native groves new painted on the eye,   290
Where no proud misers their gay hours molest
No lordly despots pass, unsocial, by.

See, yonder slave that slowly bends this way,
With years, and pain, and ceaseless toil opprest,
Though no complaining words his woes betray.   295
The eye dejected proves the heart distrest.

Perhaps in chains he left his native shore,
Perhaps he left a helpless offspring there,
Perhaps a wife, that he must see no more,
Perhaps a father, who his love did share.   300

Cursed be the ship, that brought him o'er the main,
And cursed the men, who from his country tore;

May she be stranded, ne'er to float again,
May they be shipwrecked on some hostile shore—

   O gold accurst, of every ill the spring,   305
For thee compassion flies the darkened mind,
Reason's plain dictates no conviction bring,
And madness merely sways all human kind.

not a typical capitalist

O gold accurst! for thee we madly run,
With murderous hearts, beyond the briny flood,   310
Seek foreign climes beneath a foreign sun,
And, there, exult to shed a brother's blood.

But thou, who ownest this sugar-bearing soil,
To whom no good the great FIRST CAUSE denies,
Let free-born hands attend thy sultry toil,   315
And fairer harvests to thy view shall rise,

The teeming earth will mightier stores disclose
Than ever struck the longing eye before,
And late content shall shed a soft repose—
Repose, so long a stranger at your door.   320

Give me some clime, the favorite of the sky,
Where cruel slavery never sought to reign—
But shun the theme, sad muse, and tell me why
These abject trees lie scattered o'er the plain?

These isles, lest Nature should have proved too kind,   325
Or man have sought his happiest heaven below,
Are torn by mighty winds, fierce hurricanes,
Nature convulsed in every shape of woe.

Nor scorn yon' lonely vale, of trees so reft:
There plantane groves late grew of liveliest green,   330
The orange flourished, and the lemon bore,
The genius of the isle dwelt there, unseen.

Wild were the skies, affrighted Nature groaned
As though approached her last decisive day.
Skies blazed around, and bellowing winds had nigh   335
Dislodged these cliffs, and tore yon' hills away.

O'er the wild main, dejected and afraid,
The trembling pilot lashed his helm a-lee
Or swiftly scudding, asked thy potent aid,
Dear *Pilot of the Galilëean Sea*.   340

Low hung the glooms, distended with the gale
The clouds, dark brooding, winged their circling flight,
Tremendous thunders joined the hurricane,
Daughter of chaos, and eternal night!

And how, alas! could these fair trees withstand   345
The wasteful madness of so fierce a blast,
That stormed along the plain, seized every grove,
And deluged with a sea this mournful waste.

That plantane grove, where oft I fondly strayed,
Thy darts, dread Phoebus, in those glooms to shun,   350
Is now no more a refuge or a shade,
Is now with rocks and deep sands over-run.

Those late proud domes of splendour, pomp, and ease
No longer strike the view, in grand attire;
But, torn by winds, flew piecemeal to the seas,   355
Nor left one nook to lodge the astonished 'squire.

But other groves the hand of Time shall raise,
Again shall Nature smile, serenely gay:
So soon each scene revives, why haste to leave
These green retreats, o'er the dark seas to stray.   360

For I must go where the mad pirate roves,
A stranger on the inhospitable main,

Lost to the scenes of Hudson's sweetest groves,
Cesarea's forests, and my native plain.

There endless waves deject the wearied eye,   365
And hostile winds incessant toil prepare;
But should loud bellowing storms all art defy,
The manly heart alone must conquer there.—

There wakes my fears, the guileful *Calenture*
Tempting the wanderer on the deep-sea main,   370
That paints gay groves upon the ocean floor,
Beckoning her victim to the faithless scene!

On these blue hills, to cull bright Fancy's flowers
Might yet awhile the dangerous work delay,
Might yet beguile the few remaining hours—   375
Ere to those waves I take my destined way.

Thy vales, *Bermuda,* and thy sea-girt groves
Can never like these southern forests please;
And, lashed by stormy waves, you court in vain
The northern shepherd to your cedar trees.   380

Not o'er those isles such equal planets rule.
All, but the cedar dreads the wintry blast,
Too well thy charms the banished *Waller*[7] sung;
Too near the *pilot's star* thy doom is cast.

Far o'er the waste of yonder surgy field   385
My native climes in fancied prospect lie,
Now hid in shades, and now by clouds concealed,
And now by tempests ravished from the eye.

There, triumphs to enjoy, are Britain, thine,
There, thy proud navy awes the pillaged shore;   390
Nor sees the day when nations shall combine
That pride to humble, and our rights restore.

7. Edmund Waller, English poet exiled by Cromwell for his royalist activities.

Yet o'er the globe shouldst thou extend thy reign,
Here may thy conquering arms one grotto spare;
Here—though thy conquests vex—in spite of pain,   395
We sip the enlivening glass, in spite of care.

What though we bend to a *tyrannic crown;*
Still Nature's charms in varied beauty shine—
What though we own the rude, imperious *Dane,*
Gold is his sordid care, the Muses mine.   400

Winter, and winter's glooms are far removed,
Eternal spring with smiling summer joined:—
Absence, and death, and heart-corroding care,
Why should they cloud the sun-shine of the mind?

But, shepherd, haste, and leave behind thee far   405
Thy bloody plains and iron glooms above;
Quit the cold northern star, and here enjoy,
Beneath the smiling skies, this land of love.

The drowsy pelican wings home his way,
The misty eve sits heavy on the sea,   410
And though yon' storm hangs brooding o'er the main,
Say, shall a moment's gloom discourage thee?

To-morrow's sun new paints the faded scene:
Though deep in ocean sink his western beams,
His spangled chariot shall ascend more clear,   415
More radiant from the drowsy land of dreams.

Of all the isles the neighbouring ocean bears,
None can with this their equal landscapes boast,
What could we do on SABA's cloudy height;
Or what could please on 'STATIA's barren coast?[8]   420

Couldst thou content on rough TORTOLA[9] stray,

8. St. Eustatius, islands in the Antilles chain near Santa Cruz.
9. One of the Virgin Islands.

Confest the fairest of the *Virgin* train;
Or couldst thou on those rocky summits play
Where high St. John stands frowning o'er the main?

Haste, shepherd, haste—Hesperian fruits[10] for thee   425
And clustered grapes from mingled boughs depend—
What pleasure in thy forests can there be
That, leafless now, to every tempest bend?

To milder stars, and skies of clearer blue,
Sworn foe to tyrants, for a time repair: 430
And 'till to mightier force proud Britain bends—
Despise her triumphs, and forget your care.

Soon shall the genius of this fertile soil
A new creation to the view unfold—
Admire the works of Nature's magic hand,   435
But scorn that vulgar bait—the thirst of gold.—

   Yet, if persuaded by no verse of mine,
You still admire your lands of frost and snow,
And pleased, prefer above these southern groves,
The darksome forests that around you grow: 440

Still there remain—your native air enjoy,
Repel the TYRANT, who your peace invades:
While charmed, we trace the vales of Santa Cruz.
And paint, with rapture, her inspiring shades.

   (1779; 1786)
10. The golden apples of Greek myth.

GEORGE THE THIRD'S SOLILOQUY

What mean these dreams, and hideous forms that rise
Night after night, tormenting to my eyes—
No real foes these horrid shapes can be,
But thrice as much they vex and torture me.

How cursed is he,—how doubly cursed am I—   5
Who lives in pain, and yet who dares not die;
To him no joy this world of Nature brings,
In vain the wild rose blooms, the daisy springs.
Is this a prelude to some new disgrace,
Some baleful omen to my name and race!—   10
It may be so—ere mighty Cesar died
Presaging Nature felt his doom, and sighed;
A bellowing voice through midnight groves was heard,
And threatening ghosts at dusk of eve appeared—
Ere Brutus fell, to adverse fates a prey,   15
His evil genius met him on the way,
And so may mine!—but who would yield so soon
A prize, some luckier hour may make my own?
Shame seize my crown, ere such a deed be mine—
No—to the last my squadrons shall combine,   20
And slay my foes, while foes remain to slay,
Or *heaven* shall grant me one successful day.
    Is there a robber close in Newgate[1] hemmed,
Is there a cut-throat, fettered and condemned?
Haste, loyal slaves, to George's standard come,   25
Attend his lectures when you hear the drum;
Your chains I break—for better days prepare,
Come out, my friends, from prison and from care,
Far to the west I plan your desperate sway,
There, 'tis no sin to ravage, burn, and slay   30
There, without fear, your bloody aims pursue,
And shew mankind what English thieves can do.
    That day, when first I mounted to the throne,
I swore to let all foreign foes alone.
Through love of peace to terms did I advance,   35
And made, they say, a shameful league with France.
But different scenes rise horrid to my view,
I charged my hosts to plunder and subdue—
At first, indeed, I thought short wars to wage
And sent some jail-birds to be led by *Gage*.[2]   40

1. London prison.
2. General Thomas Gage, the last royal governor of Massachusetts; he was
ordered back to England in October 1775, after the battles of Concord, Lexington,
and Bunker Hill.

For 'twas but right, that those we marked for slaves
Should be reduced by cowards, fools, and knaves;
Awhile, directed by his feeble hand,
Those *troops* were kicked and pelted through the land,
Or starved in Boston, cursed the unlucky hour   45
They left their dungeons for that fatal shore.
    France aids them now, a desperate game I play,
And hostile Spain will do the same, they say;
My armies vanquished, and my heroes fled,
My people murmuring, and my commerce dead,   50
My shattered navy pelted, bruised, and clubbed,
By Dutchmen bullied, and by Frenchmen drubbed,
My name abhorred, my nation in disgrace,
How should I act in such a mournful case!
My hopes and joys are vanished with my coin,   55
My ruined army, and my lost Burgoyne![3]
What shall I do—confess my labours vain,
Or whet my tusks, and to the charge again!
But where's my force—my choicest troops are fled,
Some thousands crippled, and a myriad dead—   60
If I were owned the boldest of mankind,
And hell with all her flames inspired my mind,
Could I at once with Spain and France contend,
And fight the *rebels*, on the world's green end?—
The pangs of *parting* I can ne'er endure,   65
Yet *part* we must, and part to meet no more!
Oh, blast this *Congress*, blast each upstart STATE,
On whose commands ten thousand captains wait;
From various climes that dire *Assembly*[4] came,
True to their trust, as hostile to my fame;   70
'Tis these, ah these, have ruined half my sway,
Disgraced my arms, and led my slaves astray—
Cursed be the day, when first I saw the sun,
Cursed be the hour, when I these wars begun:
The fiends of darkness then possessed my mind,   75
And powers unfriendly to the human kind.

    3. General John Burgoyne, leader of British forces marching south from Montreal; he was defeated by the American army at Saratoga in 1777.
    4. The Continental Congress.

To wasting grief, and sullen rage a prey,
To *Scotland's* utmost verge I'll take my way,
There with eternal storms due concert keep,
And while the billows rage, as fiercely weep—   80
Ye highland lads, my rugged fate bemoan,
Assist me with one sympathizing groan;
For late I find the nations are my foes,
I must submit, and that with bloody nose,
Or, like our James,[5] fly basely from the state,   85
Or share, what still is worse—old *Charles's*[6] fate.

    (1779; 1786)

5. King James II, exiled after the defeat of his army by William of Orange at the Battle of the Boyne, 1688.
6. King Charles I, beheaded by order of the Rump Parliament in 1649.

THE BRITISH PRISON SHIP

THE HESSIAN DOCTOR (CANTO III, PART 2)

From *Brooklyn* heights a Hessian doctor came,
Not great his skill, nor greater much his fame;
Fair Science never called the wretch her son,
And Art disdained the stupid man to own;—
Can you admire that Science was so coy,   5
Or Art refused his genius to employ!—
Do men with brutes an equal dullness share,
Or cuts yon' grovelling mole the midway air—
In polar worlds can Eden's blossoms blow,
Do trees of God in barren deserts grow.   10
Are loaded vines to Etna's summit known,
Or swells the peach beneath the frozen zone—
Yet still he put his genius to the rack;
And, as you may suppose, was owned a *quack*.
    He on his charge the healing work begun   15
With antimonial mixtures;[1] by the tun,

1. Drugs containing antimony, a salt used as an emetic to cure intestinal ailments.

Ten minutes was the time he deigned to stay,
The time of grace allotted once a day.—
He drenched us well with bitter draughts, 'tis true,
Nostrums from hell, and *cortex* from Peru—
Some with his pills he sent to Pluto's reign,[2]
And some he blistered with his flies of Spain;[3]
His Tartar doses walked their deadly round,
Till the lean patient at the potion frowned,
And swore that hemlock, death, or what you will,   25
Were nonsense to the drugs that stuffed his bill.—
On those refusing, he bestowed a kick,
Or menaced vengeance with a walking stick;—
Here, uncontrouled, he exercised his trade,
And grew experienced by the deaths he made,   30
By frequent blows we from his cane endured
He killed at least as many as he cured,
On our lost comrades built his future fame,
And scattered fate, where'er his footsteps came.

    Some did not bend, submissive to his skill,   35
And swore he mingled poison with his pill,
But we acquit him by a fair confession,
He was no *Myrmidon*[4]—he was a Hessian—
Although a beast, he had some sense of sin
Or else the Lord knows where we now had been;   40
No doubt, in that far country sent to range
Where never prisoner meets with an exchange—
No centries stand, to guard the midnight posts,
Nor seal down hatch-ways on a crowd of ghosts.

    Knave though he was, yet candour must confess   45
Not chief physician was this man of Hesse—
One master o'er the murdering tribe was placed,
By him the rest were honoured or disgraced;
Once, and but once, by some strange fortune led
He came to see the dying and the dead—   50
He came—but anger so deformed his eye,

2. Hell.
3. Blister beetles used to bleed patients.
4. An unscrupulously faithful military follower, like the Myrmidon tribesmen
Achilles led to Troy.

And such a faulcheon[5] glittered on his thigh,
And such a gloom his visage darkened o'er,
And two such pistols in his hands he bore!
That, by the gods!—with such a load of steel,   55
He came, we thought, to murder, not to heal—
Rage in his heart, and mischief in his head,
He gloomed destruction, and had smote us dead,
Had he so dared—but fear with-held his hand—
He came—blasphemed—and turned again to land.   60

      (1781; 1786)

5. Sword.

TO THE MEMORY OF THE BRAVE AMERICANS,

UNDER *GENERAL GREENE,* IN SOUTH CAROLINA, WHO FELL IN THE ACTION OF SEPTEMBER 8, 1781

At EUTAW springs the valiant died:
Their limbs with dust are covered o'er—
Weep on, ye springs, your tearful tide;
How many heroes are no more!

If in this wreck of ruin, they   5
Can yet be thought to claim a tear,
O smite your gentle breast, and say
The friends of freedom slumber here!

Thou who shalt trace this bloody plain,
If goodness rules thy generous breast,   10
Sigh for the wasted rural reign;
Sigh for the shepherds, sunk to rest!

Stranger, their humble graves adorn;
You too may fall, and ask a tear:
'Tis not the beauty of the morn   15
That proves the evening shall be clear—

They saw their injured country's woe;
The flaming town, the wasted field;
Then rushed to meet the insulting foe;
They took the spear—but left the shield.   20

Led by thy conquering genius, GREENE,
The Britons they compelled to fly:
None distant viewed the fatal plain,
None grieved, in such a cause to die—

But, like the Parthian,[1] famed of old,   25
Who, flying, still their arrows threw;
These routed Britons, full as bold,
Retreated, and retreating slew.

Now rest in peace, our patriot band;
Though far from Nature's limits thrown,   30
We trust, they find a happier land,
A brighter sun-shine of their own.

(1781; 1786)

1. Cavalry of ancient Parthia, known for their strategy of shooting at enemies
while seeming to retreat.

A PICTURE OF THE TIMES,

WITH OCCASIONAL REFLECTIONS[1]

Still round the world triumphant Discord flies,
Still angry kings to bloody contests rise;
Hosts bright with steel, in dreadful order placed,
And ships contending on the watery waste;
Distracting demons every breast engage,   5
Unwearied nations glow with mutual rage;
Still to the charge the routed Briton turns,
The war still rages and the battle burns;

1. Freneau called this poem "Philosophical Reflections" in his 1786 volume,
but retitled it in 1795 and 1809.

See, man with man in deadly combat join,
See, the black navy form the flaming line;   10
Death smiles alike at battles lost or won—
Art does for him what Nature would have done.
　　　　Can scenes like these delight the human breast?—
Who sees with joy humanity distrest?
Such tragic scenes fierce passion might prolong,   15
But slighted Reason says, they must be wrong,
　　　　Cursed be the day, how bright soe'er it shined,
That first made kings the masters of mankind;
And cursed the wretch who first with regal pride
Their equal rights to equal men denied;   20
But cursed, o'er all, who first to slavery broke,
Submissive bowed, and owned a monarch's yoke:
Their servile souls his arrogance adored
And basely owned a brother for a lord;
Hence wrath, and blood, and feuds, and wars began,   25
And man turned monster to his fellow man.
　　　　Not so that age of innocence and ease
When men, yet social, knew no ills like these;
Then dormant yet, Ambition (half unknown)
No rival murdered to possess a throne;   30
No seas to guard, no empires to defend—
Of some small tribe the father and the friend.
The hoary sage beneath his sylvan shade
Imposed no laws but those which reason made;
On peace, not war; on good, not ill, intent,   35
He judged his brethren by their own consent;
Untaught to spurn those brethren to the dust;
In virtue firm, and obstinately just,
For him no navies roved from shore to shore,
No slaves were doomed to dig the glittering ore;   40
Remote from all the vain parade of state,
No slaves in scarlet sauntered at his gate,
Nor did his breast the angry passions tear,
He knew no murder, and he felt no fear.

Was this the patriarch sage—Then turn your eyes   45
And view the contrast that our age supplies;
Touched from the life, we trace no ages fled,
We draw no curtain that conceals the dead;
To distant Britain let the view be cast,
And say, the present far exceeds the past;   50
Of all the plagues that e'er the world have cursed,
Name George, the tyrant, and you name the worst!
       What demon, hostile to the human kind,
Planted these fierce disorders in the mind?
All, urged alike, one phantom we pursue,   55
But what has war with human kind to do?
In death's black shroud our bliss can ne'er be found;
'Tis madness aims the life-destroying wound,
Sends fleets and armies to these ravaged shores
Plots constant ruin, but no peace restores.   60
       O dire ambition!—thee these horrors suit:
Lost to the human, she assumes the brute;
She, proudly vain, or insolently bold,
Her heart revenge, her eye intent on gold,
Swayed by the madness of the present hour   65
Lays worlds in ruin for *extent of power;*
That shining bait, which dropt in folly's way
Tempts the weak mind, and leads the heart astray.
       Thou happiness! still sought but never found,
We, in a circle, chace thy shadow round;   70
Meant all mankind in different forms to bless,
Which, yet possessing, we no more possess:
Thus far removed and painted on the eye
Smooth verdant fields seem blended with the sky,
But where they both in fancied contact join   75
In vain we trace the visionary line;
Still, as we chace, the empty circle flies,
Emerge new mountains, or new oceans rise.

       (1782; 1786)

230 **Philip Freneau**

THE DESERTED FARM-HOUSE

[handwritten: loss of agrarian society]

This antique dome the insatiate tooth of time *a*
Now level with the dust has almost laid;— *b*
Yet ere 'tis gone, I seize my humble theme *a*
From these low ruins, that his years have made. *b*

Behold the unsocial hearth!—where once the fires *a*   5
Blazed high, and soothed the storm-stay'd traveller's woes; *b*
See the weak roof, that abler props requires, *a*
Admits the winds, and swift descending snows. *b*

Here, to forget the labours of the day,
No more the swains at evening hours repair,   10
But wandering flocks assume the well known way
To shun the rigours of the midnight air.

In yonder chamber, half to ruin gone,
Once stood the ancient housewife's curtained bed—
Timely the prudent matron has withdrawn,   15
And each domestic comfort with her fled.

The trees, the flowers that her own hands had reared,
The plants, the vines, that were so verdant seen,—   *[handwritten: desert / deserted]*
The trees, the flowers, the vines have disappear'd,
And every plant has vanish'd from the green.   20

So sits in tears on wide Campania's plain
Rome, once the mistress of a world enslaved;
[handwritten: transitions] That triumph'd o'er the land, subdued the main,
And Time himself, in her wild transports, braved.

So sits in tears on Palestina's shore   25
The Hebrew town, of splendour once divine—
Her kings, her lords, her triumphs are no more;
Slain are her priests, and ruin'd every shrine.

Once, in the bounds of this deserted room,
Perhaps some swain nocturnal courtship made,   30

Perhaps some *Sherlock*[1] mused amidst the gloom;
Since Love and Death forever seek the shade.

Perhaps some miser, doom'd to discontent,
Here counted o'er the heaps acquired with pain;
He to the dust—his gold, on traffick sent,
Shall ne'er disgrace these mouldering walls again.

35

attack on commercialism

Nor shall the glow-worm fopling, sunshine bred,
Seek, at the evening hour this wonted dome—
Time has reduced the fabrick to a shed,
Scarce fit to be the wandering beggar's home.

40

And none but I its dismal case lament—
None, none but I o'er its cold relics mourn,
Sent by the muse—(the time perhaps mispent—)
To write dull stanzas on this dome forlorn.

(1785; 1786)

1. Probably a reference to William Sherlock, author of *A Practical Discourse Concerning Death* (1689) and *A Practical Discourse Concerning a Future Judgment* (1692).

From *The Miscellaneous Works*

THE WILD HONEY SUCKLE

Fair flower, that dost so comely grow,
Hid in this silent, dull retreat,
Untouched thy honied blossoms blow,
Unseen thy little branches greet:
　　No roving foot shall crush thee here,
　　No busy hand provoke a tear.

5

By Nature's self in white arrayed,
She bade thee shun the vulgar eye,

And planted here the guardian shade,
And sent soft waters murmuring by;   10
    Thus quietly thy summer goes,
    Thy days declining to repose.

Smit with those charms, that must decay,
I grieve to see your future doom;
They died—nor were those flowers more gay,   15
The flowers that did in Eden bloom;
    Unpitying frosts, and Autumn's power
    Shall leave no vestige of this flower.

From morning suns and evening dews
At first thy little being came: 20
If nothing once, you nothing lose,
For when you die you are the same;
    The space between, is but an hour,
    The frail duration of a flower.

    (1786; 1788)

THE INDIAN BURYING GROUND

In spite of all the learned have said,
I still my old opinion keep;
The *posture*, that *we* give the dead,
Points out the soul's eternal sleep.

Not so the ancients of these lands—   5
The Indian, when from life released,
Again is seated with his friends,
And shares again the joyous feast.[1]

His imaged birds, and painted bowl,
And venison, for a journey dressed,   10

---

1. The North American Indians bury their dead in a sitting posture; decorating the corpse with wampum, the images of birds, quadrupeds, &c: And (if that of a warrior) with bows, arrows, tomhawks and other military weapons (Freneau's note).

Bespeak the nature of the soul,
ACTIVITY, that knows no rest.

His bow, for action ready bent,
And arrows, with a head of stone,
Can only mean that life is spent,   15
And not the old ideas gone.

Thou, stranger, that shalt come this way,
No fraud upon the dead commit—
Observe the swelling turf, and say
They do not *lie*, but here they *sit*.   20

Here still a lofty rock remains,
On which the curious eye may trace
(Now wasted, half, by wearing rains)
The fancies of a ruder race.

Here still an aged elm aspires,   25
Beneath whose far-projecting shade
(And which the shepherd still admires)
The children of the forest played!

There oft a restless Indian queen
(Pale *Shebah*, with her braided hair)   30
And many a barbarous form is seen
To chide the man that lingers there.

By midnight moons, o'er moistening dews,
In habit for the chase arrayed,
The hunter still the deer pursues,   35
The hunter and the deer, a shade!

And long shall timorous fancy see
The painted chief, and pointed spear,
And Reason's self shall bow the knee
To shadows and delusions here.   40

(1787; 1788)

TO AN AUTHOR

Your leaves bound up compact and fair,
In neat array at length prepare,
To pass their hour on learning's stage,
To meet the surly critic's rage;
The statesman's slight, the smatterer's sneer—   5
Were these, indeed, your only fear,
You might be tranquil and resigned:
What most should touch your fluttering mind;
Is that, few critics will be found
To sift your works, and deal the wound.   10

    Thus, when one fleeting year is past
On some bye-shelf *your* book is cast—
Another comes, with *something new*,
And drives you fairly out of view:

With some to praise, *but more to blame*,   15
The mind returns to—whence it came;
And some alive, who *scarce could read*
Will publish satires on the dead.

    Thrice happy DRYDEN[1], who could meet
Some rival bard in every street!   20
When all were bent on writing well
It was some credit to excel:—

Thrice happy Dryden, who could find
A *Milbourne*[2] for his sport designed—
And *Pope*, who saw the harmless rage   25
Of *Dennis*[3] bursting o'er his page
Might justly spurn the *critic's aim*,
Who only helped to swell his fame.

    On these bleak climes by Fortune thrown,
Where rigid *Reason* reigns alone,   30

1. See Johnson's lives of the English Poets (Freneau's note).
2. Luke Milbourne, an English author who criticized Dryden's translation of Virgil as inferior to his own.
3. John Dennis, neoclassical English poet, dramatist, and critic, famous for his attacks on Pope.

Where lovely *Fancy* has no sway,
Nor magic forms about us play—
Nor nature takes her summer hue
Tell me, what has the muse to do?—

An age employed in edging steel   35
Can no poetic raptures feel;
No solitude's attracting power,
No leisure of the noon day hour,
No shaded stream, no quiet grove
Can this fantastic century move,   40

The muse of love in no request—
Go—try your fortune with the rest,
One of the nine you should engage,
To meet the follies of the age:—

On *one*, we fear, your choice must fall—   45
The least engaging of them all—
Her visage stern—an angry style—
A clouded brow—malicious smile—
A mind on *murdered victims* placed—
She, only she, can please the taste!   50

      (1788; 1788)

From *Poems Written between the Years 1768 & 1794*

THE VANITY OF EXISTENCE

TO THYRSIS

In youth, gay scenes attract our eyes,
    And not suspecting their decay
Life's flowery fields before us rise,
    Regardless of its winter day.

But vain pursuits, and joys as vain,   5
    Convince us life is but a dream.
Death is to wake, to rise again
    To that true life you best esteem.

So nightly on some shallow tide,
    Oft have I seen a splendid show;   10
Reflected stars on either side,
    And glittering moons were seen below.

But when the tide had ebbed away,
    The scene fantastic with it fled,
A bank of mud around me lay,   15
    And sea-weed on the river's bed.

    (1781; 1795)

THE HURRICANE[1]

Happy the man who, safe on shore,
Now trims, at home, his evening fire;
Unmoved, he hears the tempests roar,
That on the tufted groves expire:
Alas! on us they doubly fall,   5
Our feeble barque must bear them all.

Now to their haunts the birds retreat,
The squirrel seeks his hollow tree,
Wolves in their shaded caverns meet,
All, all are blest but wretched we—   10
Foredoomed a stranger to repose,
No rest the unsettled ocean knows.

While o'er the dark abyss we roam,
Perhaps, with last departing gleam,

---

1. Near the east end of Jamaica. July 30, 1784 (Freneau's note).

We saw the sun descend in gloom,   15
No more to see his morning beam;
But buried low, by far too deep,
On coral beds, unpitied, sleep!

But what a strange, uncoasted strand
Is that, where fate permits no day—   20
No charts have we to mark that land,
No compass to direct that way—
What Pilot shall explore that realm,
What new COLUMBUS take the helm!

While death and darkness both surround,   25
And tempests rage with lawless power,
Of friendship's voice I hear no sound,
No comfort in this dreadful hour—
What friendship can in tempests be,
What comfort on this raging sea?   30

The barque, accustomed to obey,
No more the trembling pilots guide:
Alone she gropes her trackless way,
While mountains burst on either side—
Thus, skill and science both must fall;   35
And ruin is the lot of all.

      (1785; 1795)

ELEGIAC LINES

ON THE DEATH OF A FIDDLER,

CALLED BLIND JACOB

In Life's fair morn, a FIDDLE, was his choice,
This he preferr'd to Reason's sober voice;
Some scores of tunes, on cat-gut taught to play,

Sweetly he scraped the dream of life away:
From house to house (the joy of all) he ran,   5
Welcome to all, this music-making man;
Where'er he went, he bade all *discord* cease
And howling brats by him were hush'd to peace:
Where'er he went, to play for beau or belle,
Much they admired the GOD *within the shell;*   10
Each grey-hair'd dame for *that* postpon'd all care,
And own'd this fiddle was a sweet affair.—
No foe had he ('twas worthy of remark),
Except, perhaps, the preacher and his clerk
Some deacon grave, who lived by looking sad,   15
Some rival wight, who no such fiddle had:
These were, indeed, disgusted with its tone;
Because—the world preferr'd it to their own.
        But, mark the event—with all his fiddling skill,
This man of tunes went capering down the hill: 20
From endless mirth, an idle habit sprung,
And years advanced, in spite of all he sung!—
Despising home, and absent day from day,
Perplext with weeds his little garden lay:—
Hence plagues came on, and hence, too soon arose   25
From midnight drams the diamonds on his nose;
Hence, saucy cares, that would no longer wait,
Seiz'd all the man, and pictured out his fate,
New artists rose, that each became his foe,
Play'd livelier tunes (or people thought them so);   30
Soon out of date the grey-hair'd scraper grew,
(The truth was this, they wanted something NEW:
Surpriz'd he saw full seventy years were past—
"And do I wake!—(the fiddler cry'd) at last?
"While other's toil'd, *to bless the rainy day.*   35
"Ye powers! have I done nothing else but *play?*"—
With grief he felt the patches on his coat,
Himself—his fiddle—on the world afloat;
His hat, a slouch, that beggars might abuse,
And toes, uncouth, that peep'd from both his shoes—   40
Then curs'd his strings, his rosin, and his art,

And said—" 'Tis so! your fiddler must depart!"
    Now he is dead!—ye few that prized him still,
That once admired—nay, once adored his skill:
And THOU, to whom I dedicate my lay,   45
Ah! for the joys he gave, some tribute pay!
You—at whose wedding he so finely play'd,
That night, when JULIA was to heaven conveyed,
Whose charms, THAT NIGHT, bade every bosom glow,
Charms, that were toasted twenty years ago!—   50
For *him*—that once you deem'd out-done by none,
For *him*, provide the monumental stone!
From other worlds he had not much to hope,
No friend to Luther, Calvin, or the Pope.
(Perhaps some better work employs him there—   55
Perhaps on Pluto's coast no fiddles are!—)
Howe'er that be, allow me to advise,
Plant some memorial where his carcase lies.
A NEWARK STONE, companion of repose,
Should tell the inscription that the muse bestows: 60
And ere that STONE his mouldering dust confines,
You give me but the HINT—I'll write the lines!

The Epitaph

Here lies a man, whom music call'd her own,
Who in a fiddling world possess'd the throne:
His strains from Nature he, 'tis certain, caught,   65
Yet from his fiddle never saved a groat—
The heavenly muse was, to the last, his friend,
But to his wants none would a shilling lend.
Blind as he was, and tho' *Euterpe*[1] fired,
Yet empty as his fiddle he retired.   70
Why did she lend him her celestial strains?
Go, ask the fiddle why it had not brains.—
    Shall we say more?—yes—what we say we mean—
Indeed a fiddle made him very lean!—
They who, like JACOB, put their trust in sound,   75

---

1. Greek muse of lyric poetry and music.

Like him, must meet the poor-house under ground,
With not a dollar to bequeath their heirs,
With not a groat to meet the churches prayers.—
Sweet be his sleep!—and truely, now, a shade,
May his bad debts for music all be paid,   80
May his old fiddle change into a harp,
And his NEW EYES distinguish FLAT from SHARP.

   (1791; 1795)

THE DISH OF TEA

Let some in beer place their delight,
O'er bottled porter waste the night,
     Or sip the rosy wine:
A dish of TEA more pleases me,
Yields softer joys, provokes less noise,   5
     And breeds no base design.

From China's groves, this present brought,
Enlivens every power of thought,
     Riggs many a ship for sea:
Old maids it warms, young widows charms;   10
And ladies' men, not one in ten
     But courts them for their TEA.

When throbbing pains assail my head,
And dullness o'er my brain is spread,
     (The muse no longer kind)   15
A single sip dispels the hyp:[1]
To chace the gloom, fresh spirits come,
     The flood-tide of the mind.

When worn with toil, or vext with care,
Let *Susan* but this draught prepare,   20
     And I forget my pain.

   1. Hypochondria; depression.

This magic bowl revives the soul;
With gentlest sway, bids care be gay;
    Nor mounts, to cloud the brain.—

If learned men the truth would speak   25
They prize it far beyond their GREEK,
    More fond attention pay;
No HEBREW root so well can suit;
More quickly taught, less dearly bought,
    Yet *studied* twice a day.   30

This leaf, from distant regions sprung,
Puts life into the female tongue,
    And aids the cause of love.
Such power has TEA o'er bond and free;
Which *priests* admire, delights the *'squire,*   35
    And *Galen's* sons [2] approve.

      (1791; 1795)

2. Doctors.

ODE[1]

God save the Rights of Man!
Give us a heart to scan
Blessings so dear:
Let them be spread around
Wherever man is found,   5
And with the welcome sound
Ravish his ear.

Let us with France agree,
And bid the world be free,
While tyrants fall!   10

1. This song celebrating egalitarian ideals was written for public performance at the time of the Genêt Affair and could be sung to the tune of "God Save the King." Freneau published it in the 1795 edition of his poems but omitted it from later collections, probably because of its unqualified support for the French Revolution.

Let the rude savage host
Of their vast numbers boast—
Freedom's almighty trust
Laughs at them all!

Though hosts of slaves conspire   15
To quench fair Gallia's fire,
Still shall they fail:
Though traitors round her rise,
Leagu'd with her enemies,
To war each patriot flies,   20
And will prevail.

No more is valour's flame
Devoted to a name,
Taught to adore—
Soldiers of LIBERTY   25
Disdain to bow the knee,
But teach EQUALITY
To every shore.

The world at last will join
To aid thy grand design,   30
Dear Liberty!
To Russia's frozen lands
The generous flame expands;
On Afric's burning sands
Shall man be free!   35

In this our western world
Be Freedom's flag unfurl'd
Through all its shores!
May no destructive blast
Our heaven of joy o'ercast,   40
May Freedom's fabric last
While time endures.

If e'er her cause require!—
Should tyrants e'er aspire

To aim their stroke,   45
May no proud despot daunt—
Should he his standard plant,
Freedom will never want
Her hearts of oak!

     (1793; 1795)

From *A Collection of Poems on American Affairs*

LINES ADDRESSED TO MR. JEFFERSON ON HIS RETIREMENT FROM THE PRESIDENCY OF THE UNITED STATES.—1809

PRAESENTI TIBI MATUROS LARGIMUR
HONORES—HOR.

To you, great sir, our heartfelt praise we give,
And your ripe honors yield you—while you live.

    At length the year, which marks his course, expires,
And JEFFERSON from public life retires;
That year, the close of years, which own his claim,
And give him all his honors, all his fame.
Far in the heaven of fame I see him fly,   5
Safe in the realms of immortality:
On EQUAL WORTH his honor'd mantle falls,
Him,[1] whom Columbia her true patriot calls;
Him, whom we saw her codes of freedom plan,
To none inferior in the ranks of man.   10

    When to the helm of state your country call'd

---

1. James Madison, fourth President of the United States and Freneau's college classmate.

No danger awed you and no fear appall'd;
Each bosom, faithful to its country's claim,
Hail'd JEFFERSON, that long applauded name;
All, then, was dark, and wrongs on wrongs accrued   15
Our treasures wasted, and our strength subdued;
What seven long years of war and blood had gain'd,
Was lost, abandon'd, squander'd, or restrain'd:
Britannia's tools had schemed their *easier* way,
To conquer, ruin, pillage, or betray;   20
Domestic traitors,[2] with exotic, join'd,
To shackle this *last refuge* of mankind;
Wars were provoked, and FRANCE[3] was made our foe,
That George's race might govern all below,
O'er this wide world, uncheck'd, unbounded, reign,   25
Seize every clime, and subjugate the main.

    All this was seen—and rising in your might,
By genius aided, you reclaim'd our right,
That RIGHT, which conquest, arms, and valor gave
To this young nation—not to live a slave.   30

    And what but toil has your long service seen
Dark tempests gathering o'er a sky serene—
For wearied years no mines of wealth can pay,
No fame, nor all the plaudits of that day,
Which now returns you to your rural shade,   35
The sage's heaven, for contemplation made,
Who, like the ROMAN[4] in their country's cause
Exert their valor, or enforce its laws,
And late retiring, every wrong redress'd,
Give their last days to solitude and rest.   40

    This great reward a generous nation yields—
REGRET attends you to your native fields;

2. Freneau attacks the Federalist administration here, with particular reference to the Alien and Sedition Laws.
3. Freneau interpreted Federalist unwillingness to support the revolutionary French government as evidence of continued loyalty to England.
4. Cincinnatus.

Their grateful thanks for every service done,
And hope, your thorny race of care is run.

    From your sage counsels what effects arise!   45
The vengeful briton from our waters flies;
His thundering ships no more our coasts assail,
But seize the advantage of the western gale.
Though bold and bloody, warlike, proud, and fierce,
They shun your vengeance for a MURDERED PEARCE,[5]   50
And starved, dejected, on some meagre shore,
Sigh for the country they shall rule no more.

    Long in the councils of your native land,
We saw you cool, unchanged, intrepid, stand:
When the firm CONGRESS, still too firm to yield,   55
Stay'd masters of the long contested field,
Your wisdom aided, what their counsels framed—
By you the murdering savages were tamed—
That INDEPENDENCE we had sworn to gain,
By you asserted (nor DECLARED in vain)   60
We seized, triumphant, from a tyrant's throne,
And Britain totter'd when the work was done.

    You, when an angry *faction* vex'd the age,
Rose to your place at once, and check'd their rage;
The envenom'd shafts of malice you defied,   65
And turn'd all projects of revolt aside:—
We saw you libell'd by the *worst of men*,[6]
While hell's red lamp hung quivering o'er his pen,
And fiends congenial every effort try
To blast that merit which shall never die—   70

    5. John Pearce, mate of an American vessel, killed in 1806 when the British ship *Leander* fired on his sloop. The ensuing public uproar forced the English consul to leave New York.
    6. Freneau's journalistic rival John Fenno, editor of the *Gazette of the United States*. Fenno's paper, supported by Hamilton, systematically attacked the Jeffersonian positions of Freneau's *National Gazette*.

These had their hour, and traitors wing'd their flight,
To aid the screechings of distracted night.

Vain were their hopes—the poison'd darts of hell,
Glanced from your flinty shield, and harmless fell.

All this you bore—beyond it all you rose,   75
Nor ask'd despotic laws to crush your foes.
Mild was your language, temperate though severe,
And not less potent than ITHURIEL's spear[7]
To touch the infernals in their loathsome guise,
Confound their slanders and detect their lies.—   80

All this you braved—and, now, what task remains,
But silent walks on solitary plains
To bid the vast luxuriant harvest grow,
The slave be happy and secured from woe—
To illume the statesmen of the times to come   85
With the bold spirit of primeval Rome;
To taste the joys your long tried service brings,
And look, with pity, on the cares of kings:—
Whether, with NEWTON, you the heavens explore,
And trace through nature the creating power,   90
Or, if with morals you reform the age,
(Alike, in all, the patriot and the sage)
May peace and soft repose, attend you still,
In the lone vale, or on the cloud-capp'd hill,
While smiling plenty decks the abundant plain,   95
And hails ASTREA[8] to the world again.

(1809; 1815)

7. In *Paradise Lost* the angel Ithuriel fights with a sword capable of exposing deceit at the slightest touch.

8. The goddess of Justice in classical mythology, who withdrew from earth to the heavens in reaction to human wickedness.

ON THE UNIFORMITY AND PERFECTION OF NATURE

On one fix'd point all nature moves,
Nor deviates from the track she loves;
Her system, drawn from reason's source,
She scorns to change her wonted course.

Could she descend from that great plan   5
To work unusual things for man,
To suit the insect of an hour—
This would betray a want of power.

Unsettled in its first design
And erring, when it did combine   10
The parts that form the vast machine,
The figures sketch'd on nature's scene.

Perfections of the great first cause
Submit to no contracted laws,
But all-sufficient, all-supreme,   15
Include no trivial views in them.

Who looks through nature with an eye
That would the scheme of heaven descry,
Observes her constant, still the same,
In all her laws, through all her frame.   20

No imperfection can be found
In all that is, above, around,—
All, nature made, in reason's sight
Is order all, and *all is right*.

     (1815; 1815)

248   **Philip Freneau**

ON THE UNIVERSALITY AND OTHER ATTRIBUTES OF THE GOD OF NATURE

All that we see, about, abroad,
What is it all, but nature's God?
In meaner works discover'd here
No less than in the starry sphere.

Deism or Pantheism

In seas, on earth, this God is seen;   5
All that exist, upon him lean;
He lives in all, and never stray'd
A moment from the works he made:

His system fix'd on general laws
Bespeaks a wise creating cause;   10
Impartially he rules mankind,
And all that on this globe we find.

Unchanged in all that seems to change,
Unbounded space is his great range;
To one vast purpose always true,   15
No time, with him, is old or new.

In all the attributes divine
Unlimited perfections shine;
In these enwrapt, in these complete,
All virtues in that centre meet.   20

This power who doth all powers transcend,
To all intelligence a friend,
Exists, the *greatest and the best*[1]
Throughout all worlds, to make them blest.

All that he did he first approved   25
He all things into *being* loved;
O'er all he made he still presides,
For them in life, or death provides.

(1815; 1815)

1. Jupiter, optimus, maximus.—Cicero (Freneau's note).

ON THE RELIGION OF NATURE

The power, that gives with liberal hand
    The blessings man enjoys, while here,
And scatters through a smiling land
    The abundant products of the year;
        That power of nature, ever bless'd,   5
        Bestow'd religion with the rest.

Born with ourselves, her early sway
    Inclines the tender mind to take
The path of right, fair virtue's way
    Its own felicity to make.   10
        This universally extends
        And leads to no mysterious ends.

Religion, such as nature taught,
    With all divine perfection suits;
Had all mankind this system sought   15
    Sophists would cease their vain disputes,
        And from this source would nations know
        All that can make their heaven below.

This deals not curses to mankind,
    Or dooms them to perpetual grief,   20
If from its aid no joys they find,
    It damns them not for unbelief;
        Upon a more exalted plan
        Creatress nature dealt with man—

Joy to the day, when all agree   25
    On such grand systems to proceed,
From fraud, design, and error free,
    And which to truth and goodness lead:
        Then persecution will retreat
        And man's religion be complete.   30

    (1815; 1815)

250 Philip Freneau

TO A CATY-DID[1]

In a branch of willow hid
Sings the evening Caty-did:
From the lofty locust bough
Feeding on a drop of dew,
In her suit of green array'd   5
Hear her singing in the shade
      Caty-did, Caty-did, Caty-did!

onomatopoeia

While upon a leaf you tread,
Or repose your little head,
On your sheet of shadows laid,   10
All the day you nothing said:
Half the night your cheery tongue
Revell'd out its little song,
      Nothing else but Caty-did.

From your lodgings on the leaf   15
Did you utter joy or grief—?
Did you only mean to say,
I have had my summer's day,
And am passing, soon, away   *grave*
To the grave of Caty-did:—   20
      Poor, unhappy Caty-did!   *sadness*

But you would have utter'd more
Had you known of nature's power—
From the world when you retreat,
And a leaf's your winding sheet,   25
Long before your spirit fled,
Who can tell but nature said,   *cycle of nature*
Live again, my Caty-did!
      Live, and chatter Caty-did.

1. A well known insect, when full grown, about two inches length, and of the exact color of a green leaf. It is of the genus cicada, or grasshopper kind, inhabiting the green foliage of trees and singing such a note as *Caty-did* in the evening, towards Autumn (Freneau's note).

Tell me, what did Caty[2] do?   *daughter or*   30
Did she mean to trouble you?—   *granddaughter.*
Why was Caty not forbid
To trouble little Caty-did?—
Wrong, indeed at you to fling,
Hurting no one while you sing   35
      Caty-did! Caty-did! Caty-did!

    Why continue to complain?
Caty tells me, she again
Will not give you plague or pain:—
Caty says you may be hid   40
Caty will not go to bed
While you sing us Caty-did.
       Caty-did! Caty-did! Caty-did!

    But, while singing, you forgot
To tell us what did Caty *not:*   45
Caty-did not think of cold,
Flocks retiring to the fold,
Winter, with his wrinkles old;
Winter, that yourself foretold
      When you gave us Caty-did.   50
    Stay securely in your nest;

Caty now, will do her best,
All she can, to make you blest;
But, you want no human aid—
Nature, when she form'd you, said,   55
"Independent you are made,
My dear little Caty-did:
Soon yourself must disappear
With the verdure of the year,"—
And to go, we know not where,   60
      With your song of Caty-did.

(1815?; 1815)

2. The poet's third daughter, Catherine Freneau, or his grandchild, Catherine Ledyard.

Carlyle — All of being is infinite conjugation of the verb to do.

From *The Fredonian* (November 28, 1822)

A FRAGMENT OF BION[1]

My verses please—I thank you, friend,
That such as you my lines commend:
But is that all?—Mere empty fame
Is but an echo of a name.
To write, was my sad destiny,   5
The worst of trades, we all agree.
Why should I toil upon a page
That soon must vanish from the stage,
Lest in oblivion's dreary gloom,
The immensity of things to come!—   10
In that *abyss* I claim no part,
Is mine, indeed!—this beating heart
Must with the mass of atoms rest,
My fancy dead, my fires repress'd.

If God, or fate to man would give   15
In two succeeding states to live,
The first, in pain and sorrow pass'd,
In ease, content, and bliss, the last,
I then would rack my anxious brain
With study how that state to gain;   20
Each day, my toiling mind employ,
In hopes to share the promised joy.

But, since to all, impartial heaven
One fleeting life has only given,

1. The preceding lines, in the original, were written by Bion, a celebrated
pagan philosopher of Smyrna, in the Lesser Asia, and commonly classed among
the minor Greek poets. He is very ancient, and not long after the time of Homer.
From the few fragments of his writings that remain, it appears he believed that
the soul and body died together.—Yet, it is remarkable, he here declares that
if he could persuade himself, there was to be a future state of happiness, he
should think no diligence or pains too much to be a partaker of that eternal
inheritance. What a lesson to the professors of Christianity, from the pen of a
mere moralist, a child of nature and hedonism! (Freneau's note).

'Twere madness, sure, that time to waste   25
In search of joys I ne'er can taste;
My little is enough for me,
Content with mediocrity:
It never sinks into the heart
How soon from hence we all must part.   30
What hope can bloom on life's last stage,
When every sense declines with age,
The eye be-dimm'd, the fancy dead,
The frost of *sixty* on my head,
What hope remains?—*one debt* I pay,   35
Then mingle with my native clay . . .

    (1789; 1822)

FIVE

William Cullen Bryant

(1794-1878)

THE LAST of our five early American poets, William Cullen Bryant, is often paradoxically remembered as his country's first major poet, not because he came earliest chronologically or was the first to write memorable verses but because he initiated that romantic tradition of nineteenth-century writing which has dominated popular and scholarly perceptions of this country's literature. For generations of students, Bryant's portrait on the schoolroom wall—surrounded by Emerson, Whittier, Holmes, Lowell, and Longfellow—both established his importance and limited the cultural context in which he would be considered. Yet his poetry relates to the Puritan and neoclassical traditions from which it emerged as well as to the romantic patterns it introduced. Reading Bryant in the context of earlier poetry, one gains insights which might be obscured by identifying him only with the artistic achievements of the American Renaissance. Renaissance, after all, means rebirth; the beginning, or genesis, of this nation's poetry came almost two centuries earlier, with Anne Bradstreet.

The latently Puritan aspects of his New England tradition reached Bryant through the atmosphere of Cummington, Massachusetts, where he was born in 1794 and spent his boyhood. A small farming town in the mountains west of the Connecticut River, Cummington maintained the conservative Congregational and Federalist principles of its settlers. Bryant grew up on a family farm belonging to his maternal grandfather, Deacon Ebenezer Snell (sentimentally remembered in "The Old Man's Counsel" [1840]) and received steady moral and religious instruction from his grandparents and his mother. He attended the Congregational church, participated in family prayer, and wrote his first childish verses on biblical subjects. Although he never formally subscribed to orthodox Calvinist doctrine, he gained from this early experience a habit of moral earnestness, a concern for spiritual values, and a love for the sonorous, rhythmic, elevated language which he found even in the informal family prayer of Bible-reading farmers.

His father, Dr. Peter Bryant, introduced young Cullen to more liberal Unitarian religious views while reinforcing the Federalist political attitudes which dominated Cummington. A country doctor with a busy if not lucrative practice, Peter Bryant felt literary ambitions; he kept in touch with cultural leaders in Boston and occasionally submitted verses to literary journals. When his second son showed precocious poetic talent, then, Dr. Bryant was ready to encourage ambition, correct careless thought or expression, provide models from his extensive library of classical and English poetry, and assist publication. He trained the young poet in the rational conventions of neoclassical writing and guided him in translation of classical poetry, especially the *Aeneid*.

With his father's help, Bryant published his first poem in the local newspaper in 1807 and a satiric verse pamphlet, *The Embargo*, the next year. An anti-Jeffersonian satire attacking the shipping embargo as a menace to New England commerce and agriculture, the verses recall Freneau's political writing in manner though not in party allegiance. An excerpt may demonstrate both the neoclassical conventions and the conservative opinions with which Bryant began his career:

> As Johnson deep, as Addison refin'd,
> And skill'd to pour conviction o'er the mind,
> Oh might some Patriot rise! the gloom dispel,
> Chase error's mist, and break her magic spell!
>
> But vain the wish, for hark! the murmuring meed
> Of hoarse applause, from yonder shed proceed;
> Enter, and view the thronging concourse there,
> Intent, with gaping mouth, and stupid stare,
> While in the midst their supple leader stands,

Harangues aloud, and flourishes his hands;
To adulation tunes his servile throat,
And sues, successful, for each blockhead's vote.[1]

The Embargo won considerable local celebrity for its fourteen-year-old author and encouraged his ambition for literary achievement.

Bryant's formal education was limited, consisting of preparatory studies with neighboring clergymen and less than a year at Williams College. Family financial pressures prevented him from transferring to Yale and forced him to read law instead, in preparation for the legal practice he opened in 1815 and effectively concluded in 1825. He practiced law in Great Barrington, Massachusetts, but continued to write poetry, publishing whatever he could. His reputation grew dramatically in 1817, when the *North American Review* published an early version of "Thanatopsis," which his father copied from the manuscript he found in his desk and carried to Boston to submit to the editors. That such a poem could be written by any American impressed the editors and reading public; that it had first been drafted by a boy of sixteen or seventeen amazed them. In 1821 Bryant published *Poems*, a modest anthology of his early work. He read the Phi Beta Kappa poem at Harvard that same year and gradually came to know other literary people in New England and New York, but he was still a country lawyer when he married Frances Fairchild in 1821. A few years later, however, he left the Berkshires for New York City and abandoned law for journalism while continuing his work as a poet. Bryant became a celebrated writer, acclaimed in the last decades of his long life as the father of American poetry. He lectured on poetry, wrote, revised, read, and published it for over seventy years, but his best and most characteristic work was, for the most part, written early, either in Cummington or Great Barrington. The congenial literary climate he later enjoyed provided him a receptive audience but failed to stimulate better poetry.

1. "The Embargo, or Sketches of the Times; A Satire," *William Cullen Bryant: Representative Selections* . . . , ed. Tremaine McDowell, American Writers Series (New York: American Book Co., 1935), pp. 344-345, ll. 111-122.

Like Freneau, Bryant found journalism a suitable profession for a writer, but his career was more stable and successful. In 1827 he joined the New York *Evening Post*. In 1829 he became editor-in-chief and part owner and continued to run the paper until his death in 1878. He brought high editorial standards to the paper and made it a respected voice for liberal ideas, including abolition and trade unionism. A Democrat for most of his career, Bryant was an early convert to the Republican Party and an influential supporter of Lincoln. His editorials reflect the seriousness of his thinking on a wide variety of topics; they, better than the poetry, demonstrate Bryant's public concerns.

Whenever he could withdraw for a while from the *Evening Post*, Bryant liked to travel. He made several extended trips to Europe, where he lived in Spain, Italy, Germany, and other countries, learning the language and literature of each place. One trip took him to the Middle East and the holy land. His brothers and eventually his mother moved west from Massachusetts to Illinois, and Bryant's visits to them introduced him to the prairies and growing towns of the frontier, which he increasingly perceived as the hope of America and which he described in "The Prairies" (1832) and "The Painted Cup" (1842). His interest in the American landscape encouraged a complementary concern with native American peoples: the history and traditions of successive Indian populations.

In Bryant's last years he was celebrated, even lionized, as one of the greatest, oldest, and wisest American writers. He spoke at all sorts of public gatherings as a representative of culture in a materialistic society, and he probably acceded too readily to demands for new speeches, poems, editions, and personal appearances—especially after his wife's death in 1866, which left him with a need for activity to quiet his grief. The acclaim he enjoyed as an artist would have dazzled Freneau and Dwight, who found their republic unreceptive to poetry, and would have saddened Bradstreet and Taylor for the inversion of values it suggested. It deflected attention from his better youthful poetry, written in solitude, and made Bryant pose as counselor and comforter of the people. Even his death became a public event. When he collapsed after a meeting in honor of Mazzini, the poet suffered a concussion which left him comatose for three weeks—with newspapers reporting regularly on his condition and finally on his death. A mob of admirers stormed the church and thronged the street on the morning of his funeral.

Considering Bryant's lengthy journalistic career and his intense concern with civic issues, it is surprising that public affairs had so little influence on his poetry. Aside from a few poems related to the Civil War, an elegy for Lincoln, and the patriotic hymn, " 'Oh Mother of a Mighty Race' " (1846), he wrote little about political issues in the United States. Several poems supported independence movements in Europe. Nothing distinguished Bryant's more clearly from Freneau's poetic practice than this diminished emphasis on public life. Similarly, in all but a few poems, he neglected New York City, though he spent most of his life there. "Hymn of the City" (1830) recognizes God's presence even in an urban environment but depends on natural imagery for its force, while "To a Mosquito" (1825) satirizes urban society from the perspective of the rural poet addressing the country-born insect.

Bryant's themes were established before he moved to New York or became an editor. They emerged from his rural experiences as a boy and young man, and they happened also to be the themes of the romantic poets then dominant in English literature: nature, mutability, death, poetry, and the self. Freneau had considered some of these topics, but it remained for the more fully romantic poet to explore them in depth.

Nature dominated Bryant's poetry as a subject of description and as a source of insight, as a point of comparison for human growth, and as a revelation of God. In "Inscription for the Entrance to a Wood" (1815) Bryant praised nature as a refuge from worldly cares, a source of refreshment and spiritual renewal. In "A Forest Hymn" (1825) he hailed it as God's temple, the most fitting place for worship. He approached nature with love and reverence and associated it with everything he found good. He used a forest landscape to stimulate reflections on liberty in "The Antiquity of Freedom" (1842), in preference to the more conventional battlefields or civic shrines.

The landscape of Bryant's poetry is that of the Berkshires:

forests, rivers, mountains, and changing seasons. It is the wilderness just beyond the farms, an area accessible to ordinary people but frequently neglected. Later he discovered and celebrated the prairies with their vast grasslands and unbroken skies. Bryant's love of nature was strongly felt, an innate gift, and his knowledge was exacting. His poems identify an amazing variety of plants, birds, and animals and show familiarity with the forest habitat in all seasons and weather conditions. His footnotes often supplied botanical references and alternative names for wildlife, with comments on the characteristics of some rare plant. He was the first American poet to record his native landscape with such intimate awareness, and he won even Emerson's respect for his presentation of native scenery in an American language—the woodlands of New England as well as the prairies "for which the speech of England has no name." Bryant's commitment to the American landscape as a stimulus to art inspired his verses "To Cole, the Painter, Departing for Europe" (1829), in which he cautioned Thomas Cole, an artist associated with the Hudson River School of painting, to remember the wild beauty of his own country when confronted with the more formal, humanized, and frequently depicted landscapes of Europe.[2]

His awareness of natural cycles stimulated Bryant's concern with mutability, another characteristic theme. He noted the transitions in the forest landscape with changing seasons or weather in "A Winter Piece" (1820), "The Hurricane" (1827), and similar poems. He observed the succession of flowers in "The Yellow Violet" (1814). And he was equally concerned with transitions in human experience: from youth to age in "The Old Man's Counsel" (1840) and from life to death in "The Death of the Flowers" (1825). Nature reminded him also of the cyclic quality of history in which whole civilizations grow to maturity and

2. Resemblances between Bryant's poetic landscapes and Hudson River painting have been explored by a number of scholars, including Donald A. Ringe in "Kindred Spirits: Bryant and Cole," *American Quarterly* 6 (1954): 233-244; and Charles L. Sanford in "The Concept of the Sublime in the Works of Thomas Cole and William Cullen Bryant," *American Literature* 28 (1957): 434-448. Asher Durand, another Hudson River artist, saluted the closeness of poetry and painting to the mountainous northeastern landscape in "Kindred Spirits," an etching which shows Bryant and Cole on a rocky precipice overlooking a Catskill gorge.

crumble into decay. In "The Prairies," for instance, he recalled the mound-builders, overcome by the Indians, who were themselves gradually yielding to the successive waves of white exploration and settlement. But those farming communities, still in the poet's dreams of the future, would be equally subject to annihilation. "And the mound-builders vanished from the earth . . ."

Although he defended change as stimulating in "Mutation" (1824), Bryant habitually conceived transition, in human terms, as it related to death. In his early poems particularly, he worried about death and showed a compulsive concern with personal annihilation. "Thanatopsis," his first major poem and still his most famous, is a meditation on death, an effort to find a way of accepting mortality in rational rather than religious terms. Confronting the question of how the wise man might reconcile himself to the certainty of death, Bryant offered several perspectives in the various versions of the poem.[3] Even in the final version, there are several approaches to death: the apprehensions of the shuddering mortal, afraid "of the stern agony, and shroud, and pall"; the naturalistic voice of nature promising resolution of organic matter into new if senseless forms so that the man becomes "a brother to the insensible rock"; and a more humanistic voice promising fellowship with all men who have yet lived or ever will. The meditator, then, is finally enjoined to go calmly to his final rest in confidence rather than fear, "Like one who wraps the drapery of his couch / About him, and lies down to pleasant dreams." All the perspectives are simultaneously true; and, if the reader finally responds to death with serenity, he does so because he chooses fortitude over fear. The rhetoric of the poem is comforting and the sonorous language soothing, but the argument in no way proves the hope of pleasant dreams nor promises an awakening.

Bryant wrestled again with the problem in "Hymn to Death" (1820), where he praised death as deliverer from human evil, only to confront the irony of death's equally inevitable destruction of goodness, painfully discovered here through the loss of the poet's father. Later he linked human mortality with the cycles

3. The history of "Thanatopsis," as Bryant worked it out and revised it over a period of years, may be found in Albert F. McLean, Jr., *William Cullen Bryant* (New York: Twayne Publishers, 1964), chap. 3; and Charles H. Brown, *William Cullen Bryant* (New York: Charles Scribner's Sons, 1971), chap. 5-6.

of the natural year in "The Death of the Flowers," an elegy for his favorite sister. This theme, which dominated Bryant's early writing, gradually lost force in his poetry as he overcame the early sickness of his consumptive constitution, accepted the consolations of religion, and came to terms with his own mortality.

With his constant awareness of transition, Bryant tended to view life in terms of a journey toward death and whatever lay beyond it, and his poems occasionally recall Bradstreet's theme of pilgrimage. "To a Waterfowl" (1815), for instance, observes the flight of a solitary bird at nightfall, "lone wandering, but not lost," and urges the flier, symbolic of the isolated human pilgrim, to trust the Power which guides its course and to persevere, faithfully, in a journey toward ultimate safe repose. It is the poet himself, not a surrogate, who wanders in "The Journey of Life" (1826), isolated, melancholy, faltering, but still hopeful.

Bryant's romanticism encouraged him to write about self-exploration and personal growth in poems like " 'I Cannot Forget with What Fervid Devotion' " (1815). Other themes relate to the self and encourage psychological awareness. Nature contributes to personal discovery; mutability and death force confrontation with the self and its progress on the journey of life. An "I" speaks in Bryant's poems, as in Bradstreet's and Taylor's; the poet no longer attempts neoclassical objectivity but uses his art instead as a means of revealing himself to himself and to his most sensitive readers. Bryant's poems are not fully autobiographical, of course, and personal reserve kept him from publishing intimate revelations of his family, though two poems in this anthology, " 'Oh Fairest of the Rural Maids' " (1820) and "The Twenty-seventh of March" (1853) reveal the love he felt for his wife.

The last major theme of Bryant's writing was poetry itself, in such poems as " 'I Cannot Forget with What Fervid Devotion,' " which links the poetic vocation with closeness to nature and a primal vision of youth, and "The Poet" (1863), which tries to define his art. His emphasis, unlike Dwight's or Freneau's, was on those passionate feelings which could inspire song and enflame the reader; he measured poetry by its source and effect rather than its content. He idealized the poet as a person of special insight, given from childhood. Although Bryant himself was a meticulous craftsman in his poetic practice and was occasionally criticized by other poets for his latently neoclassical lack of verbal roughness, he stressed passion and power over formal correctness and articulated a decidedly romantic theory of his art.

Bryant was strongly influenced early in his career by the English romantic poets, but he never neglected the biblical and neoclassical readings which fired his imagination even earlier. Throughout his life, he wrote hymns in the familiar Christian language of his grandparents, and his last major poetic project was a blank-verse translation of the *Iliad* and the *Odyssey*. As a boy, he admired Pope and the neoclassical writers his father enjoyed. In adolescence, however, he discovered Lord Byron, imitating him in various ways. Later, he read the Graveyard Poets and Shelley, Keats, and Halleck, but the strongest influence on his writing was that of Wordsworth's and Coleridge's *Lyrical Ballads,* which he discovered in 1815. Wordsworth encouraged Bryant's responsiveness to nature, his sensitivity to language, and his concern for the complex pattern of feeling, conception, memory, and sensory image awakened by an experience of nature. Bryant was influenced also by the romantic traditions of other European literatures and regularly translated works from the Provencal, Spanish, Portuguese, Italian, and German languages, many of them by contemporary poets.

The romantic revolution encouraged Bryant to experiment with more literary forms than his neoclassical predecessors. He tried odes, hymns, ballads, and sonnets as well as the heroic couplets of his earlier poems, but his characteristic form was a sonorous blank verse notable for its run-on lines and long, rounded vowel tones. At its best, as in "Thanatopsis," his blank verse proved elevating and calming—encouraging to serene reflection. At times, however, it degenerated into a soporific mannerism and deflected attention from his ideas. His most successful poems were meditations, although he experimented with narrative verse in "Monument Mountain" (1824) and other poems telling Gothic or sentimental tales, often dealing with strange journeys into imaginary worlds.

Bryant's tone, even more than his forms, marked a new departure for American poetry. Where the Puritan had written as a soul directly to God and the neoclassicist as one reasonable man

to another member of his society, Bryant wrote as the romantic
poet, a man of special sensitivity communing with himself, nature,
God, and other men similarly attuned to reverential feelings. The
"I" of the poems is more dominant than before and the "you"
differently conceived.

Acclaimed as a major poet from the first appearance of "Thana-
topsis" and regularly saluted with each new edition of his work,
Bryant received the attention, criticism, and even the competition
which Freneau said he wanted. Contemporary writers evaluated
his work repeatedly and recognized its principal merits and de-
fects. In "A Fable for Critics" (1848) James Russell Lowell iden-
tified Bryant's faults, even while exaggerating them for the sake
of satiric wit:

> There is Bryant, as quiet, as cool, and as dignified,
> As a smooth, silent iceberg, that never is ignified,
> Save when by reflection 'tis kindled o' nights
> With a semblance of flame by the chill Northern Lights.
> He may rank (Griswold says so) first bard of your nation
> (There's no doubt that he stands in supreme iceolation),
> Your topmost Parnassus he may set his heel on,
> But no warm applauses come, peal following peal on,—
> He's too smooth and too polished to hang any zeal on:
> Unqualified merits, I'll grant, if you choose, he has 'em,
> But he lacks the one merit of kindling enthusiasm;
> If he stir you at all, it is just, on my soul,
> Like being stirred up with the very North Pole.
> ....
>
> But, deduct all you can, there's enough that's right good in him,
> He has a true soul for field, river, and wood in him;
> And his heart, in the midst of brick walls, or where'er it is,
> Glows, softens, and thrills with the tenderest charities—
> To you mortals that delve in this trade-ridden planet?
> No, to old Berkshire's hills, with their limestone and granite.[4]

His poems explored too narrow a range, concentrated too intently
on the natural world at the expense of human awareness and
even, Lowell felt, political concern. The lack of character study

4. "A Fable for Critics," *The Poetical Works of James Russell Lowell*, vol. 3
(Boston: Houghton, Mifflin & Co., 1890), pp. 51-52.

and of dramatic sense prevented success in the development of a long narrative poem; those he attempted had value chiefly for their imaginative natural descriptions.

Yet Bryant's literary powers evoked more comment than his faults and drew praise from a surprising variety of writers, including those whose poetry differed most markedly from his. Poe, for instance, praised Bryant's polish and stylistic correctness, valued the selectivity of his themes, and found in him "genius . . . of a marked character." [5] Emerson admired his detailed knowledge of the Berkshire landscape and his innovative use of American names. Whitman hailed Bryant's evocative exploration of themes which would become the heart of American poetry:

> Bryant pulsing the first interior verse—throbs of a mighty world— bard of the river and wood, ever conveying a taste of the open air, with scents as from hay fields, grapes, birch-borders—always lurking fond of threnodies—beginning and ending his long career with chants of death, with here and there through all, poems or passages of poems, touching the highest universal truths, enthusiasms, duties—morals as grim and eternal, if not as stormy and fateful, as anything in Aeschylus.[6]

There was general agreement that Bryant was a notable poet, though not among the very greatest, and that he deserved recognition for his achievement in writing poems of lasting value and for establishing a public position for the poet in the United States. He introduced in poetry an American romanticism similar to that which his friends Irving and Cooper introduced in prose, and he represented the beginning of a new literary era even while drawing to a conclusion some patterns of Puritanism and neoclassicism which had characterized earlier periods. Like the speaker of "The Path" (1863), Bryant cut a trail from settled areas into the wilderness of imagination, starting a process of movement for others to complete.

5. "Review of Complete Poetical Works (New York: 1846)," *Godey's Magazine and Lady's Book* 32 (April 1846): 182-186; included by McDowell in *William Cullen Bryant: Representative Selections*, pp. 384-386.

6. "My Tribute to Four Poets," from *Specimen Days;* cited in McLean, *William Cullen Bryant*, p. 135.

BIBLIOGRAPHIC NOTE

The standard edition remains *Poems by William Cullen Bryant* (New York: D. Appleton & Co., 1876), but the later collection, edited by Parke Godwin, the poet's son-in-law, is more readily available: *The Poetical Works of William Cullen Bryant*, 2 vols. (New York: D. Appleton & Co., 1883; reprinted, 1967). Louis Untermeyer's anthology, *The Poems of William Cullen Bryant, Selected and Edited* (New York: Heritage Press, 1947), presents a wide range of the poetry in an attractive, convenient format, as does Tremaine McDowell's *William Cullen Bryant: Representative Selections*, American Writers Series (New York: American Book Co., 1935).

The most recent and authoritative biography is Charles H. Brown's *William Cullen Bryant* (New York: Charles Scribner's Sons, 1971). Two earlier biographies provide a more contemporary view of the poet: Parke Godwin, ed., *A Biography of William Cullen Bryant, with Extracts from His Private Correspondence*, 2 vols. (New York: D. Appleton & Co., 1883), and John Bigelow, *William Cullen Bryant*, American Men of Letters Series (Boston: Houghton Mifflin Co. 1890).

A good critical introduction to Bryant's poetry is offered by Albert F. McLean, Jr., in *William Cullen Bryant*, Twayne's United States Authors Series (New York: Twayne Publishers, 1964). Helpful chapters on Bryant's achievement in the perspective of other American poetry may be found in Gay Wilson Allen's study, *American Prosody* (New York: American Book Co., 1935), and in Hyatt H. Waggoner's survey, *American Poets: From the Puritans to the Present* (Boston: Houghton Mifflin Co., 1968). William Cullen Bryant II provides detailed analysis of Bryant's most famous poem in his article, "The Genesis of 'Thanatopsis,' " *New England Quarterly* 21 (1948): 163-184.

THE TEXT

Bryant's poems are arranged chronologically by order of composition, according to the poet's usual practice. The text follows *Poems by William Cullen Bryant* (New York: D. Appleton & Company, 1876), the last edition Bryant actually supervised.

Poems

THE YELLOW VIOLET

emblematic

When beechen buds begin to swell,
　　And woods the blue-bird's warble know,
The yellow violet's modest bell
　　Peeps from the last year's leaves below.

Ere russet fields their green resume,　　　　　　　5
　　Sweet flower, I love, in forest bare,
To meet thee, when thy faint perfume
　　Alone is in the virgin air.

Of all her train, the hands of Spring
　　First plant thee in the watery mould,　　　　10
And I have seen thee blossoming
　　Beside the snow-bank's edges cold.

painterly method

Thy parent sun, who bade thee view
　　Pale skies, and chilling moisture sip,
Has bathed thee in his own bright hue,　　　　15
　　And streaked with jet thy glowing lip.

Yet slight thy form, and low thy seat,
　　And earthward bent thy gentle eye,
Unapt the passing view to meet,
　　When loftier flowers are flaunting nigh.　　20

Oft, in the sunless April day,
　　Thy early smile has stayed my walk;
But midst the gorgeous blooms of May,
　　I passed thee on thy humble stalk.

moral —
lack of objectivity

So they, who climb to wealth, forget　　　　25
　　The friends in darker fortunes tried.
I copied them—but I regret
　　That I should ape the ways of pride.

And when again the genial hour
  Awakes the painted tribes of light,   30
I'll not o'erlook the modest flower
  That made the woods of April bright.

  (1814; 1821)

one flower reveals implications for universe

INSCRIPTION FOR THE ENTRANCE TO A WOOD[1]

Stranger, if thou hast learned a truth which needs
No school of long experience, that the world
Is full of guilt and misery, and hast seen
Enough of all its sorrows, crimes, and cares,
To tire thee of it, enter this wild wood   5
And view the haunts of Nature. The calm shade
Shall bring a kindred calm, and the sweet breeze
That makes the green leaves dance, shall waft a balm
To thy sick heart. Thou wilt find nothing here
Of all that pained thee in the haunts of men,   10
And made thee loathe thy life. The primal curse
Fell, it is true, upon the unsinning earth,
But not in vengeance. God hath yoked to guilt
Her pale tormentor, misery. Hence, these shades
Are still the abodes of gladness; the thick roof   15
Of green and stirring branches is alive
And musical with birds, that sing and sport
In wantonness of spirit; while below
The squirrel, with raised paws and form erect,
Chirps merrily. Throngs of insects in the shade   20
Try their thin wings and dance in the warm beam
That waked them into life. Even the green trees
Partake the deep contentment; as they bend
To the soft winds, the sun from the blue sky
Looks in and sheds a blessing on the scene.   25

1. Reversing the message of the famous inscription Dante found at the entrance
to the Inferno, Bryant counsels the reader to abandon discouragement rather
than hope, while opening himself to the healing power of nature.

Scarce less the cleft-born wild-flower seems to enjoy
Existence, than the wingèd plunderer
That sucks its sweets. The mossy rocks themselves,
And the old and ponderous trunks of prostrate trees
That lead from knoll to knoll a causey rude   30
Or bridge the sunken brook, and their dark roots,
With all their earth upon them, twisting high,
Breathe fixed tranquillity. The rivulet
Sends forth glad sounds, and tripping o'er its bed
Of pebbly sands, or leaping down the rocks,   35
Seems, with continuous laughter, to rejoice
In its own being. Softly tread the marge,
Lest from her midway perch thou scare the wren
That dips her bill in water. The cool wind,
That stirs the stream in play, shall come to thee,   40
Like one that loves thee nor will let thee pass
Ungreeted, and shall give its light embrace.

(1815; 1817)

TO A WATERFOWL

Whither, midst falling dew,
While glow the heavens with the last steps of day,
Far, through their rosy depths, dost thou pursue
    Thy solitary way?

Vainly the fowler's eye   5
Might mark thy distant flight to do thee wrong,
As, darkly seen against the crimson sky,[1]
    Thy figure floats along.

1. Earlier versions describing the bird's figure as "darkly painted on," "Limned
upon," and "shadowed on" the sky indicated the pictorial quality, directly related
to painting, which Bryant tried to achieve in this poem.

    Seek'st thou the plashy brink
Of weedy lake, or marge of river wide,   10
Or where the rocking billows rise and sink
    On the chafed ocean-side?

    There is a Power whose care
Teaches thy way along that pathless coast—
The desert and illimitable air—   15
    Lone wandering, but not lost.

    All day thy wings have fanned,
At that far height, the cold, thin atmosphere,
Yet stoop not, weary, to the welcome land,
    Though the dark night is near.   20

    And soon that toil shall end;
Soon shalt thou find a summer home, and rest,
And scream among thy fellows; reeds shall bend,
    Soon, o'er thy sheltered nest.

    Thou'rt gone, the abyss of heaven   25
Hath swallowed up thy form; yet, on my heart
Deeply has sunk the lesson thou hast given,
    And shall not soon depart.

    He who, from zone to zone,
Guides through the boundless sky thy certain flight,   30
In the long way that I must tread alone,
    Will lead my steps aright.

    (1815; 1818)

"I CANNOT FORGET WITH WHAT FERVID DEVOTION"

I cannot forget with what fervid devotion
    I worshipped the visions of verse and of fame;
Each gaze at the glories of earth, sky, and ocean,
    To my kindled emotions, was wind over flame.

And deep were my musings in life's early blossom,   5
    'Mid the twilight of mountain-groves wandering long;
How thrilled my young veins, and how throbbed my full
    bosom,
    When o'er me descended the spirit of song!

'Mong the deep-cloven fells that for ages had listened
    To the rush of the pebble-paved river between,   10
Where the kingfisher screamed and gray precipice glistened,
    All breathless with awe have I gazed on the scene;

Till I felt the dark power o'er my reveries stealing,
    From the gloom of the thickets that over me hung,
And the thoughts that awoke, in that rapture of feeling,   15
    Were formed into verse as they rose to my tongue.

Bright visions! I mixed with the world, and ye faded,
    No longer your pure rural worshipper now;
In the haunts your continual presence pervaded,
    Ye shrink from the signet of care on my brow.   20

In the old mossy groves on the breast of the mountain,
    In deep lonely glens where the waters complain,
By the shade of the rock, by the gush of the fountain,
    I seek your loved footsteps, but seek them in vain.

Oh, leave not forlorn and forever forsaken,   25
    Your pupil and victim to life and its tears!
But sometimes return, and in mercy awaken
    The glories ye showed to his earlier years.

(1815; 1826)

Serious tone (handwritten)

THANATOPSIS[1]

To him who in the love of Nature holds
Communion with her visible forms, she speaks
A various language; for his gayer hours
She has a voice of gladness, and a smile
And eloquence of beauty, and she glides
Into his darker musings, with a mild
And healing sympathy, that steals away
Their sharpness, ere he is aware. When thoughts
Of the last bitter hour come like a blight
Over thy spirit, and sad images   10
Of the stern agony, and shroud, and pall,
And breathless darkness, and the narrow house,
Make thee to shudder, and grow sick at heart;—
Go forth, under the open sky, and list
To Nature's teachings, while from all around—   15
Earth and her waters, and the depths of air—
Comes a still voice.—Yet a few days, and thee
The all-beholding sun shall see no more
In all his course; nor yet in the cold ground,
Where thy pale form was laid, with many tears,   20
Nor in the embrace of ocean, shall exist
Thy image. Earth, that nourished thee, shall claim
Thy growth, to be resolved to earth again,
And, lost each human trace, surrendering up
Thine individual being, shalt thou go   25
To mix for ever with the elements,
To be a brother to the insensible rock
And to the sluggish clod, which the rude swain
Turns with his share, and treads upon. The oak
Shall send his roots abroad, and pierce thy mould.   30

Marginal handwritten notes:
Perception of senses vs. thought
Landscape vs. inscape
organic cycle
Surrender individuality
pantheism

1. The title means a meditation on death (*Thanatos*, in Greek); it was chosen
by the editors of the *North American Review* in 1817, when they put together
two manuscript poems written by young Bryant at intervals since 1811 and printed
them as the first published version of this, his best-known poem. The *North
American Review* "Thanatopsis" began with line 17 of the poem as it appears
here (following Bryant's 1821 text) and continued, with variations from the later
version, to line 66. Bryant added the comforting framework to the poem in 1821
and retained it thereafter.

Yet not to thine eternal resting-place
Shalt thou retire alone, nor couldst thou wish
Couch more magnificent. Thou shalt lie down
With patriarchs of the infant world—with kings,
The powerful of the earth—the wise, the good,   35
Fair forms, and hoary seers of ages past,
All in one mighty sepulchre. The hills
Rock-ribbed and ancient as the sun,—the vales
Stretching in pensive quietness between;
The venerable woods—rivers that move   40
In majesty, and the complaining brooks
That make the meadows green; and, poured round all,
Old Ocean's gray and melancholy waste,—
Are but the solemn decorations all
Of the great tomb of man. The golden sun,   45
The planets, all the infinite host of heaven,
Are shining on the sad abodes of death,
Through the still lapse of ages. All that tread
The globe are but a handful to the tribes
That slumber in its bosom.—Take the wings   50
Of morning, pierce the Barcan wilderness,[2]
Or lose thyself in the continuous woods
Where rolls the Oregon,[3] and hears no sound,
Save his own dashings—yet the dead are there:
And millions in those solitudes, since first   55
The flight of years began, have laid them down
In their last sleep—the dead reign there alone.
So shalt thou rest, and what if thou withdraw
In silence from the living, and no friend
Take note of thy departure? All that breathe   60
Will share thy destiny. The gay will laugh
When thou art gone, the solemn brood of care
Plod on, and each one as before will chase
His favorite phantom; yet all these shall leave

2. A desert in North Africa.
3. The Columbia River.

Their mirth and their employments, and shall come   65
And make their bed with thee. As the long train
Of ages glides away, the sons of men,
The youth in life's green spring, and he who goes
In the full strength of years, matron and maid,
The speechless babe, and the gray-headed man—   70
Shall one by one be gathered to thy side
By those, who in their turn shall follow them.

    So live, that when thy summons comes to join
The innumerable caravan, which moves
To that mysterious realm, where each shall take   75
His chamber in the silent halls of death,
Thou go not, like the quarry-slave at night,
Scourged to his dungeon, but, sustained and soothed
By an unfaltering trust, approach thy grave,
Like one who wraps the drapery of his couch   80
About him, and lies down to pleasant dreams.

    (1817; 1821)

A WINTER PIECE

    The time has been that these wild solitudes,
Yet beautiful as wild, were trod by me
Oftener than now; and when the ills of life
Had chafed my spirit—when the unsteady pulse
Beat with strange flutterings—I would wander forth   5
And seek the woods. The sunshine on my path
Was to me as a friend. The swelling hills,
The quiet dells retiring far between,
With gentle invitation to explore
Their windings, were a calm society   10
That talked with me and soothed me. Then the chant
Of birds, and chime of brooks, and soft caress
Of the fresh sylvan air, made me forget

The thoughts that broke my peace, and I began
To gather simples[1] by the fountain's brink,   15
And lose myself in day-dreams. While I stood
In Nature's loneliness, I was with one
With whom I early grew familiar, one
Who never had a frown for me, whose voice
Never rebuked me for the hours I stole   20
From cares I loved not, but of which the world
Deems highest, to converse with her. When shrieked
The bleak November winds, and smote the woods,
And the brown fields were herbless, and the shades,
That met above the merry rivulet,   25
Were spoiled, I sought, I loved them still; they seemed
Like old companions in adversity.
Still there was beauty in my walks; the brook,
Bordered with sparkling frost-work, was as gay
As with its fringe of summer flowers. Afar,   30
The village with its spires, the path of streams
And dim receding valleys, hid before
By interposing trees, lay visible
Through the bare grove, and my familiar haunts
Seemed new to me. Nor was I slow to come   35
Among them, when the clouds, from their still skirts,
Had shaken down on earth the feathery snow,
And all was white. The pure keen air abroad,
Albeit it breathed no scent of herb, nor heard
Love-call of bird nor merry hum of bee,   40
Was not the air of death. Bright mosses crept
Over the spotted trunks, and the close buds,
That lay along the boughs, instinct with life,
Patient, and waiting the soft breath of Spring,
Feared not the piercing spirit of the North.   45
The snow-bird twittered on the beechen bough,
And 'neath the hemlock, whose thick branches bent
Beneath its bright cold burden, and kept dry
A circle, on the earth, of withered leaves,

---

1. Medicinal herbs.

The partridge found a shelter. Through the snow   50
The rabbit sprang away. The lighter track
Of fox, and the raccoon's broad path, were there,
Crossing each other. From his hollow tree
The squirrel was abroad, gathering the nuts
Just fallen, that asked the winter cold and sway   55
Of winter blast, to shake them from their hold.

    But Winter has yet brighter scenes—he boasts
Splendors beyond what gorgeous Summer knows;
Or Autumn with his many fruits, and woods
All flushed with many hues. Come when the rains   60
Have glazed the snow and clothed the trees with ice,
While the slant sun of February pours
Into the bowers a flood of light. Approach!
The incrusted surface shall upbear thy steps,
And the broad arching portals of the grove   65
Welcome thy entering. Look! the massy trunks
Are cased in the pure crystal; each light spray,
Nodding and tinkling in the breath of heaven,
Is studded with its trembling water-drops,
That glimmer with an amethystine light.   70
But round the parent-stem the long low boughs
Bend, in a glittering ring, and arbors hide
The glassy floor. Oh! you might deem the spot
The spacious cavern of some virgin mine,
Deep in the womb of earth—where the gems grow,   75
And diamonds put forth radiant rods and bud
With amethyst and topaz—and the place
Lit up, most royally, with the pure beam
That dwells in them. Or haply the vast hall
Of fairy palace, that outlasts the night,   80
And fades not in the glory of the sun;—
Where crystal columns send forth slender shafts
And crossing arches; and fantastic aisles
Wind from the sight in brightness, and are lost
Among the crowded pillars. Raise thine eye;   85
Thou seest no cavern roof, no palace vault;

There the blue sky and the white drifting cloud
Look in. Again the wildered fancy dreams
Of spouting fountains, frozen as they rose,
And fixed, with all their branching jets, in air,   90
And all their sluices sealed. All, all is light;
Light without shade. But all shall pass away
With the next sun. From numberless vast trunks
Loosened, the crashing ice shall make a sound
Like the far roar of rivers, and the eve   95
Shall close o'er the brown woods as it was wont.

     And it is pleasant, when the noisy streams
Are just set free, and milder suns melt off
The plashy snow, save only the firm drift
In the deep glen or the close shade of pines—   100
'Tis pleasant to behold the wreaths of smoke
Roll up among the maples of the hill,
Where the shrill sound of youthful voices wakes
The shriller echo, as the clear pure lymph,[2]
That from the wounded trees, in twinkling drops,   105
Falls, mid the golden brightness of the morn,
Is gathered in with brimming pails, and oft,
Wielded by sturdy hands, the stroke of axe
Makes the woods ring. Along the quiet air,
Come and float calmly off the soft light clouds,   110
Such as you see in summer, and the winds
Scarce stir the branches. Lodged in sunny cleft,
Where the cold breezes come not, blooms alone
The little wind-flower, whose just opened eye
Is blue as the spring heaven it gazes at—   115
Startling the loiterer in the naked groves
With unexpected beauty, for the time
Of blossoms and green leaves is yet afar.
And ere it comes, the encountering winds shall oft
Muster their wrath again, and rapid clouds   120
Shade heaven, and bounding on the frozen earth

     2. Maple sap.

Shall fall their volleyed stores, rounded like hail
And white like snow, and the loud North again
Shall buffet the vexed forest in his rage.

   (1820; 1821)

HYMN TO DEATH

    Oh! could I hope the wise and pure in heart
Might hear my song without a frown, nor deem
My voice unworthy of the theme it tries,—
I would take up the hymn to Death, and say
To the grim power, The world hath slandered thee   5
And mocked thee. On thy dim and shadowy brow
They place an iron crown, and call thee king
Of terrors, and the spoiler of the world,
Deadly assassin, that strik'st down the fair,
The loved, the good—that breathest on the lights   10
Of virtue set along the vale of life,
And they go out in darkness. I am come,
Not with reproaches, not with cries and prayers,
Such as have stormed thy stern, insensible ear
From the beginning; I am come to speak   15
Thy praises. True it is, that I have wept
Thy conquests, and may weep them yet again,
And thou from some I love will take a life
Dear to me as my own. Yet while the spell
Is on my spirit, and I talk with thee   20
In sight of all thy trophies, face to face,
Meet is it that my voice should utter forth
Thy nobler triumphs; I will teach the world
To thank thee. Who are thine accusers?—Who?
The living!—they who never felt thy power,   25
And know thee not. The curses of the wretch
Whose crimes are ripe, his sufferings when thy hand
Is on him, and the hour he dreads is come,
Are writ among thy praises. But the good—

Does he whom thy kind hand dismissed to peace,   30
Upbraid the gentle violence that took off
His fetters, and unbarred his prison-cell?

    Raise then the hymn to Death. Deliverer!
God hath anointed thee to free the oppressed
And crush the oppressor. When the armed chief,   35
The conqueror of nations, walks the world,
And it is changed beneath his feet, and all
Its kingdoms melt into one mighty realm—
Thou, while his head is loftiest and his heart
Blasphemes, imagining his own right hand   40
Almighty, thou dost set thy sudden grasp
Upon him, and the links of that strong chain
Which bound mankind are crumbled; thou dost break
Sceptre and crown, and beat his throne to dust.
Then the earth shouts with gladness, and her tribes   45
Gather within their ancient bounds again.
Else had the mighty of the olden time,
Nimrod,[1] Sesostris,[2] or the youth[3] who feigned
His birth from Libyan Ammon, smitten yet
The nations with a rod of iron, and driven   50
Their chariot o'er our necks. Thou dost avenge,
In thy good time, the wrongs of those who know
No other friend. Nor dost thou interpose
Only to lay the sufferer asleep,
Where he who made him wretched troubles not   55
His rest—thou dost strike down his tyrant too.
Oh, there is joy when hands that held the scourge
Drop lifeless, and the pitiless heart is cold.
Thou too dost purge from earth its horrible
And old idolatries;—from the proud fanes   60
Each to his grave their priests go out, till none
Is left to teach their worship; then the fires
Of sacrifice are chilled, and the green moss

1. A great hunter and ruler in the early days of creation (Gen. 10.8).
2. The Egyptian conqueror-king, Ramses.
3. Alexander the Great.

O'ercreeps their altars; the fallen images
Cumber the weedy courts, and for loud hymns,   65
Chanted by kneeling multitudes, the wind
Shrieks in the solitary aisles. When he
Who gives his life to guilt, and laughs at all
The laws that God or man has made, and round
Hedges his seat with power, and shines in wealth,—   70
Lifts up his atheist front to scoff at Heaven,
And celebrates his shame in open day,
Thou, in the pride of all his crimes, cutt'st off
The horrible example. Touched by thine,
The extortioner's hard hand foregoes the gold   75
Wrung from the o'er-worn poor. The perjurer,
Whose tongue was lithe, e'en now, and voluble
Against his neighbor's life, and he who laughed
And leaped for joy to see a spotless fame
Blasted before his own foul calumnies,   80
Are smit with deadly silence. He, who sold
His conscience to preserve a worthless life,
Even while he hugs himself on his escape,
Trembles, as, doubly terrible, at length,
Thy steps o'ertake him, and there is no time   85
For parley, nor will bribes unclench thy grasp.
Oft, too, dost thou reform thy victim, long
Ere his last hour. And when the reveller,
Mad in the chase of pleasure, stretches on,
And strains each nerve, and clears the path of life   90
Like wind, thou point'st him to the dreadful goal,
And shak'st thy hour-glass in his reeling eye,
And check'st him in mid course. Thy skeleton hand
Shows to the faint of spirit the right path,
And he is warned, and fears to step aside.   95
Thou sett'st between the ruffian and his crime
Thy ghastly countenance, and his slack hand
Drops the drawn knife. But, oh, most fearfully
Dost thou show forth Heaven's justice, when thy shafts
Drink up the ebbing spirit—then the hard   100
Of heart and violent of hand restores

The treasure to the friendless wretch he wronged.
Then from the writhing bosom thou dost pluck
The guilty secret; lips, for ages sealed,
Are faithless to their dreadful trust at length,   105
And give it up; the felon's latest breath
Absolves the innocent man who bears his crime;
The slanderer, horror-smitten, and in tears,
Recalls the deadly obloquy he forged
To work his brother's ruin. Thou dost make   110
Thy penitent victim utter to the air
The dark conspiracy that strikes at life,
And aims to whelm the laws; ere yet the hour
Is come, and the dread sign of murder given.

    Thus, from the first of time, hast thou been found   115
On virtue's side; the wicked, but for thee,
Had been too strong for the good; the great of earth
Had crushed the weak for ever. Schooled in guile
For ages, while each passing year had brought
Its baneful lesson, they had filled the world   120
With their abominations; while its tribes,
Trodden to earth, imbruted, and despoiled,
Had knelt to them in worship; sacrifice
Had smoked on many an altar, temple-roofs
Had echoed with the blasphemous prayer and hymn: 125
But thou, the great reformer of the world,
Tak'st off the sons of violence and fraud
In their green pupilage, their lore half learned—
Ere guilt had quite o'errun the simple heart
God gave them at their birth, and blotted out   130
His image. Thou dost mark them flushed with hope,
As on the threshold of their vast designs
Doubtful and loose they stand, and strik'st them down.

....

    Alas! I little thought that the stern power,
Whose fearful praise I sang, would try me thus   135
Before the strain was ended. It must cease—

For he[4] is in his grave who taught my youth
The art of verse, and in the bud of life
Offered me to the Muses. Oh, cut off
Untimely! when thy reason in its strength,   140
Ripened by years of toil and studious search,
And watch of Nature's silent lessons, taught
Thy hand to practise best the lenient art
To which thou gavest thy laborious days,
And, last, thy life. And, therefore, when the earth   145
Received thee, tears were in unyielding eyes
And on hard cheeks, and they who deemed thy skill
Delayed their death-hour, shuddered and turned pale
When thou wert gone. This faltering verse, which thou
Shalt not, as wont, o'erlook, is all I have   150
To offer at thy grave—this—and the hope
To copy thy example, and to leave
A name of which the wretched shall not think
As of an enemy's, whom they forgive
As all forgive the dead. Rest, therefore, thou   155
Whose early guidance trained my infant steps—
Rest, in the bosom of God, till the brief sleep
Of death is over, and a happier life
Shall dawn to waken thine insensible dust.

    Now thou art not—and yet the men whose guilt   160
Has wearied Heaven for vengeance—he who bears
False witness—he who takes the orphan's bread,
And robs the widow—he who spreads abroad
Polluted hands in mockery of prayer,
Are left to cumber earth. Shuddering I look   165
On what is written, yet I blot not out
The desultory numbers; let them stand,
The record of an idle revery.

    (1820; 1826)

4. The poet's father, Dr. Peter Bryant.

"OH, FAIREST OF THE RURAL MAIDS"

Oh, fairest of the rural maids![1]
Thy birth was in the forest shades;
Green boughs, and glimpses of the sky,
Were all that met thine infant eye.

Thy sports, thy wanderings, when a child,   5
Were ever in the sylvan wild;
And all the beauty of the place
Is in thy heart and on thy face.

The twilight of the trees and rocks
Is in the light shade of thy locks;   10
Thy step is as the wind, that weaves
Its playful way among the leaves.

Thine eyes are springs, in whose serene
And silent waters heaven is seen;
Their lashes are the herbs that look   15
On their young figures in the brook.

The forest depths, by foot unpressed,
Are not more sinless than thy breast;
The holy peace, that fills the air
Of those calm solitudes, is there.   20

(1820; 1832)

1. This love poem was addressed to Bryant's future wife, Frances Fairchild, whose surname may be discovered in the opening lines of the first two stanzas.

MONUMENT MOUNTAIN[1]

Thou who wouldst see the lovely and the wild
Mingled in harmony on Nature's face,
Ascend our rocky mountains. Let thy foot
Fail not with weariness, for on their tops
The beauty and the majesty of earth,   5
Spread wide beneath, shall make thee to forget
The steep and toilsome way. There, as thou stand'st,
The haunts of men below thee, and around
The mountain-summits, thy expanding heart
Shall feel a kindred with that loftier world   10
To which thou art translated, and partake
The enlargement of thy vision. Thou shalt look
Upon the green and rolling forest-tops,
And down into the secrets of the glens,
And streams that with their bordering thickets strive   15
To hide their windings. Thou shalt gaze, at once,
Here on white villages, and tilth, and herds,
And swarming roads, and there on solitudes
That only hear the torrent, and the wind,
And eagle's shriek. There is a precipice   20

1. Bryant's note indicates the origin of this story: "The mountain called by
this name is a remarkable precipice in Great Barrington, overlooking the rich
and picturesque valley of the Housatonic, in the western part of Massachusetts.
At the southern extremity is, or was a few years since, a conical pile of small
stones, erected, according to the tradition of the surrounding country, by the
Indians, in memory of a woman of the Stockbridge tribe who killed herself by
leaping from the edge of the precipice. Until within a few years past, small parties
of that tribe used to arrive from their settlement in the western part of the State
of New York, on visits to Stockbridge, the place of their nativity and former
residence. A young woman belonging to one of these parties related, to a friend
of the author, the story on which the poem of Monument Mountain is founded.
An Indian girl had formed an attachment for her cousin, which, according to
the customs of the tribe, was unlawful. She was, in consequence, seized with
a deep melancholy, and resolved to destroy herself. In company with a female
friend, she repaired to the mountain, decked out for the occasion in all her
ornaments, and, after passing the day on the summit in singing with her companion
the traditional songs of her nation, she threw herself headlong from the rock,
and was killed."

That seems a fragment of some mighty wall,
Built by the hand that fashioned the old world,
To separate its nations, and thrown down
When the flood drowned them. To the north, a path
Conducts you up the narrow battlement.   25
Steep is the western side, shaggy and wild
With mossy trees, and pinnacles of flint,
And many a hanging crag. But, to the east,
Sheer to the vale go down the bare old cliffs—
Huge pillars, that in middle heaven upbear   30
Their weather-beaten capitals, here dark
With moss, the growth of centuries, and there
Of chalky whiteness where the thunderbolt
Has splintered them. It is a fearful thing
To stand upon the beetling verge, and see   35
Where storm and lightning, from that huge gray wall,
Have tumbled down vast blocks, and at the base
Dashed them in fragments, and to lay thine ear
Over the dizzy depth, and hear the sound
Of winds, that struggle with the woods below,   40
Come up like ocean-murmurs. But the scene
Is lovely round; a beautiful river there
Wanders amid the fresh and fertile meads,
The paradise he made unto himself,
Mining the soil for ages. On each side   45
The fields swell upward to the hills; beyond,
Above the hills, in the blue distance, rise
The mountain-columns with which earth props heaven.

There is a tale about these reverend rocks,
A sad tradition of unhappy love,   50
And sorrows borne and ended, long ago,
When over these fair vales the savage sought
His game in the thick woods. There was a maid
The fairest of the Indian maids, bright-eyed,
With wealth of raven tresses, a light form,   55
And a gay heart. About her cabin-door
The wide old woods resounded with her song

And fairy laughter all the summer day.
She loved her cousin; such a love was deemed,
By the morality of those stern tribes,   60
Incestuous, and she struggled hard and long
Against her love, and reasoned with her heart,
As simple Indian maiden might. In vain.
Then her eye lost its lustre, and her step
Its lightness, and the gray-haired men that passed
Her dwelling, wondered that they heard no more   65
The accustomed song and laugh of her, whose looks
Were like the cheerful smile of Spring, they said,
Upon the Winter of their age. She went
To weep where no eye saw, and was not found   70
When all the merry girls were met to dance.
And all the hunters of the tribe were out;
Nor when they gathered from the rustling husk
The shining ear; nor when, by the river's side,
They pulled the grape and startled the wild shades   75
With sounds of mirth. The keen-eyed Indian dames
Would whisper to each other, as they saw
Her wasting form, and say, *The girl will die.*

One day into the bosom of a friend,
A playmate of her young and innocent years,   80
She poured her griefs, "Thou know'st, and thou alone,"
She said, "for I have told thee, all my love,
And guilt, and sorrow. I am sick of life.
All night I weep in darkness, and the morn
Glares on me, as upon a thing accursed,   85
That has no business on the earth. I hate
The pastimes and the pleasant toils that once
I loved; the cheerful voices of my friends
Sound in my ear like mockings, and, at night,
In dreams, my mother, from the land of souls,   90
Calls me and chides me. All that look on me
Do seem to know my shame; I cannot bear
Their eyes; I cannot from my heart root out
The love that wrings it so, and I must die."

It was a summer morning, and they went   95
To this old precipice. About the cliffs
Lay garlands, ears of maize, and shaggy skins
Of wolf and bear, the offerings of the tribe
Here made to the Great Spirit, for they deemed,
Like worshippers of the elder time, that God   100
Doth walk on the high places and affect
The earth-o'erlooking mountains. She had on
The ornaments with which her father loved
To deck the beauty of his bright-eyed girl,
And bade her wear when stranger warriors came   105
To be his guests. Here the friends sat them down,
And sang, all day, old songs of love and death,
And decked the poor wan victim's hair with flowers,
And prayed that safe and swift might be her way
To the calm world of sunshine, where no grief   110
Makes the heart heavy and the eyelids red.
Beautiful lay the region of her tribe
Below her—waters resting in the embrace
Of the wide forest, and maize-planted glades
Opening amid the leafy wilderness.   115
She gazed upon it long, and at the sight
Of her own village peeping through the trees,
And her own dwelling, and the cabin-roof
Of him she loved with an unlawful love,
And came to die for, a warm gush of tears   120
Ran from her eyes. But when the sun grew low
And the hill-shadows long, she threw herself
From the steep rock and perished. There was scooped,
Upon the mountain's southern slope, a grave;
And there they laid her, in the very garb   125
With which the maiden decked herself for death,
With the same withering wild-flowers in her hair.
And o'er the mould that covered her, the tribe
Built up a simple monument, a cone
Of small loose stones. Thenceforward all who passed,   130
Hunter, and dame, and virgin, laid a stone
In silence on the pile. It stands there yet.

And Indians from the distant West, who come
To visit where their fathers' bones are laid,
Yet tell the sorrowful tale, and to this day   135
The mountain where the hapless maiden died
Is called the Mountain of the Monument.

      (1824; 1824)

MUTATION

They talk of short-lived pleasure—be it so—
    Pain dies as quickly: stern, hard-featured Pain
Expires, and lets her weary prisoner go.
    The fiercest agonies have shortest reign;
    And after dreams of horror, comes again   5
The welcome morning with its rays of peace.
    Oblivion, softly wiping out the stain,
Makes the strong secret pangs of shame to cease:
Remorse is virtue's root; its fair increase
    Are fruits of innocence and blessedness: 10
Thus joy, o'erborne and bound, doth still release
    His young limbs from the chains that round him press.
Weep not that the world changes—did it keep
A stable, changeless state, 'twere cause indeed to weep.

      (1824; 1824)

A FOREST HYMN

    The groves were God's first temples. Ere man learned
To hew the shaft, and lay the architrave,
And spread the roof above them—ere he framed
The lofty vault, to gather and roll back
The sound of anthems; in the darkling wood,   5
Amid the cool and silence, he knelt down,
And offered to the Mightiest solemn thanks
And supplication. For his simple heart

Might not resist the sacred influences
Which, from the stilly twilight of the place,   10
And from the gray old trunks that high in heaven
Mingled their mossy boughs, and from the sound
Of the invisible breath that swayed at once
All their green tops, stole over him, and bowed
His spirit with the thought of boundless power   15
And inaccessible majesty. Ah, why
Should we, in the world's riper years, neglect
God's ancient sanctuaries, and adore
Only among the crowd, and under roofs
That our frail hands have raised? Let me, at least,   20
Here, in the shadow of this aged wood,
Offer one hymn—thrice happy, if it find
Acceptance in His ear.

                         Father, thy hand
Hath reared these venerable columns, thou   25
Didst weave this verdant roof. Thou didst look down
Upon the naked earth, and, forthwith, rose
All these fair ranks of trees. They, in thy sun,
Budded, and shook their green leaves in thy breeze,
And shot toward heaven. The century-living crow   30
Whose birth was in their tops, grew old and died
Among their branches, till, at last, they stood,
As now they stand, massy, and tall, and dark,
Fit shrine for humble worshipper to hold
Communion with his Maker. These dim vaults,   35
These winding aisles, of human pomp or pride
Report not. No fantastic carvings show
The boast of our vain race to change the form
Of thy fair works. But thou art here—thou fill'st
The solitude. Thou art in the soft winds   40
That run along the summit of these trees
In music; thou art in the cooler breath
That from the inmost darkness of the place   *animism?*
Comes, scarcely felt; the barky trunks, the ground,
The fresh moist ground, are all instinct with thee.   45

Here is continual worship;—Nature, here,
In the tranquillity that thou dost love,
Enjoys thy presence. Noiselessly, around,
From perch to perch, the solitary bird
Passes; and yon clear spring, that, midst its herbs,   50
Wells softly forth and wandering steeps the roots
Of half the mighty forest, tells no tale
Of all the good it does. Thou has not left
Thyself without a witness, in these shades,
Of thy perfections. Grandeur, strength, and grace,   55
Are here to speak of thee. This mighty oak—
By whose immovable stem I stand and seem
Almost annihilated—not a prince,
In all that proud old world beyond the deep,
E'er wore his crown as loftily as he   60
Wears the green coronal of leaves with which
Thy hand has graced him. Nestled at his root
Is beauty, such as blooms not in the glare
Of the broad sun. That delicate forest flower,
With scented breath and look so like a smile,
Seems, as it issues from the shapeless mould,   65
An emanation of the indwelling Life,
A visible token of the upholding Love,
That are the soul of this great universe.

    My heart is awed within me when I think   70
Of the great miracle that still goes on,
In silence, round me—the perpetual work
Of thy creation, finished, yet renewed
Forever. Written on thy works I read
The lesson of thy own eternity.
Lo! all grow old and die—but see again,   75
How on the faltering footsteps of decay
Youth presses—ever-gay and beautiful youth
In all its beautiful forms. These lofty trees
Wave not less proudly that their ancestors   80
Moulder beneath them. Oh, there is not lost
One of earth's charms: upon her bosom yet,

After the flight of untold centuries,
The freshness of her far beginning lies
And yet shall lie. Life mocks the idle hate   85
Of his arch-enemy Death—yea, seats himself
Upon the tyrant's throne—the sepulchre,
And of the triumphs of his ghastly foe
Makes his own nourishment. For he came forth
From thine own bosom, and shall have no end.   90

There have been holy men who hid themselves
Deep in the woody wilderness, and gave
Their lives to thought and prayer, till they outlived
The generation born with them, nor seemed
Less aged than the hoary trees and rocks   95
Around them;—and there have been holy men
Who deemed it were not well to pass life thus.
But let me often to these solitudes
Retire, and in thy presence reassure
My feeble virtue. Here its enemies,
The passions, at thy plainer footsteps shrink   100
And tremble and are still. O God! when thou
Dost scare the world with tempests, set on fire
The heavens with falling thunderbolts, or fill,
With all the waters of the firmament,   105
The swift dark whirlwind that uproots the woods
And drowns the villages; when, at thy call,
Uprises the great deep and throws himself
Upon the continent, and overwhelms
Its cities—who forgets not, at the sight   110
Of these tremendous tokens of thy power,
His pride, and lays his strifes and follies by?
Oh, from these sterner aspects of thy face
Spare me and mine, nor let us need the wrath
Of the mad, unchained elements to teach   115
Who rules them. Be it ours to meditate,
In these calm shades, thy milder majesty,
And to the beautiful order of thy works
Learn to conform the order of our lives.

(1825; 1825)

TO A MOSQUITO

Fair insect! that, with threadlike legs spread out,
    And blood-extracting bill and filmy wing,
Dost murmur, as thou slowly sail'st about,
    In pitiless ears full many a plaintive thing,
And tell how little our large veins would bleed,   5
Would we but yield them to thy bitter need.

Unwillingly, I own, and, what is worse,
    Full angrily men hearken to thy plaint;
Thou gettest many a brush, and many a curse,
    For saying thou art gaunt, and starved, and faint;   10
Even the old beggar, while he asks for food,
Would kill thee, hapless stranger, if he could.

I call thee stranger, for the town, I ween,
    Has not the honor of so proud a birth—
Thou com'st from Jersey meadows, fresh and green,   15
    The offspring of the gods, though born on earth;
For Titan[1] was thy sire, and fair was she,
The ocean-nymph that nursed thy infancy.

Beneath the rushes was thy cradle swung,
    And when at length thy gauzy wings grew strong,   20
Abroad to gentle airs their folds were flung.
    Rose in the sky and bore thee soft along;
The south wind breathed to waft thee on thy way,
And danced and shone beneath the billowy bay.

Calm rose afar the city spires, and thence   25
    Came the deep murmur of its throng of men,
And as its grateful odors met thy sense,
    They seemed the perfumes of thy native fen.
Fair lay its crowded streets, and at the sight
Thy tiny song grew shriller with delight.   30

1. This name, usually applied to an ancient race of giant deities in ancient mythology, occasionally identifies the sun god; hence, the mosquito is a child of heat and water in the New Jersey marshes.

At length thy pinions fluttered in Broadway—
    Ah! there were fairy steps, and white necks kissed
By wanton airs, and eyes whose killing ray
    Shone through the snowy veils like stars through mist;
And fresh as morn, on many a cheek and chin,   35
Bloomed the bright blood through the transparent skin.

Sure these were sights to touch an anchorite!
    What! do I hear thy slender voice complain?
Thou wailest when I talk of beauty's light,
    As if it brought the memory of pain;   40
Thou art a wayward being—well—come near,
And pour thy tale of sorrow in my ear.

What sayst thou—slanderer!—rouge makes thee sick?
    And China bloom at best is sorry food?
And Rowland's Kalydor, if laid on thick,   45
    Poisons the thirsty wretch that bores for blood?
Go! 'twas a just reward that met thy crime—
But shun the sacrilege another time.

That bloom was made to look at, not to touch;
    To worship, not approach, that radiant white;   50
And well might sudden vengeance light on such
    As dared, like thee, most impiously to bite.
Thou shouldst have gazed at distance and admired,
Murmured thy adoration, and retired.

Thou'rt welcome to the town; but why come here   55
    To bleed a brother poet, gaunt like thee?
Alas! the little blood I have is dear,
    And thin will be the banquet drawn from me.
Look round—the pale-eyed sisters in my cell,
Thy old acquaintance, Song and Famine, dwell.   60

Try some plump alderman, and suck the blood
    Enriched by generous wine and costly meat;
On well-filled skins, sleek as thy native mud,
    Fix thy light pump and press thy freckled feet.
Go to the men for whom, in ocean's halls,   65
The oyster breeds, and the green turtle sprawls.

There corks are drawn, and the red vintage flows
    To fill the swelling veins for thee, and now
The ruddy cheek and now the ruddier nose
    Shall tempt thee, as thou flittest round the brow.   70
And when the hour of sleep its quiet brings,
No angry hand shall rise to brush thy wings.

       (1825; 1826)

THE DEATH OF THE FLOWERS

The melancholy days have come, the saddest of the year,
Of wailing winds, and naked woods, and meadows brown
    and sere;
Heaped in the hollows of the grove, the autumn leaves lie
    dead;
They rustle to the eddying gust, and to the rabbit's tread;
The robin and the wren are flown, and from the shrubs
    the jay,   5
And from the wood-top calls the crow through all the
    gloomy day.

Where are the flowers, the fair young flowers, that lately
    sprang and stood
In brighter light and softer airs, a beauteous sisterhood?
Alas! they all are in their graves, the gentle race of flowers

Are lying in their lowly beds, with the fair and good
   of ours.   10
The rain is falling where they lie, but the cold November
   rain
Calls not from out the gloomy earth the lovely ones again.

The wind-flower and the violet, they perished long ago,
And the brier-rose and the orchis died amid the summer
   glow;
But on the hill the golden-rod, and the aster in the wood,   15
And the yellow sunflower by the brook in autumn beauty
   stood,
Till fell the frost from the clear cold heaven, as falls the
   plague on men,
And the brightness of their smile was gone, from upland,
   glade, and glen.

And now, when comes the calm mild day, as still such days
   will come,
To call the squirrel and the bee from out their winter
   home;   20
When the sound of dropping nuts is heard, though all the
   trees are still,
And twinkle in the smoky light the waters of the rill,
The south wind searches for the flowers whose fragrance late
   he bore,
And sighs to find them in the wood and by the stream no
   more.

And then I think of one[1] who in her youthful beauty died,   25
The fair meek blossom that grew up and faded by my side.
In the cold moist earth we laid her, when the forests cast the
   leaf,
And we wept that one so lovely should have a life so brief:
Yet not unmeet it was that one, like that young friend
   of ours,
So gentle and so beautiful, should perish with the flowers.   30

     (1825; 1826)

   1. The poet's sister, Sarah Bryant Shaw.

THE JOURNEY OF LIFE

Beneath the waning moon I walk at night,
    And muse on human life—for all around
Are dim uncertain shapes that cheat the sight,
    And pitfalls lurk in shade along the ground,
And broken gleams of brightness, here and there,   5
Glance through, and leave unwarmed the death-like air.

The trampled earth returns a sound of fear—
    A hollow sound, as if I walked on tombs;
And lights, that tell of cheerful homes, appear
    Far off, and die like hope amid the glooms.   10
A mournful wind across the landscape flies,
And the wide atmosphere is full of sighs.

And I, with faltering footsteps, journey on,
    Watching the stars that roll the hours away,
Till the faint light that guides me now is gone,   15
    And, like another life, the glorious day
Shall open o'er me from the empyreal height,
With warmth, and certainty, and boundless light.

    (1826; 1832)

THE HURRICANE [1]

    Lord of the winds! I feel thee nigh,
I know thy breath in the burning sky!
And I wait, with a thrill in every vein,
For the coming of the hurricane!

    And lo! on the wing of the heavy gales,   5
Through the boundless arch of heaven he sails;
Silent and slow, and terribly strong,
The mighty shadow is borne along,

---

1. Bryant identified this poem as essentially a translation of one by José Maria de Heredia, a Cuban poet who published a volume in New York in 1825.

Like the dark eternity to come;
While the world below, dismayed and dumb,   10
Through the calm of the thick hot atmosphere,
Looks up at its gloomy folds with fear.

They darken fast; and the golden blaze
Of the sun is quenched in the lurid haze,
And he sends through the shade a funeral ray—   15
A glare that is neither night nor day,
A beam that touches, with hues of death,
The clouds above and the earth beneath.
To its covert glides the silent bird,
While the hurricane's distant voice is heard   20
Uplifted among the mountains round,
And the forests hear and answer the sound.

He is come! he is come! do ye not behold
His ample robes on the wind unrolled?
Giant of air! we bid thee hail!—   25
How his gray skirts toss in the whirling gale;
How his huge and writhing arms are bent
To clasp the zone of the firmament,
And fold at length, in their dark embrace,
From mountain to mountain the visible space!   30

Darker—still darker! the whirlwinds bear
The dust of the plains to the middle air:
And hark to the crashing, long and loud,
Of the chariot of God in the thunder-cloud!
You may trace its path by the flashes that start   35
From the rapid wheels where'er they dart,
As the fire-bolts leap to the world below,
And flood the skies with a lurid glow.

What roar is that?—'tis the rain that breaks
In torrents away from the airy lakes,   40
Heavily poured on the shuddering ground,
And shedding a nameless horror round.
Ah! well-known woods, and mountains, and skies,

With the very clouds!—ye are lost to my eyes.
I seek ye vainly, and see in your place   45
The shadowy tempest that sweeps through space,
A whirling ocean that fills the wall
Of the crystal heaven, and buries all.
And I, cut off from the world, remain
Alone with the terrible hurricane.   50

(1827; 1827)

TO COLE, THE PAINTER, DEPARTING FOR EUROPE

Thine eyes shall see the light of distant skies;
    Yet, COLE! thy heart shall bear to Europe's strand
    A living image of our own bright land,
Such as upon thy glorious canvas lies;
Lone lakes—savannas where the bison roves—   5
    Rocks rich with summer garlands—solemn streams—
    Skies, where the desert eagle wheels and screams—
Spring bloom and autumn blaze of boundless groves.
Fair scenes shall greet thee where thou goest—fair,
    But different—everywhere the trace of men,   10
    Paths, homes, graves, ruins, from the lowest glen
To where life shrinks from the fierce Alpine air—
    Gaze on them, till the tears shall dim thy sight,
    But keep that earlier, wilder image bright.

(1829; 1829)

HYMN OF THE CITY

    Not in the solitude
Alone may man commune with Heaven, or see,
    Only in savage wood
And sunny vale, the present Deity;
    Or only hear his voice
Where the winds whisper and the waves rejoice.   5

Even here do I behold
Thy steps, Almighty!—here, amid the crowd,
    Through the great city rolled,
With everlasting murmur deep and loud—
    Choking the ways that wind
'Mong the proud piles, the work of human kind.

[handwritten: God is imminent in city]
[handwritten: buildings]

    Thy golden sunshine comes
From the round heaven, and on their dwellings lies
    And lights their inner homes;   15
For them thou fill'st with air the unbounded skies,
    And givest them the stores
Of ocean, and the harvests of its shores.

    Thy Spirit is around,
Quickening the restless mass that sweeps along;   20
    And this eternal sound—
Voices and footfalls of the numberless throng—
    Like the resounding sea,
Or like the rainy tempest, speaks of thee.

    And when the hour of rest   25
Comes, like a calm upon the mid-sea brine,
    Hushing its billowy breast—
The quiet of that moment too is thine;
    It breathes of Him who keeps
The vast and helpless city while it sleeps.   30

        (1830; 1830)

THE PRAIRIES

    These are the gardens of the Desert, these
The unshorn fields, boundless and beautiful,
For which the speech of England has no name—
The Prairies. I behold them for the first,

[handwritten: Most American of early American poems]

[handwritten: affecting picture - sublime - Picturesque]

Romantic

And my heart swells, while the dilated sight
Takes in the encircling vastness. Lo! they stretch   *Edmund Burke*
In airy undulations, far away,   *(Aesthetic of Sublime)*
As if the Ocean, in his gentlest swell,
Stood still, with all his rounded billows fixed,
And motionless forever. Motionless?—   10
No—they are all unchained again. The clouds
Sweep over with their shadows, and, beneath,
The surface rolls and fluctuates to the eye;[1]
Dark hollows seem to glide along and chase
The sunny ridges. Breezes of the South!   15
Who toss the golden and the flame-like flowers,
And pass the prairie-hawk that, poised on high,
Flaps his broad wings, yet moves not—ye have played
Among the palms of Mexico and vines
Of Texas, and have crisped the limited brooks   20
That from the fountains of Sonora glide
Into the calm Pacific—have ye fanned
A nobler or a lovelier scene than this?
Man hath no part in all this glorious work:
The hand that built the firmament hath heaved   25
And smoothed these verdant swells, and sown their slopes   *God as*
With herbage, planted them with island-groves,   *farmer...*
And hedged them round with forests. Fitting floor
For this magnificent temple of the sky—
With flowers whose glory and whose multitude   30
Rival the constellations! The great heavens
Seem to stoop down upon the scene in love,—
A nearer vault, and of a tenderer blue,
Than that which bends above our Eastern hills.

As o'er the verdant waste I guide my steed,   35
Among the high rank grass that sweeps his sides

1. The prairies of the West, with an undulating surface, *rolling prairies,* as
they are called, present to the unaccustomed eye a singular spectacle when the
shadows of the clouds are passing rapidly over them. The face of the ground
seems to fluctuate and toss like billows of the sea (Bryant's note).

The hollow beating of his footstep seems
A sacrilegious sound. I think of those
Upon whose rest he tramples. Are they here—
The dead of other days?—and did the dust   40
Of these fair solitudes once stir with life
And burn with passion? Let the mighty mounds
That overlook the rivers, or that rise
In the dim forest crowded with old oaks,
Answer. A race, that long has passed away,   45
Built them; a disciplined and populous race
Heaped, with long toil, the earth, while yet the Greek
Was hewing the Pentelicus[2] to forms
Of symmetry, and rearing on its rock
The glittering Parthenon. These ample fields   50
Nourished their harvests, here their herds were fed,
When haply by their stalls the bison lowed,
And bowed his manèd shoulder to the yoke.
All day this desert murmured with their toils,
Till twilight blushed, and lovers walked, and wooed   55
In a forgotten language, and old tunes,
From instruments of unremembered form,
Gave the soft winds a voice. The red-man came—
The roaming hunter-tribes, warlike and fierce,
And the mound-builders vanished from the earth.   60
The solitude of centuries untold
Has settled where they dwelt. The prairie-wolf
Hunts in their meadows, and his fresh-dug den
Yawns by my path. The gopher mines the ground
Where stood their swarming cities. All is gone;   65
All—save the piles of earth that hold their bones,
The platforms where they worshipped unknown gods,
The barriers which they builded from the soil
To keep the foe at bay—till o'er the walls
The wild beleaguerers broke, and, one by one,   70
The strongholds of the plain were forced, and heaped
With corpses. The brown vultures of the wood
Flocked to those vast uncovered sepulchres,

2. A mountain near Athens, famous for marble.

And sat, unscared and silent, at their feast.
Haply some solitary fugitive,   75
Lurking in marsh and forest, till the sense
Of desolation and of fear became
Bitterer than death, yielded himself to die.
Man's better nature triumphed then. Kind words
Welcomed and soothed him; the rude conquerors   80
Seated the captive with their chiefs; he chose
A bride among their maidens, and at length
Seemed to forget—yet ne'er forgot—the wife
Of his first love, and her sweet little ones,
Butchered, amid their shrieks, with all his race.   85

Thus change the forms of being. Thus arise
Races of living things, glorious in strength,
And perish, as the quickening breath of God
Fills them, or is withdrawn. The red-man, too,
Has left the blooming wilds he ranged so long,   90
And, nearer to the Rocky Mountains, sought
A wilder hunting-ground. The beaver builds
No longer by these streams, but far away,
On waters whose blue surface ne'er gave back
The white man's face—among Missouri's springs,   95
And pools whose issues swell the Oregon—
He rears his little Venice. In these plains
The bison feeds no more. Twice twenty leagues
Beyond remotest smoke of hunter's camp,
Roams the majestic brute, in herds that shake   100
The earth with thundering steps—yet here I meet
His ancient footprints stamped beside the pool.

Still this great solitude is quick with life.
Myriads of insects, gaudy as the flowers
They flutter over, gentle quadrupeds,   105
And birds, that scarce have learned the fear of man,
Are here, and sliding reptiles of the ground,
Startlingly beautiful. The graceful deer
Bounds to the wood at my approach. The bee,

A more adventurous colonist than man,   110
With whom he came across the eastern deep,
Fills the savannas with his murmurings,
And hides his sweets, as in the golden age,
Within the hollow oak. I listen long
To his domestic hum, and think I hear   115
The sound of that advancing multitude
Which soon shall fill these deserts. From the ground
Comes up the laugh of children, the soft voice
Of maidens, and the sweet and solemn hymn
Of Sabbath worshippers. The low of herds   120
Blends with the rustling of the heavy grain
Over the dark-brown furrows. All at once
A fresher wind sweeps by, and breaks my dream,
And I am in the wilderness alone.

(1832; 1834)

THE OLD MAN'S COUNSEL

Among our hills and valleys, I have known
Wise and grave men, who, while their diligent hands
Tended or gathered in the fruits of earth,
Were reverent learners in the solemn school
Of Nature. Not in vain to them were sent   5
Seed-time and harvest, or the vernal shower
That darkened the brown tilth, or snow that beat
On the white winter hills. Each brought, in turn,
Some truth, some lesson on the life of man,
Or recognition of the Eternal mind   10
Who veils his glory with the elements.

One such I knew long since, a white-haired man,
Pithy of speech, and merry when he would;
A genial optimist, who daily drew
From what he saw his quaint moralities.   15
Kindly he held communion, though so old,

With me a dreaming boy, and taught me much
That books tell not, and I shall ne'er forget.

   The sun of May was bright in middle heaven,
And steeped the sprouting forests, the green hills,   20
And emerald wheat-fields, in his yellow light.
Upon the apple-tree, where rosy buds
Stood clustered, ready to burst forth in bloom,
The robin warbled forth his full clear note
For hours, and wearied not. Within the woods,   25
Whose young and half-transparent leaves scarce cast
A shade, gay circles of anemones
Danced on their stalks; the shad-bush, white with flowers,
Brightened the glens; the new-leaved butternut
And quivering poplar to the roving breeze   30
Gave a balsamic fragrance. In the fields
I saw the pulses of the gentle wind
On the young grass. My heart was touched with joy
At so much beauty, flushing every hour
Into a fuller beauty; but my friend,   35
The thoughtful ancient, standing at my side,
Gazed on it mildly sad. I asked him why.

   "Well mayst thou join in gladness," he replied,
"With the glad earth, her springing plants and flowers,
And this soft wind, the herald of the green   40
Luxuriant summer. Thou art young like them,
And well mayst thou rejoice. But while the flight
Of seasons fills and knits thy spreading frame,
It withers mine, and thins my hair, and dims
These eyes, whose fading light shall soon be quenched   45
In utter darkness. Hearest thou that bird?"

   I listened, and from midst the depth of woods
Heard the love-signal of the grouse, that wears
A sable ruff around his mottled neck;
Partridge they call him by our northern streams,   50
And pheasant by the Delaware. He beat

His barred sides with his speckled wings, and made
A sound like distant thunder; slow the strokes
At first, then fast and faster, till at length
They passed into a murmur and were still.   55

  "There hast thou," said my friend, "a fitting type
Of human life. 'Tis an old truth, I know,
But images like these revive the power
Of long-familiar truths. Slow pass our days
In childhood, and the hours of light are long   60
Betwixt the morn and eve; with swifter lapse
They glide in manhood, and in age they fly;
Till days and seasons flit before the mind
As flit the snow-flakes in a winter storm,
Seen rather than distinguished. Ah! I seem   65
As if I sat within a helpless bark,
By swiftly-running waters hurried on
To shoot some mighty cliff. Along the banks
Grove after grove, rock after frowning rock,
Bare sands and pleasant homes, and flowery nooks,   70
And isles and whirlpools in the stream, appear
Each after each, but the devoted skiff
Darts by so swiftly that their images
Dwell not upon the mind, or only dwell
In dim confusion; faster yet I sweep   75
By other banks, and the great gulf is near.

  "Wisely, my son, while yet thy days are long,
And this fair change of seasons passes slow,
Gather and treasure up the good they yield—
All that they teach of virtue, of pure thoughts   80
And kind affections, reverence for thy God
And for thy brethren; so when thou shalt come
Into these barren years, thou mayst not bring
A mind unfurnished and a withered heart."

  Long since that white-haired ancient slept—but still,   85
When the red flower-buds crowd the orchard-bough,

And the ruffed grouse is drumming far within
The woods, his venerable form again
Is at my side, his voice is in my ear.

    (1840; 1840)

THE PAINTED CUP

    The fresh savannas of the Sangamon[1]
Here rise in gentle swells, and the long grass
Is mixed with rustling hazels. Scarlet tufts
Are glowing in the green, like flakes of fire:
The wanderers of the prairie know them well,   5
And call that brilliant flower the Painted Cup.

    Now, if thou art a poet, tell me not
That these bright chalices were tinted thus
To hold the dew for fairies, when they meet
On moonlight evenings in the hazel-bowers,   10
And dance till they are thirsty. Call not up,
Amid this fresh and virgin solitude,
The faded fancies of an elder world;
But leave these scarlet cups to spotted moths
Of June, and glistening flies, and humming-birds,   15
To drink from, when on all these boundless lawns
The morning sun looks hot. Or let the wind
O'erturn in sport their ruddy brims, and pour
A sudden shower upon the strawberry-plant,
To swell the reddening fruit that even now   20
Breathes a slight fragrance from the sunny slope.

    But thou art of a gayer fancy. Well—
Let then the gentle Manitou[2] of flowers,
Lingering amid the bloomy waste he loves,

1. A river in central Illinois.
2. The Great Spirit of the American Indians.

Though all his swarthy worshippers are gone— 25
Slender and small, his rounded cheek all brown
And ruddy with the sunshine; let him come
On summer mornings, when the blossoms wake,
And part with little hands the spiky grass,
And touching, with his cherry lips, the edge 30
Of these bright beakers, drain the gathered dew.

    (1842; 1842)

THE ANTIQUITY OF FREEDOM

    Here are old trees, tall oaks, and gnarlèd pines,
That stream with gray-green mosses; here the ground
Was never trenched by spade, and flowers spring up
Unsown, and die ungathered. It is sweet
To linger here, among the flitting birds 5
And leaping squirrels, wandering brooks, and winds
That shake the leaves, and scatter, as they pass,
A fragrance from the cedars, thickly set
With pale-blue berries. In these peaceful shades—
Peaceful, unpruned, immeasurably old— 10
My thoughts go up the long dim path of years,
Back to the earliest days of liberty.

    O Freedom! thou art not, as poets dream,
A fair young girl, with light and delicate limbs,
And wavy tresses gushing from the cap 15
With which the Roman master crowned his slave
When he took off the gyves. A bearded man,
Armed to the teeth, art thou; one mailèd hand
Grasps the broad shield, and one the sword; thy brow,
Glorious in beauty though it be, is scarred 20
With tokens of old wars; thy massive limbs
Are strong with struggling. Power at thee has launched
His bolts, and with his lightnings smitten thee;
They could not quench the life thou hast from heaven;

Merciless Power has dug thy dungeon deep,   25
And his swart armorers, by a thousand fires,
Have forged thy chain; yet, while he deems thee bound,
The links are shivered, and the prison-walls
Fall outward; terribly thou springest forth,
As springs the flame above a burning pile,   30
And shoutest to the nations, who return
Thy shoutings, while the pale oppressor flies.

  Thy birthright was not given by human hands:
Thou wert twin-born with man. In pleasant fields,
While yet our race was few, thou sat'st with him,   35
To tend the quiet flock and watch the stars,
And teach the reed to utter simple airs.
Thou by his side, amid the tangled wood,
Didst war upon the panther and the wolf,
His only foes; and thou with him didst draw   40
The earliest furrow on the mountain-side,
Soft with the deluge. Tyranny himself,
Thy enemy, although of reverend look,
Hoary with many years, and far obeyed,
Is later born than thou; and as he meets   45
The grave defiance of thine elder eye,
The usurper trembles in his fastnesses.

  Thou shalt wax stronger with the lapse of years,
But he shall fade into a feeble age—
Feebler, yet subtler. He shall weave his snares,   50
And spring them on thy careless steps, and clap
His withered hands, and from their ambush call
His hordes to fall upon thee. He shall send
Quaint maskers, wearing fair and gallant forms
To catch thy gaze, and uttering graceful words   55
To charm thy ear; while his sly imps, by stealth,
Twine round thee threads of steel, light thread on thread,
That grow to fetters; or bind down thy arms
With chains concealed in chaplets. Oh! not yet
Mayst thou unbrace thy corslet, nor lay by   60

Thy sword; nor yet, O Freedom! close thy lids,
In slumber; for thine enemy never sleeps,
And thou must watch and combat till the day
Of the new earth and heaven. But wouldst thou rest
Awhile from tumult and the frauds of men,   65
These old and friendly solitudes invite
Thy visit. They, while yet the forest-trees
Were young upon the unviolated earth,
And yet the moss-stains on the rock were new,
Beheld thy glorious childhood, and rejoiced.   70

    (1842; 1842)

"OH MOTHER OF A MIGHTY RACE"

Oh mother of a mighty race,
Yet lovely in thy youthful grace!
The elder dames, thy haughty peers,
Admire and hate thy blooming years.
     With words of shame   5
And taunts of scorn they join thy name.

For on thy cheeks the glow is spread
That tints thy morning hills with red;
Thy step—the wild-deer's rustling feet,
Within thy woods are not more fleet;   10
     Thy hopeful eye
Is bright as thine own sunny sky.

Ay, let them rail—those haughty ones,
While safe thou dwellest with thy sons.
They do not know how loved thou art,   15
How many a fond and fearless heart
     Would rise to throw
Its life between thee and the foe.

They know not, in their hate and pride,
What virtues with thy children bide;   20
How true, how good, thy graceful maids
Make bright, like flowers, the valley-shades;
          What generous men
Spring, like thine oaks, by hill and glen.

What cordial welcomes greet the guest   25
By thy lone rivers of the West;
How faith is kept, and truth revered.
And man is loved, and God is feared,
          In woodland homes,
And where the ocean-border foams.   30

There's freedom at thy gates and rest
For Earth's down-trodden and opprest,
A shelter for the hunted head,
For the starved laborer toil and bread.
          Power, at thy bounds,   35
Stops and calls back his baffled hounds.

Oh, fair young mother! on thy brow
Shall sit a nobler grace than now.
Deep in the brightness of thy skies
The thronging years in glory rise,   40
          And, as they fleet,
Drop strength and riches at thy feet.

Thine eye, with every coming hour,
Shall brighten, and thy form shall tower;
And when thy sisters, elder born,   45
Would brand thy name with words of scorn,
          Before thine eye,
Upon their lips the taunt shall die.

     (1846?; 1847)

THE TWENTY-SEVENTH OF MARCH

Oh, gentle one,[1] thy birthday sun should rise
Amid a chorus of the merriest birds
That ever sang the stars out of the sky
In a June morning. Rivulets should send
A voice of gladness from their winding paths,   5
Deep in o'erarching grass, where playful winds,
Stirring the loaded stems, should shower the dew
Upon the grassy water. Newly-blown
Roses, by thousands, to the garden-walks
Should tempt the loitering moth and diligent bee.   10
The longest, brightest day in all the year
Should be the day on which thy cheerful eyes
First opened on the earth, to make thy haunts
Fairer and gladder for thy kindly looks.

    Thus might a poet say; but I must bring   15
A birthday offering of an humbler strain,
And yet it may not please thee less. I hold
That 'twas the fitting season for thy birth
When March, just ready to depart, begins
To soften into April. Then we have   20
The delicatest and most welcome flowers,
And yet they take least heed of bitter wind
And lowering sky. The periwinkle then,
In an hour's sunshine, lifts her azure blooms
Beside the cottage-door; within the woods   25
Tufts of ground-laurel, creeping underneath
The leaves of the last summer, send their sweets
Up to the chilly air, and, by the oak,
The squirrel-cups, a graceful company,
Hide in their bells, a soft aërial blue—   30
Sweet flowers, that nestle in the humblest nooks,
And yet within whose smallest bud is wrapped
A world of promise! Still the north wind breathes
His frost, and still the sky sheds snow and sleet;

1. Frances Fairchild Bryant.

Yet ever, when the sun looks forth again,   35
The flowers smile up to them from their low seats.
    Well hast thou borne the bleak March day of life.
Its storms and its keen winds to thee have been
Most kindly tempered, and through all its gloom
There has been warmth and sunshine in thy heart;   40
The griefs of life to thee have been like snows,
That light upon the fields in early spring,
Making them greener. In its milder hours,
The smile of this pale season, thou hast seen
The glorious bloom of June, and in the note   45
Of early bird, that comes a messenger
From climes of endless verdure, thou hast heard
The choir that fills the summer woods with song.
    Now be the hours that yet remain to thee
Stormy or sunny, sympathy and love,
That inextinguishably dwell within   50
Thy heart, shall give a beauty and a light
To the most desolate moments, like the glow
Of a bright fireside in the wildest day;
And kindly words and offices of good   55
Shall wait upon thy steps, as thou goest on,
Where God shall lead thee, till thou reach the gates
Of a more genial season, and thy path
Be lost to human eye among the bowers
And living fountains of a brighter land.   60

    (1853; 1856)

ROBERT OF LINCOLN

Merrily swinging on brier and weed,
    Near to the nest of his little dame,
Over the mountain-side or mead,
    Robert of Lincoln is telling his name:
        Bob-o'-link, bob-o'-link,   5
           Spink, spank, spink;

Snug and safe is that nest of ours,
Hidden among the summer flowers.
          Chee, chee, chee.

Robert of Lincoln is gayly drest,   10
    Wearing a bright black wedding-coat;
White are his shoulders and white his crest,
    Hear him call in his merry note:
        Bob-o'-link, bob-o'-link,
        Spink, spank, spink;   15
Look, what a nice new coat is mine,
Sure there was never a bird so fine.
          Chee, chee, chee.

Robert of Lincoln's Quaker wife,
    Pretty and quiet, with plain brown wings,   20
Passing at home a patient life,
    Broods in the grass while her husband sings:
        Bob-o'-link, bob-o'-link,
        Spink, spank, spink.
Brood, kind creature; you need not fear   25
Thieves and robbers while I am here.
          Chee, chee, chee.

Modest and shy as a nun is she;
    One weak chirp is her only note.
Braggart and prince of braggarts is he,   30
    Pouring boasts from his little throat:
        Bob-o'-link, bob-o'-link,
        Spink, spank, spink;
Never was I afraid of man;
Catch me, cowardly knaves, if you can!   35
          Chee, chee, chee.

Six white eggs on a bed of hay,
    Flecked with purple, a pretty sight!
There as the mother sits all day,
    Robert is singing with all his might: 40

      Bob-o'-link, bob-o'-link,
        Spink, spank, spink;
Nice good wife, that never goes out,
Keeping house while I frolic about.
           Chee, chee, chee.   45

Soon as the little ones chip the shell,
      Six wide mouths are open for food;
Robert of Lincoln bestirs him well,
      Gathering seeds for the hungry brood.
      Bob-o'-link, bob-o'-link,   50
        Spink, spank, spink;
This new life is likely to be
Hard for a gay young fellow like me.
           Chee, chee, chee.

Robert of Lincoln at length is made   55
      Sober with work, and silent with care;
Off is his holiday garment laid,
      Half forgotten that merry air:
      Bob-o'-link, bob-o'-link,
        Spink, spank, spink;   60
Nobody knows but my mate and I
Where our nest and our nestlings lie.
           Chee, chee, chee.

Summer wanes; the children are grown;
      Fun and frolic no more he knows;   65
Robert of Lincoln's a humdrum crone;
      Off he flies, and we sing as he goes;
      Bob-o'-link, bob-o'-link,
        Spink, spank, spink;
When you can pipe that merry old strain,   70
Robert of Lincoln, come back again.
           Chee, chee, chee.

(1855; 1855)

THE POET

Thou, who wouldst wear the name
   Of poet mid thy brethren of mankind,
And clothe in words of flame
   Thoughts that shall live within the general mind!
Deem not the framing of a deathless lay   5
The pastime of a drowsy summer day.

But gather all thy powers,
   And wreak them on the verse that thou dost weave,
And in thy lonely hours,
   At silent morning or at wakeful eve,   10
While the warm current tingles through thy veins,
Set forth the burning words in fluent strains.

No smooth array of phrase,
   Artfully sought and ordered though it be,
Which the cold rhymer lays   15
   Upon his page with languid industry,
Can wake the listless pulse to livelier speed,
Or fill with sudden tears the eyes that read.

The secret wouldst thou know
   To touch the heart or fire the blood at will?   20
Let thine own eyes o'erflow;
   Let thy lips quiver with the passionate thrill;
Seize the great thought, ere yet its power be past,
And bind, in words, the fleet emotion fast.

Then, should thy verse appear   25
   Halting and harsh, and all unaptly wrought,
Touch the crude line with fear,
   Save in the moment of impassioned thought;
Then summon back the original glow, and mend
The strain with rapture that with fire was penned.   30

Yet let no empty gust

Of passion find an utterance in thy lay,
A blast that whirls the dust
    Along the howling street and dies away;
But feelings of calm power and mighty sweep,   35
Like currents journeying through the windless deep.

Seek'st thou, in living lays,
    To limn the beauty of the earth and sky?
Before thine inner gaze
    Let all that beauty in clear vision lie;   40
Look on it with exceeding love, and write
The words inspired by wonder and delight.

Of tempests wouldst thou sing,
    Or tell of battles—make thyself a part
Of the great tumult; cling
    To the tossed wreck with terror in thy heart;   45
Scale, with the assaulting host, the rampart's height,
And strike and struggle in the thickest fight.

So shalt thou frame a lay
    That haply may endure from age to age,
And they who read shall say: 50
    "What witchery hangs upon this poet's page!
What art is his the written spells to find
That sway from mood to mood the willing mind!"

    (1863; 1864)

THE PATH

The path we planned beneath October's sky,
    Along the hill-side, through the woodland shade,
Is finished; thanks to thee, whose kindly eye
    Has watched me, as I plied the busy spade;
Else had I wearied, ere this path of ours   5
Had pierced the woodland to its inner bowers.

Yet, 'twas a pleasant toil to trace and beat,
    Among the glowing trees, this winding way,
While the sweet autumn sunshine, doubly sweet,
    Flushed with the ruddy foliage, round us lay,   10
As if some gorgeous cloud of morning stood,
In glory, mid the arches of the wood.

A path! what beauty does a path bestow
    Even on the dreariest wild! its savage nooks
Seem homelike where accustomed footsteps go,   15
    And the grim rock puts on familiar looks.
The tangled swamp, through which a pathway strays,
Becomes a garden with strange flowers and sprays.

See, from the weedy earth a rivulet break
    And purl along the untrodden wilderness;   20
There the shy cuckoo comes his thirst to slake,
    There the shrill jay alights his plumes to dress;
And there the stealthy fox, when morn is gray,
Laps the clear stream and lightly moves away.

But let a path approach that fountain's brink,   25
    And nobler forms of life, behold! are there:
Boys kneeling with protruded lips to drink,
    And slender maids that homeward slowly bear
The brimming pail, and busy dames that lay
Their webs to whiten in the summer ray.   30

Then know we that for herd and flock are poured
    Those pleasant streams that o'er the pebbles slip;
Those pure sweet waters sparkle on the board;
    Those fresh cool waters wet the sick man's lip;
Those clear bright waters from the font are shed,   35
In dews of baptism, on the infant's head.

What different steps the rural footway trace!
    The laborer afield at early day;
The schoolboy sauntering with uneven pace;

The Sunday worshipper in fresh array;   40
And mourner in the weeds of sorrow drest;
And, smiling to himself, the wedding guest.

There he who cons a speech and he who hums
    His yet unfinished verses, musing walk.
There, with her little brood, the matron comes,   45
    To break the spring flower from its juicy stalk;
And lovers, loitering, wonder that the moon
Has risen upon their pleasant stroll so soon.

Bewildered in vast woods, the traveller feels
    His heavy heart grow lighter, if he meet   50
The traces of a path, and straight he kneels,
    And kisses the dear print of human feet,
And thanks his God, and journeys without fear,
For now he knows the abodes of men are near.

Pursue the slenderest path across a lawn: 55
    Lo! on the broad highway it issues forth,
And, blended with the greater track, goes on,
    Over the surface of the mighty earth,
Climbs hills and crosses vales, and stretches far,
Through silent forests, toward the evening star—   60

And enters cities murmuring with the feet
    Of multitudes, and wanders forth again,
And joins the climes of frost to climes of heat,
    Binds East to West, and marries main to main,
Nor stays till at the long-resounding shore   65
Of the great deep, where paths are known no more.

O mighty instinct, that dost thus unite
    Earth's neighborhoods and tribes with friendly bands,
What guilt is theirs who, in their greed or spite,
    Undo thy holy work with violent hands!   70
And post their squadrons, nursed in war's grim trade,
To bar the ways for mutual succor made.

    (1863; 1864)

APPENDIX

Michael
Wigglesworth
(1631-1705)

UNLIKE BRADSTREET and Taylor, Michael Wigglesworth used his versifying talents for public instruction in Puritan ideas and attitudes rather than for private reflection on his own spiritual state. As minister to the church at Malden, Massachusetts, Wigglesworth suffered health problems which limited his pastoral activities, but he discovered that didactic poems could teach and even entertain believers throughout New England.

His most famous poem, *The Day of Doom* (1662), reviews Puritan beliefs about predestination and moral theology in a rather mechanical narrative presenting the end of the world and Christ's judgment on successive categories of saints and sinners—from hypocrites to unbaptized infants. With its insistent meter and emphatic rhymes, the poem hurtles through two hundred and twenty-four stanzas like the following:

> *Rom. 6:23*
> Earths dwellers all, both great and small,
>   have wrought iniquity,
> And suffer must, for it is just,
>   Eternal misery.
> Amongst the many there come not any,
>   before the Judge's face,

> That able are themselves to clear,
> of all this cursed race.[1]

The Day of Doom became an immediate best-seller: it was re-printed for over a century in England and America, memorized by generations of New England children, and used continually as a supplement to the Bible and catechism.

"God's Controversy with New-England" (1662) reveals another aspect of Wigglesworth's sermonizing in verse. It is a jeremiad, threatening the Puritan colonies with destruction if they should continue their decline from the ideals of the founding generation. The poem reveals the emergence of a mythic sense of the colonial past as early as 1662, with the light of the gospel carried across the ocean by the heroic fathers to irradiate the wilderness, only to be dimmed by the sinfulness and worldly values of the younger generations of the Puritan community itself. It shows Wiggles-worth's love for New England as well as his disappointment and fear and reveals the tension he felt between the ideals of the original religious mission and the realities of an increasingly com-plex social organization. He interpreted the drought of 1662 as God's cautionary rebuke to an ungrateful people.

BIBLIOGRAPHIC NOTE

Although there is no collected edition of Wigglesworth's writings, his major poems are frequently anthologized (often, unfortunately, in severely abbreviated form). Complete texts of *The Day of Doom*, as well as "God's Controversy With New-England," appear in *Seventeenth-Century American Poetry*, edited by Harrison T. Meserole (Garden City, N.Y.: Doubleday & Co., 1968; reprinted, New York: W. W. Norton & Co., 1972).

Readers interested in Wigglesworth himself and in the evidence his life gives about Puritan psychological, spiritual, and practical experience should examine his diary, edited by Edmund S. Morgan: *The Diary of Michael Wigglesworth, 1653-1657: The Conscience of a Puritan* (New York: Harper Press, 1965). There are also a modern biography written by Richard Crowder, *No Featherbed to Heaven: a Biography of Michael Wigglesworth* (East Lansing: Michigan State University Press, 1962), and a chapter on Wiggles-worth in Austin Warren's book, *The New England Conscience*

---

1. "The Day of Doom," *Seventeenth-Century American Poetry*, ed. Harrison T. Meserole (Garden City, N.Y.: Doubleday & Co., 1968), p. 72, stanza 67.

(Ann Arbor: University of Michigan Press, 1966).

Perspective on "God's Controversy With New-England" may be gained from examining the social and historical contexts of seventeenth-century Massachusetts and the literary context of the Puritan jeremiad. The following works provide valuable insights into the myths of New England's foundation and decline which Wigglesworth articulates in his poem: Perry Miller, *The New England Mind: From Colony to Province* (Cambridge, Mass.: Harvard University Press, 1953; reprinted Boston, Mass.: Beacon Press, 1961); Emory Elliott, *Power and the Pulpit in Puritan New England* (Princeton, N.J.: Princeton University Press, 1975); and David Minter, "The Puritan Jeremiad as a Literary Form," included in *The American Puritan Imagination: Essays in Revaluation,* ed. Sacvan Bercovitch (London: Cambridge University Press, 1974).

THE TEXT

This edition of "God's Controversy With New-England" adopts the text in Harrison T. Meserole's anthology, *Seventeenth-Century American Poetry* (Garden City, N.Y.: Doubleday & Co., 1968; reprinted, New York: W. W. Norton & Co., 1972). Meserole follows the manuscript version in the collection of the Massachusetts Historical Society, which published the poem for the first time in *Proceedings of the Massachusetts Historical Society:* 12 (1871-1873): 83-93.

"GOD'S CONTROVERSY WITH NEW-ENGLAND"

Written in the time of the great drought Anno 1662.
By a lover of New England's prosperity.

Isaiah, 5.4.—What could have been done more to my vineyard that I have not done in it? wherefore when I looked that it should bring forth grapes, brought it forth wilde grapes?

The Authors Request Unto the Reader.

Good christian Reader judge me not
    As too censorious,
For pointing at those faults of thine

Which are notorious.
For if those faults be none of thine   5
   I do not thee accuse:
But if they be, to hear thy faults
   Why shouldest thou refuse.

I blame not thee to spare my self:
   But first at home begin,   10
And judge my self, before that I
   Reproove anothers sin.
Nor is it I that thee reproove
   Let God himself be heard
Whose awfull providence's voice   15
   No man may disregard.

Quod Deus omnipotens regali voce minatur,
Quod tibi proclamant uno simul ore prophetae,
Quodq' ego cum lachrymis testor de numinis irâ,
Tu leve comentu ne ducas, Lector Amice.[1]   20

New-England Planted, Prospered, Declining, Threatned, Punished.

Beyond the great Atlantick flood
   There is a region vast,
A country where no English foot
   In former ages past:
A waste and howling wilderness,   25
   Where none inhabited
But hellish fiends, and brutish men
   That Devils worshiped.

This region was in darkness plac't
   Far off from heavens light,   30
Amidst the shaddows of grim death

1. What almighty God warns with a ruler's voice,
What the prophets proclaim to you, crying all together,
And what I testify tearfully about the wrath of God
Do not reflect upon lightly, Dear Reader.

And of eternal night.
For there the Sun of righteousness
    Had never made to shine
The light of his sweet countenance,   35
    And grace which is divine:

Until the time drew nigh wherein
    The glorious Lord of hostes
Was pleasd to lead his armies forth
    Into those forrein coastes.   40
At whose approach the darkness sad
    Soon vanished away,
And all the shaddows of the night
    Were turnd to lightsome day.

The dark and dismal western woods   45
    (The Devils den whilere)
Beheld such glorious gospel-shine,
    As none beheld more cleare.
Where sathan had his scepter sway'd
    For many generations,   50
The Kings of Kings set up his throne
    To rule amongst the nations.

The stubborn he in pieces brake,
    Like vessels made of clay:
And those that sought his peoples hurt   55
    He turned to decay.
Those curst Amalekites,[2] that first
    Lift up their hand on high
To fight against Gods Israel,
    Were ruin'd fearfully.   60

Thy terrours on the Heathen folk,

2. Marauding biblical tribesmen, who robbed and attacked the Israelites from the time of Moses until David overcame them. Wigglesworth applies the name typologically here to the hostile Indian tribes encountered by the New England colonists.

    O Great Jehovah, fell:
The fame of thy great acts, o Lord,
    Did all the nations quell.
Some hid themselves for fear of thee   65
    In forrests wide & great:
Some to thy people croutching came,
    For favour to entreat.

Some were desirous to be taught
    The knowledge of thy wayes,   70
And being taught, did soon accord
    Therein to spend their dayes.
Thus were the fierce & barbarous
    Brought to civility,
And those that liv'd like beasts (or worse)   75
    To live religiously.

O happiest of dayes wherein
    The blind received sight,
And those that had no eyes before
    Were made to see the light!   80
The wilderness hereat rejoyc't,
    The woods for joy did sing,
The vallys & the little hills
    Thy praises ecchoing.

Here was the hiding place, which thou,   85
    Jehovah, didst provide
For thy redeemed ones, and where
    Thou didst thy jewels hide
In per'lous times, and saddest dayes
    Of sack-cloth and of blood,   90
When th'overflowing scourge did pass
    Through Europe, like a flood.

While almost all the world beside
    Lay weltring in their gore:
We, only we, enjoyd such peace   95

As none enjoyd before.
No forrein foeman did us fray,
    Nor threat'ned us with warrs:
We had no enemyes at home,
    Nor no domestick jarrs.   100

The Lord had made (such was his grace)
    For us a Covenant
Both with the men, and with the beasts,
    That in this desart haunt:
So that through places wilde and waste   105
    A single man, disarm'd,
Might journey many hundred miles,
    And not at all be harm'd.

Amidst the solitary woods
    Poor travellers might sleep   110
As free from danger as at home,
    Though no man watch did keep.
Thus were we priviledg'd with peace,
    Beyond what others were.
Truth, Mercy, Peace, with Righteousness.   115
    Took up their dwelling here.

Our Governour was of our selves.
    And all his Bretheren,
For wisdom & true piety,
    Select, & chosen men.   120
Who, Ruling in ye fear of God,
    The righteous cause maintained,
And all injurious violence,
    And wickedness, restrained.

Our temp'rall blessings did abound: 125
    But spirituall good things
Much more abounded, to the praise
    Of that great King of Kings.
Gods throne was here set up; here was

His tabernacle pight: 130
This was the place, and these the folk
    In whom he took delight.

Our morning starrs shone all day long:
    Their beams gave forth such light,
As did the noon-day sun abash,   135
    And's glory dazle quite.
Our day continued many yeers,
    And had no night at all:
Yea many thought the light would last,
    And be perpetuall.   140

Such, o New-England, was thy first,
    Such was thy best estate:
But, Loe! a strange and suddain change
    My courage did amate.
The brightest of our morning starrs   145
    Did wholly disappeare:
And those that tarried behind [3]
    With sack-cloth covered were.

Moreover, I beheld & saw
    Our welkin[4] overkest,   150
And dismal clouds for sun-shine late
    O'respread from east to west.
The air became tempestuous;
    The wilderness gan quake:
And from above with awfull voice   155
    Th' Almighty thundring spake.

Are these the men that erst at my command
    Forsook their ancient seats and native soile,

3. Deaths of prominent Puritans of the first generation were often interpreted as divine judgments on New England's sins. The mythology of the founding fathers was already well established in Wigglesworth's time, although it was not to reach its most extreme literary expression until Cotton Mather's epic history, *Magnalia Christi Americana* (1702).
    4. Sky.

To follow me into a desart land,
    Contemning all the travell and the toile,   160
Whose love was such to purest ordinances
    As made them set at nought their fair inheritances?

Are these the men that prized libertee
    To walk with God according to their light,
To be as good as he would have them bee,   165
    To serve and worship him with all their might,
Before the pleasures which a fruitfull field,
    And country flowing-full of all good things, could yield,

Are these the folk whom from the brittish Iles,
    Through the stern billows of the watry main,   170
I safely led so many thousand miles,
    As if their journey had been through a plain?
Whom having from all enemies protected,
    And through so many deaths and dangers well directed,

I brought and planted on the western shore,   175
    Where nought but bruits and salvage wights did swarm
(Untaught, untrain'd, untam'd by vertue's lore)
    That sought their blood, yet could not do them harm?
My fury's flaile them thresht, my fatall broom
    Did sweep them hence, to make my people
        elbow-room.   180

Are these the men whose gates with peace I crown'd,
    To whom for bulwarks I salvation gave,
Whilst all things else with rattling tumults sound,
    And mortall frayes send thousands to the grave?
Whilest their own brethren bloody hands embrewed   185
    In brothers blood, and fields with carcases bestrewed?

Is this the people blest with bounteous store,
    By land and sea full richly clad and fed,
Whom plenty's self stands waiting still before,
    And powreth out their cups well tempered?   190

For whose dear sake an howling wildernes
    I lately turned into a fruitfull paradeis?

Are these the people in whose hemisphere
    Such bright-beam'd, glist'ring, sun-like starrs I placed,
As by their influence did all things cheere,   195
    As by their light blind ignorance defaced,
As errours into lurking holes did fray,
    As turn'd the late dark night into a lightsome day?

Are these the folk to whom I milked out
    And sweetnes stream'd from consolations brest;   200
Whose soules I fed and strengthened throughout
    With finest spirituall food most finely drest?
On whom I rained living bread from Heaven,
    Withouten Errour's bane, or Superstition's leaven?

With whom I made a Covenant of peace,   205
    And unto whom I did most firmly plight
My faithfulness, If whilst I live I cease
    To be their Guide, their God, their full delight;
Since them with cords of love to me I drew,
    Enwrapping in my grace such as should them ensew.   210

Are these the men, that now mine eyes behold,
    Concerning whom I thought, and whilome spake,
First Heaven shall pass away together scrold,
    Ere they my lawes and righteous wayes forsake,
Or that they slack to runn their heavenly race?   215
    Are these the same? or are some others come in place?

If these be they, how is it that I find
    In stead of holiness Carnality,
In stead of heavenly frames an Earthly mind,
    For burning zeal luke-warm Indifferency,   220
For flaming love, key-cold Dead-heartedness,
    For temperance (in meat, and drinke, and cloaths)
        excess?

Whence cometh it, that Pride, and Luxurie
    Debate, Deceit, Contention, and Strife,
False-dealing, Covetousness, Hypocrisie   225
    (With such like Crimes) amongst them are so rife,
That one of them doth over-reach another?
    And that an honest man can hardly trust his Brother?

How is it, that Security, and Sloth,
    Amongst the best are Common to be found?   230
That grosser sins, in stead of Graces growth,
    Amongst the many more and more abound?
I hate dissembling shews of Holiness.
    Or practise as you talk, or never more profess.

Judge not, vain world, that all are hypocrites   235
    That do profess more holiness than thou:
All foster not dissembling, guilefull sprites,
    Nor love their lusts, though very many do.
Some sin through want of care and constant watch,
    Some with the sick converse, till they the sickness
        catch.   240

Some, that maintain a reall root of grace,
    Are overgrown with many noysome weeds,
Whose heart, that those no longer may take place,
    The benefit of due correction needs.
And such as these however gone astray   245
    I shall by stripes reduce into a better way.

Moreover some there be that still retain
    Their ancient vigour and sincerity;
Whom both their own, and others sins, constrain
    To sigh, and mourn, and weep, and wail, & cry: 250
And for their sakes I have forborn to powre
    My wrath upon Revolters to this present houre.

To praying Saints I always have respect,
    And tender love, and pittifull regard:

Nor will I now in any wise neglect   255
    Their love and faithfull service to reward;
Athough I deal with others for their folly,
    And turn their mirth to tears that have been too jolly.

For thinke not, O Backsliders, in your heart,
    That I shall still your evill manners beare: 260
Your sinns me press as sheaves do load a cart,
    And therefore I will plague you for this geare
Except you seriously, and soon, repent,
    Ile not delay your pain and heavy punishment.

And who be those themselves that yonder shew?   265
    The seed of such as name my dreadfull Name!
On whom whilere compassions skirt I threw
    Whilest in their blood they were, to hide their shame!
Whom my preventing love did neer me take!
    Whom for mine own I mark't, lest they should me
        forsake!5   270

I look't that such as these to vertue's Lore
    (Though none but they) would have Enclin'd their ear:
That they at least mine image should have bore,
    And sanctify'd my name with awfull fear.
Let pagan's Bratts pursue their lusts, whose meed   275
    Is Death: For christians children are an holy seed.

But hear O Heavens! Let Earth amazed stand;
    Ye Mountaines melt, and Hills come flowing down:
Let horrour seize upon both Sea and Land;
    Let Natures self be cast into a stown.   280
I children nourisht, nurtur'd and upheld:
    But they against a tender father have rebell'd.

5. The tendency for baptized children of church members to fail to experience
grace and, therefore, to remain apart from the Lord's Supper was one of the
most serious problems of the second-generation Puritans. In the same year
Wigglesworth wrote this poem, the Synod of 1662 attempted to resolve the issue
by adopting the Half-Way Covenant.

What could have been by me performed more?
    Or wherein fell I short of your desire?
Had you but askt, I would have op't my store,   285
    And given what lawfull wishes could require.
For all this bounteous cost I lookt to see
    Heaven-reaching-hearts, & thoughts, Meekness,
        Humility.

But lo, a sensuall Heart all void of grace,
    An Iron neck, a proud presumptuous Hand;   290
A self-conceited, stiff, stout, stubborn Race,
    That fears no threats, submitts to no command:
Self-will'd, perverse, such as can beare no yoke;
    A Generation even ripe for vengeance stroke.

Such were that Carnall Brood of Israelites   295
    That Josua and the Elders did ensue,
Who growing like the cursed Cananites
    Upon themselves my heavy judgements drew.
Such also was that fleshly Generation,
    Whom I o'rewhelm'd by waters deadly inundation.   300

They darker light, and lesser meanes misused;
    They had not such Examples them to warn:
You clearer Rules, and Precepts, have abused,
    And dreadfull monuments of others harm.
My gospels glorious light you do not prize: 305
    My Gospels endless, boundless grace you clean despize.

My painfull[6] messengers you disrespect,
    Who toile and sweat and sweale[7] themselves away,
Yet nought at all with you can take effect,
    Who hurrie headlong to your own decay.   310
In vain the Founder melts, and taketh pains:
    Bellows and Lead's consum'd, but still your dross
        remains.

6. Conscientious; painstaking.
7. Burn or melt.

What should I do with such a stiff-neckt race?
  How shall I ease me of such Foes as they?
What shall befall despizers of my Grace?   315
  I'le surely beare their candle-stick[8] away,
And Lamps put out. Their glorious noon-day light
  I'le quickly turn into a dark Egyptian night.

Oft have I charg'd you by my ministers
  To gird your selves with sack cloth, and repent.   320
Oft have I warnd you by my messengers;
  That so you might my wrathfull ire prevent:
But who among you hath this warning taken?
  Who hath his crooked wayes, & wicked works
    forsaken?

Yea many grow to more and more excess;   325
  More light and loose, more Carnall and prophane.
The sins of Sodom, Pride, and Wantonness,
  Among the multitude spring up amain.
Are these the fruits of Pious Education,
  To run with greater speed and Courage to Damnation   330

If here and there some two, or three, shall steere
  A wiser course, then their Companions do,
You make a mock of such; and scoff, and jeere
  Becaus they will not be so bad as you.
Such is the Generation that succeeds   335
  The men, whose eyes have seen my great & awfull
    deeds.

Now therefore hearken and encline your ear,
  In judgement I will henceforth with you plead;
And if by that you will not learn to fear,
  But still go on a sensuall life to lead: 340
I'le strike at once an All-Consuming stroke;
  Nor cries nor tears shall then my fierce intent revoke.

8. Source of spiritual illumination. This image was frequently applied by
Wigglesworth's contemporaries to describe the first New England churches and
the most effective ministers.

Thus ceast his Dreadful-threatning voice
 The high & lofty-One.
The Heavens stood still Appal'd thereat;   345
 The Earth beneath did groane:
Soon after I beheld and saw
 A mortall dart come flying:
I lookt again, & quickly saw
 Some fainting, others dying.   350

The Heavens more began to lowre,
 The welkin Blacker grew:
And all things seemed to forebode
 Sad changes to ensew.
From that day forward hath the Lord   355
 Apparently contended
With us in Anger, and in Wrath:
 But we have not amended.

Our healthfull dayes are at an end,
 And sicknesses come on   360
From yeer to yeer, becaus our hearts
 Away from God are gone.
New-England, where for many yeers
 You scarcely heard a cough,
And where Physicians had no work,   365
 Now finds them work enough.

Now colds and coughs, Rhewms, and sore-throats,
 Do more & more abound:
Now Agues sore & feavers strong
 In every place are found.   370
How many houses have we seen
 Last Autumn, and this spring,
Wherein the healthful were too few
 To help the languishing.

One wave another followeth,   375
 And one disease begins
Before another cease, becaus

We turn not from our sins.
We stopp our ear against reproof,
    And hearken not to God: 380
God stops his ear against our prayer,
    And takes not off his rod.

Our fruitful seasons have been turnd
    Of late to barrenness,
Sometimes through great & parching drought,   385
    Sometimes through rain's excess.
Yea now the pastures & corn fields
    For want of rain do languish:
The cattell mourn, & hearts of men
    Are fill'd with fear & anguish.   390

The clouds are often gathered,
    As if we should have rain:
But for our great unworthiness
    Are scattered again.
We pray & fast, & make fair shewes,   395
    As if we meant to turn:
But whilst we turn not, God goes on
    Our field, & fruits to burn.

And burnt are all things in such sort,
    That nothing now appears,   400
But what may wound our hearts with grief,
    And draw foorth floods of teares.
All things a famine do presage
    In that extremity,
As if both men, and also beasts,   405
    Should soon be done to dy.

This O New-England hast thou got
    By riot, & excess:
This hast thou brought upon thy self
    By pride & wantonness.   410

Thus must thy worldlyness be whipt.
    They, that too much do crave,
Provoke the Lord to take away
    Such blessings as they have.

We have been also threatened   415
    With worser things then these:
And God can bring them on us still,
    To morrow if he please.
For if his mercy be abus'd,
    Which holpe us at our need   420
And mov'd his heart to pitty us,
    We shall be plagu'd indeed.

Beware, O sinful Land, beware;
    And do not think it strange
That sorer judgements are at hand,   425
    Unless thou quickly change.
Or God, or thou, must quickly change;
    Or else thou art undon:
Wrath cannot cease, if sin remain,
    Where judgement is begun.   430

Ah dear New England! dearest land to me;
    Which unto God hast hitherto been dear,
And mayst be still more dear than formerlie,
    If to his voice thou wilt incline thine ear.

Consider wel & wisely what the rod,   435
    Wherewith thou art from yeer to yeer chastized,
Instructeth thee. Repent, & turn to God,
    Who wil not have his nurture be despized.

Thou still hast in thee many praying saints,
    Of great account, and precious with the Lord,   440
Who dayly powre out unto him their plaints,
    And strive to please him both in deed & word.

Cheer on, sweet souls, my heart is with you all,
    And shall be with you, maugre[9] Sathan's might:
And whereso'ere this body be a Thrall,[10]   445
    Still in New-England shall be my delight.

    (1662; 1873)

9. Despite.
10. Slave; servant.

Ebenezer Cook
(c. 1670–c. 1732)

EBENEZER COOK (or Cooke as he sometimes signed himself)
was born in England but spent much of his life in Maryland,
where his father conducted a tobacco-exporting business and
owned a plantation at the mouth of the Choptank River. His
biography is obscure, but the few records of his activities indicate
that he sailed fairly regularly between England and America, that
he owned land in Maryland, and that he practiced law and held
minor colonial offices. Cook's reputation rests, however, almost
exclusively on his literary achievements as his colony's self-ap-
pointed poet laureate. His principal poem, *The Sot-Weed Factor,*
was published in London in 1708 and appeared in a later version
as *Sot-Weed Redivivus,* published in 1731 in Annapolis. These
works, with a few minor poems, constitute Cook's known literary
production and afford material for conjecture about his life—con-
jecture imaginatively developed in John Barth's novel, *The Sot-
Weed Factor* (1960).

Capturing the raw, rowdy aspects of colonial life, Cook recounts
the misadventures of an English tobacco agent, or sot-weed factor,
when his excursion to Maryland involves him in a succession of
disastrous encounters with rascals, whores, and savages. The poem
burlesques the pretensions of colonial society and attacks the
dishonesty of all classes in its rapid, blustering review of the
narrator's discomfitures. More notably, it introduces a comic
American folklore tradition by mocking the greenhorn speaker
himself, whose arrogance, folly, and groundless fears of the wilder-
ness make him a vulnerable target for abuse.

340 Ebenezer Cook

BIBLIOGRAPHIC NOTE

There is no complete edition of Cook's poetry available, but the poems attributed to him have all been published. *The Sot-Weed Factor* is frequently anthologized, usually following the text of the 1708 edition but occasionally adopting the 1731 version. The standard reprinting of the first edition appears in *Early Maryland Poetry*, ed. Bernard C. Steiner, Fund Publication no. 36 (Baltimore: Maryland Historical Society, 1900), pp. 11-31.

   Two books that offer useful information about Cook and helpful readings of his work are J. A. Leo Lemay's survey, *Men of Letters in Colonial Maryland* (Knoxville: University of Tennessee Press, 1972), and Edward H. Cohen's specialized study, *Ebenezer Cooke: The Sot-Weed Canon* (Athens: University of Georgia Press, 1975). Robert D. Arner analyzes the most famous Cook poem in "Ebenezer Cooke's *The Sot-Weed Factor:* The Structure of Satire," *Southern Literary Journal* 4 (1971): 33-47.

THE TEXT

This text of *The Sot-Weed Factor* is based on Kenneth Silverman's anthology, *Colonial American Poetry* (New York: Hafner Publishing Co., 1968), which follows the London edition of 1708.

THE SOT-WEED FACTOR   *Tobacco Agent*

Condemn'd by Fate to way-ward Curse,
Of Friends unkind, and empty Purse;
Plagues worse then fill'd *Pandora's* Box,
I took my leave of *Albion's* Rocks:
With heavy Heart, concern'd that I   5
Was forc'd my Native Soil to fly,
And the *Old World* must bid good-buy.
But Heav'n ordain'd it should be so,
And to repine is vain we know:
Freighted with Fools, from *Plymouth* sound,   10
To *Mary-Land* our Ship was bound;
Where we arriv'd in dreadful Pain,

Influence of Picaresque Economics / Mercantilism Couplets   *iambic tetrameter*

Shock'd by the Terrours of the Main;
For full three Months, our wavering Boat,

Did thro' the surley Ocean float,   15
And furious Storms and threat'ning Blasts,
Both tore our Sails and sprung our Masts:
Wearied, yet pleas'd, we did escape
Such Ills, we anchor'd at the *Cape;*[1]
But weighing soon, we plough'd the *Bay,*   20
To Cove it[2] in *Piscato-way,*[3]
Intending there to open Store,
I put myself and Goods a-shore:
Where soon repair'd a numerous Crew,
In Shirts and Drawers of *Scotch-cloth* Blue.[4]   25
With neither Stockings, Hat, nor Shooe.
These *Sot-weed* Planters Crowd the Shoar,
In Hue as tawny as a Moor:
Figures so strange, no God design'd,
To be a part of Humane Kind: 30
But wanton Nature, void of Rest,
Moulded the brittle Clay in Jest.
At last a Fancy very odd
Took me, this was the Land of *Nod;*
Planted at first, when Vagrant *Cain,*   35
His Brother had unjustly slain:
Then conscious of the Crime he'd done,
From Vengeance dire, he hither run;
And in a Hut supinely dwelt,
The first in *Furs* and *Sot-weed* dealt.   40
And ever since his Time, the Place,
Has harbour'd a detested Race;
Who when they cou'd not live at Home,

1. By the *Cape,* is meant the *Capes* of *Virginia,* the first Land on the Coast of *Virginia* and *Mary-Land* (Cook's note).
2. To *Cove* is to lie at Anchor safe in Harbour (Cook's note).
3. The Bay of *Piscato-way,* the usual place where our Ships come to an Anchor in *Mary-Land* (Cook's note).
4. The Planters generally wear Blue *Linnen* (Cook's note).

*New World filled
with criminals*

For Refuge to these Worlds did roam;
In hopes by Flight they might prevent,   45
The Devil and his fell intent;
Obtain from Tripple Tree⁵ repreive,
And Heav'n and Hell alike deceive:
But e're their Manners I display,   ⎫
I think it fit I open lay   ⎬   50
My Entertainment by the way;   ⎭
That Strangers well may be aware on,
What homely Diet they must fare on.
To touch that Shoar, where no good Sense is found,
But Conversation's lost, and Manners drown'd.   55
I crost unto the other side,   ⎫
A River whose impetuous Tide,   ⎬
The Savage Borders does divide;   ⎭
In such a shining odd invention,
I scarce can give its due Dimention.   60
The *Indians* call this watry Waggon
Canoo,⁶ a Vessel none can brag on;
Cut from a *Popular-Tree*, or *Pine,*
And fashion'd like a Trough for Swine:
In this most noble Fishing-Boat,   65
I boldly put myself a-float;
Standing Erect, with Legs stretch'd wide,
We paddled to the other side:
Where being Landed safe by hap,
As *Sol* fell into *Thetis* Lap.   70
A ravenous Gang bent on the stroul,
Of Wolves ⁷ for Prey, began to howl;
This put me in a pannick Fright,
Least I should be devoured quite:
But as I there a musing stood,   75
And quite benighted in a Wood,⁸
A Female Voice pierc'd thro' my Ears,

5. Gallows.
6. A *Canoo* is an *Indian* Boat, cut out of the body of a Popler-Tree (Cook's note).
7. Wolves are very numerous in *Mary-Land* (Cook's note).
8. Cook probably intended this allusion to the popular ballad, "The Babes in the Wood," to alert the reader to the narrator's helpless innocence as he enters a settled area which he mistakes for a howling wilderness.

Crying, *You Rogue drive home the Steers.*
I listen'd to th'attractive sound,
And straight a Herd of Cattel found $\Big\}$ 80
Drove by a Youth, and homewards bound:
Cheer'd with the sight, I straight thought fit,
To ask where I a Bed might get.
The surley Peasant bid me stay,
And ask'd from whom I'de run away.[9] 85
Surpriz'd at such a saucy Word,
I instantly lugg'd out my Sword;
Swearing I was no Fugitive,
But from *Great-Britain* did arrive, $\Big\}$
In hopes I better there might Thrive. 90
To which he mildly made reply,
I beg your Pardon, Sir, *that I*
Should talk to you Unmannerly;
But if you please to go with me $\Big\}$
To yonder House, you'll welcome be. 95
Encountring soon the smoaky Seat,
The Planter old did thus me greet:
"Whether you come from Goal [10] or Colledge, ~~Jail~~
"You're welcome to my certain Knowledge;
"And if you please all Night to stay, 100
"My Son shall put you in the way.
Which offer I most kindly took,
And for a Seat did round me look:
When presently amongst the rest, 105
He plac'd his unknown *English* Guest,
Who found them drinking for a whet,
A Cask of Syder [11] on the Fret,
Till Supper came upon the Table,
On which I fed whilst I was able. 110
So after hearty Entertainment,
Of Drink and Victuals without Payment;
For Planters Tables, you must know,
Are free for all that come and go.

9. 'Tis supposed by the Planters, that all unknown Persons are run away from some Master (Cook's note).

10. Jail.

11. Syder-pap is a sort of Food made of Syder and small Homine, like our Oat-meal (Cook's note).

While Pon [12] and Milk, with Mush[13] well stoar'd,   115
In wooden Dishes grac'd the Board;
With Homine[14] and Syder-pap,
(Which scarce a hungry Dog wou'd lap)
Well stuff'd with Fat, from Bacon fry'd,
Or with *Molossus* dulcify'd.   120
Then out our Landlord pulls a Pouch,
As greasy as the Leather Couch
On which he sat, and straight begun,
To load with Weed his *Indian* Gun;
In length, scarce longer than ones Finger,   125
Or that for which the Ladies linger:
His Pipe smoak'd out with aweful Grace,
With aspect grave and solemn pace;
The reverend Sire walks to a Chest,
Of all his Furniture the best,   130
Closely confin'd within a Room,
Which seldom felt the weight of Broom;
From thence he lugs a Cag of Rum,
And nodding to me, thus begun:
I find, says he, you don't much care,   135
For this our *Indian* Country Fare;
But let me tell you, Friend of mine,
You may be glad of it in time,
Tho' now your Stomach is so fine;
And if within this Land you stay,   140
You'll find it true what I do say.
This said, the Rundlet up he threw,
And bending backwards strongly drew:
I pluck'd as stoutly for my part,
Altho' it made me sick at Heart.   145
And got so soon into my Head
I scare cou'd find my way to Bed;

12. Pon is Bread made of *Indian-Corn* (Cook's note).
13. Mush is a sort of Hasty-pudding made with Water and *Indian* Flower (Cook's note).
14. Homine is a Dish that is made of boiled *Indian* Wheat, eaten with Molossus, or Bacon-Fat (Cook's note).

Where I was instantly convey'd
By one who pass'd for Chamber-Maid;
Tho' by her loose and sluttish Dress,   150
She rather seem'd a *Bedlam-Bess:*   *asylum*
Curious to know from whence she came,
I prest her to declare her Name.
She Blushing, seem'd to hide her Eyes,
And thus in Civil Terms replies;   155
In better Times, e'er to this Land,
I was unhappily Trapann'd;[15]
Perchance as well I did appear,
As any Lord or Lady here,
Not then a Slave for twice two Year.[16]   160
My Cloaths were fashionably new,
Nor were my Shifts of Linnen Blue;
But things are changed now at the Hoe,
I daily work, and Bare-foot go,
In weeding Corn or feeding Swine,   165
I spend my melancholy Time.
Kidnap'd and Fool'd, I hither fled,
To shun a hated Nuptial Bed,[17]
And to my cost already find,
Worse Plagues than those I left behind.   170
Whate'er the Wanderer did profess,
Good-faith I cou'd not choose but guess
The Cause which brought her to this place,
Was supping e'er the Priest said Grace.
Quick as my Thoughts, the Slave was fled,   175
(Her Candle left to shew my Bed)
Which made of Feathers soft and good,
Close in the Chimney-corner stood;[18]
I threw me down expecting Rest,

15. Kidnapped.
16. 'Tis the Custom for Servants to be obliged for four Years to very servile Work; after which time they have their Freedom (Cook's note).
17. These are the general Excuses made by *English* Women, which are sold, or sell themselves to *Mary-Land* (Cook's note).
18. Beds stand in the Chimney-corner in this Country (Cook's note).

To be in golden Slumbers blest: 180
But soon a noise disturb'd my quiet,
And plagu'd me with nocturnal Riot;
A Puss which in the ashes lay,
With grunting Pig began a Fray;
And prudent Dog, that Feuds might cease,   185
Most strongly bark'd to keep the Peace.
This Quarrel scarcely was decided,
By stick that ready lay provided;
But *Reynard* arch and cunning Loon,
Broke into my Appartment soon;   190
In hot pursuit of Ducks and Geese,
With fell intent the same to seize:
Their Cackling Plaints with strange surprize,
Chac'd Sleeps thick Vapours from my Eyes:
Raging I jump'd upon the Floar,   195
And like a Drunken Saylor Swore;
With Sword I fiercely laid about,
And soon dispers'd the Feather'd Rout:
The Poultry out of Window flew,
And *Reynard* cautiously withdrew: 200
The Dogs who this Encounter heard,
Fiercly themselves to aid me rear'd,
And to the Place of Combat run,
Exactly as the Field was won.
Fretting and hot as roasting Capon,   205
And greasy as a Flitch of Bacon;
I to the Orchard did repair,
To Breathe the cool and open Air;
Expecting there the rising Day,
Extended on a Bank I lay: 210
But Fortune here, that saucy Whore,
Disturb'd me worse and plagu'd me more,
Than she had done the night before.
Hoarse croaking Frogs [19] did 'bout me ring,
Such Peals the Dead to Life wou'd bring,   215
A Noise might move their Wooden King.

19. Frogs are called *Virginea* Bells, and make, (both in that Country and *Mary-Land*) during the Night, a very hoarse ungrateful Noise (Cook's note).

I stuff'd my Ears with Cotten white
For fear of being deaf out-right,
And curst the melancholy Night:
But soon my Vows I did recant,   220
And Hearing as a Blessing grant;
When a confounded Rattle-Snake,
With hissing made my Heart to ake:
Not knowing how to fly the Foe,
Or whether in the Dark to go;   225
By strange good Luck, I took a Tree,
Prepar'd by Fate to set me free;
Where riding on a Limb a-stride,
Night and the Branches did me hide,
And I the Devil and Snake defy'd.   230
Not yet from Plagues exempted quite,
The curst Muskitoes[20] did me bite;
Till rising Morn' and blushing Day,
Drove both my Fears and Ills away;
And from Night's Errors set me free.   235
Discharg'd from hospitable Tree;
I did to Planters Booth repair,
And there at Breakfast nobly Fare,
On rashier broil'd of infant Bear:
I thought the Cub delicious Meat,   240
Which ne'er did ought but Chesnuts eat;
Nor was young Orsin's flesh the worse,
Because he suck'd a Pagan Nurse.
Our Breakfast done, my Landlord stout,
Handed a Glass of Rum about;   245
Pleas'd with the Treatment I did find,
I took my leave of Oast so kind;
Who to oblige me, did provide,
His eldest Son to be my Guide,
And lent me Horses of his own,   250
A skittish Colt, and aged Rhoan,
The four-leg'd prop of his Wife *Joan.*

20. These were probably the source of the hissing noise, which the narrator
mistook for a rattlesnake.

Steering our Barks in Trot or Pace,
We sail'd directly for a place
In *Mary-Land* of high renown,   255
Known by the Name of *Battle-Town*.
To view the Crowds did there resort, ⎫
Which Justice made, and Law their sport, ⎬
In that sagacious County Court: ⎭
Scarce had we enter'd on the way,   260
Which thro' thick Woods and Marshes lay;
But *Indians* strange did soon appear,
In hot persuit of wounded Deer;
No mortal Creature can express,
His wild fantastick Air and Dress;   265
His painted Skin in colours dy'd, ⎫
His sable Hair in Satchel ty'd, ⎬
Shew'd Savages not free from Pride: ⎭
His tawny Thighs, and Bosom bare,
Disdain'd a useless Coat to wear,   270
Scorn'd Summer's Heat, and Winters Air;
His manly Shoulders such as please,
Widows and Wives, were bath'd in Grease
Of Cub and Bear, whose supple Oil,
Prepar'd his Limbs 'gainst Heat or Toil.   275
Thus naked Pict in Battel faught,
Or undisguis'd his Mistress sought;
And knowing well his Ware was good,
Refus'd to screen it with a Hood;
His Visage dun, and chin that ne'er ⎫   280
Did Raizor feel or Scissers bear, ⎬
Or know the Ornament of Hair, ⎭
Look'd sternly Grim, surpriz'd with Fear,
I spur'd my Horse, as he drew near:
But Rhoan who better knew than I,   285
The little Cause I had to fly;
Seem'd by his solemn steps and pace,
Resolv'd I shou'd the Specter face,
Nor faster mov'd, tho' spur'd and lick'd,
Than *Balaam's* Ass by Prophet kick'd.   290

Kekicknitop[21] the Heathen cry'd:
How is it *Tom*, my Friend reply'd,
Judging from thence the Brute was civel,
I boldly fac'd the Courteous Devil;
And lugging out a Dram of Rum,   295
I gave his Tawny worship some:
Who in his language as I guess, ⎫
(My Guide informing me no less,) ⎬
Implored the Devil,[22] me to bless. ⎭
I thank'd him for his good Intent,   300
And forwards on my Journey went,
Discoursing as along I rode,
Whether this Race was framed by God
Or whether some Malignant pow'r,
Contriv'd them in an evil hour   305
And from his own Infernal Look;
Their Dusky form and Image took:
From hence we fell to Argument
Whence Peopled was this Continent,
My Friend suppos'd *Tartarians* wild,   310
Or *Chinese* from their Home exiled;
Wandering thro' Mountains hid with Snow, ⎫
And Rills did in the Vallies flow, ⎬
Far to the South of *Mexico:* ⎭
Broke thro' the Barrs which Nature cast,   315
And wide unbeaten Regions past,

21. *Kekicknitop* is an *Indian* Expression, and signifies no more than this, *How do you do?* (Cook's note).

22. These *Indians* worship the Devil, and pray to him as we do to God Almighty. 'Tis suppos'd, That *America* was peopl'd from *Scythia* or *Tartaria*, which Borders on *China*, by reason the *Tartarians* and *Americans* very much agree in their Manners, Arms and Government. Other Persons are of Opinion, that the *Chinese* first peopled the *West Indies;* imagining *China* and the Southern part of *America* to be contiguous. Others believe that the *Phoenicians* who were very skilful Mariners, first planted a Colony in the Isles of *America*, and supply'd the Persons left to inhabit there with Women and all other Necessaries; till either the Death or Shipwreck of the first Discoverers, or some other Misfortune occasioned the loss of the Discovery, which had been purchased by the Peril of the first Adventurers (Cook's note).

Till near those Streams the humane deludge roll'd,
Which sparkling shin'd with glittering Sands of Gold;
And fetch *Pizarro*[23] from the *Iberian* Shoar,[24]
To Rob the Natives of their fatal Stoar.   320
I Smil'd to hear my young Logician,
Thus Reason like a Politician;
Who ne're by Fathers Pains and Earning
Had got at Mother *Cambridge* Learning;
Where Lubber youth just free from birch   325
Most stoutly drink to prop the Church;
Nor with *Grey Groat*[25] had taken Pains
To purge his Head and Cleanse his Reines:
And in obedience to the Colledge,
Had pleas'd himself with carnal Knowledge: 330
And tho' I lik'd the youngester's Wit,
I judg'd the Truth he had not hit;
And could not choose but smile to think
What they could do for Meat and Drink,
Who o'er so many Desarts ran,   335
With Brats and Wives in *Caravan;*
Unless perchance they'd got the Trick,
To eat no more than Porker sick;
Or could with well contented Maws,
Quarter like Bears[26] upon their Paws.   340
Thinking his Reasons to confute,
I gravely thus commenc'd Dispute,
And urg'd that tho' a *Chinese* Host,
Might penetrate this *Indian* Coast;
Yet this was certainly most true,   345
They never cou'd the Isles subdue;
For knowing not to steer a Boat,
They could not on the Ocean float,

23. *Pizzarro* was the Person that conquer'd *Peru;* a Man of a most bloody Disposition, base, treacherous, covetous, and revengeful (Cook's note).
24. *Spanish* Shoar (Cook's note).
25. There is a very bad Custom in some Colledges, of giving the Students A *Groat ad purgandas Rhenes,* which is usually employ'd to the use of the *Donor* (Cook's note).
26. Bears are said to live by sucking of their *Paws,* according to the Notion of some Learned Authors (Cook's note).

What is the ancestry of the Native Americans

Or plant their Sunburnt Colonies,
In Regions parted by the Seas: 350
I thence inferr'd *Phoenicians*[27] old,
Discover'd first with Vessels bold
These Western Shoars, and planted here,
Returning once or twice a Year,
With *Naval Stoars* and Lasses kind,   355
To comfort those were left behind;
Till by the Winds and Tempest toar,
From their intended Golden Shoar;
They suffer'd Ship-wreck, or were drown'd,
And lost the World so newly found.   360
But after long and learn'd Contenion,
We could not finish our dissention;
And when that both had talk'd their fill,
We had the self same Notion still.
Thus Parson grave well read and Sage,   365
Does in dispute with Priest engage;
The one protests they are not Wise,
Who judge by Sense[28] and trust their Eyes;   *empiricism*
And vows he'd burn for it at Stake,
That Man may God his Maker make;   370
The other smiles at his Religion,
And vows he's but a learned Widgeon:[29]
And when they have empty'd all their stoar ⎫
From Books and Fathers, are not more   ⎬
Convinc'd or wiser than before.   ⎭   375
      Scarce had we finish'd serious Story,
But I espy'd the Town before me,
And roaring Planters on the ground,
Drinking of Healths in Circle round:
Dismounting Steed with friendly Guide,   380

27. The *Phoenicians* were the best and boldest Saylors of Antiquity, and indeed the only *Persons*, in former Ages, who durst venture themselves on the Main Sea (Cook's note).

28. The *Priests* argue, That our Senses in the point of *Transubstantiation* ought not to be believed, for tho' the Consecrated Bread has all the accidents of Bread, yet they affirm, 'tis the Body of Christ, and not Bread but Flesh and Bones (Cook's note).

29. Simpleton; fool.

Our Horses to a Tree we ty'd,
And forwards pass'd amongst the Rout,
To chuse convenient *Quarters* out:
But being none were to be found,
We sat like others on the ground   385
Carousing Punch in open Air
Till Cryer did the Court declare;
The planting Rabble being met,
Their Drunken Worships likewise set:
Cryer proclaims that Noise shou'd cease,   390
And streight the Lawyers broke the Peace.
Wrangling for Plantiff and Defendant,
I thought they ne'er wou'd make an end on't:
With nonsense, stuff and false quotations,
With brazen Lyes and Allegations;   395
And in the splitting of the Cause,
They us'd such Motions with their Paws,
As shew'd their Zeal was strongly bent,
In Blows to end the Argument.
A reverend Judge, who to the shame   400
Of all the Bench, cou'd write his Name;[30]
At Petty-fogger took offence,
And wonder'd at his Impudence.
My Neighbour *Dash* with scorn replies,
And in the Face of Justice flies: 405
The Bench in fury streight divide,
And Scribbles take, or Judges side;
The Jury, Lawyers, and their Clyents,
Contending, fight like earth-born Gyants:
But Sheriff wily lay perdue,[31]   410
Hoping Indictments would ensue,
And when————————
A Hat or Wig fell in the way,
He seiz'd them for the *Queen* as stray:
The Court adjourn'd in usual manner,   415

30. In the County-Court of *Mary-Land*, very few of the Justices of the *Peace* can write or read (Cook's note).
31. Hidden; concealed.

In Battle Blood, and fractious Clamour;
I thought it proper to provide,
A Lodging for myself and Guide,
So to our Inn we march'd away,
Which at a little distance lay;   420
Where all things were in such Confusion,
I thought the World at its conclusion:
A Herd of Planters on the ground,
O'er-whelm'd with Punch, dead drunk we found:
Others were fighting and contending,   425
Some burnt their Cloaths to save the mending.
A few whose Heads by frequent use,
Could better bare the potent Juice,
Gravely debated State Affairs.
Whilst I most nimbly trip'd up Stairs;   430
Leaving my Friend discoursing oddly,
And mixing things Prophane and Godly:
Just then beginning to be Drunk,
As from the Company I slunk,
To every Room and Nook I crept,   435
In hopes I might have somewhere slept;
But all the bedding was possest
By one or other drunken Guest:
But after looking long about,
I found an antient Corn-loft out,   440
Glad that I might in quiet sleep,
And there my bones unfractur'd keep.
I lay'd me down secure from Fray,
And soundly snoar'd till break of Day;
When waking fresh I sat upright,   445
And found my Shoes were vanish'd quite,
Hat, Wig, and Stockings, all were fled
From this extended *Indian* Bed:
Vext at the Loss of Goods and Chattel,
I swore I'd give the Rascal battel,   450
Who had abus'd me in this sort,
And Merchant Stranger made his Sport.
I furiously descended Ladder;

No Hare in *March* was ever madder:
In vain I search'd for my Apparel,   455
And did with Oast and Servants Quarrel;
For one whose Mind did much aspire
To Mischief,[32] threw them in the Fire;
Equipt with neither Hat nor Shooe, ⎫
I did my coming hither rue,   ⎬   460
And doubtful thought what I should do: ⎭
Then looking round, I saw my Friend
Lie naked on a Tables end;
A Sight so dismal to behold,
One wou'd have judg'd him dead and cold;   465
When wringing of his bloody Nose,
By fighting got we may suppose;
I found him not so fast asleep,
Might give his Friends a cause to weep:
Rise *Oronooko*,[33] rise, said I,   470
And from this *Hell* and *Bedlam* fly.
My Guide starts up, and in amaze,
With blood-shot Eyes did round him gaze;
At length with many a sigh and groan,
He went in search of aged Rhoan;   475
But Rhoan, tho' seldom us'd to faulter,
Had fairly this time slipt his Halter;
And not content all Night to stay
Ty'd up from Fodder, ran away:
After my Guide to ketch him ran,   480
And so I lost both Horse and Man;
Which Disappointment, tho' so great,
Did only Mirth and Jests create:
Till one more Civil than the rest,
In Conversation for the best,   485
Observing that for want of Rhoan,
I should be left to walk alone;

32. 'Tis the Custom of the Planters, to throw their own, or any other Persons
Hat, Wig, Shooes or Stockings in the Fire (Cook's note).
33. Planters are usually call'd by the Name of *Oronooko*, from their Planting
Oronooko-Tobacco (Cook's note).

Most readily did me intreat,
To take a Bottle at his Seat;
A Favour at that time so great,   490
I blest my kind propitious Fate;
And finding soon a fresh supply,
Of Cloaths from Stoar-house kept hard by,
I mounted streight on such a Steed,
Did rather curb, than whipping need;   495
And straining at the usual rate,   ⎫
With spur of Punch which lay in Pate,   ⎬
E'er long we lighted at the Gate: ⎭
Where in an antient *Cedar* House,
Dwelt my new Friend, a Cockerouse;[34]   500
Whose Fabrick, tho' 'twas built of Wood,
Had many Springs and Winters stood;
When sturdy Oaks, and lofty Pines
Were level'd with Musmelion[35] Vines,
And Plants eradicated were,   505
By Hurricanes into the air;
There with good Punch and apple Juice,
We spent our Hours without abuse:
Till Midnight in her sable Vest,
Persuaded Gods and Men to rest;   510
And with a pleasing kind surprize,
Indulg'd soft Slumbers to my Eyes.
Fierce *AEthon*[36] courser of the Sun,
Had half his Race exactly run;
And breath'd on me a fiery Ray,   ⎫   515
Darting hot Beams the following Day,   ⎬
When snug in Blanket white I lay: ⎭
But Heat and *Chinces*[37] rais'd the Sinner,
Most opportunely to his Dinner;
Wild Fowl and Fish delicious Meats,   ⎫   520
As good as *Neptune's* Doxy eats,   ⎬   *mistress*
Began our Hospitable Treat;   ⎭

34. Cockerouse, is a Man of Quality (Cook's note).
35. Musmilleon Vines are what we call Muskmilleon Plants (Cook's note).
36. *AEthon* is one of the Poetical Horses of the Sun (Cook's note).
37. *Chinces* are a sort of Vermin like our *Bugs* in *England* (Cook's note).

Fat Venson follow'd in the Rear,
And Turkies[38] wild Luxurious Chear:
But what the Feast did most commend,   525
Was hearty welcom from my Friend.
Thus having made a noble Feast;
And eat as well as pamper'd Priest,
Madera strong in flowing Bowls,
Fill'd with extream, delight our Souls;   530
Till wearied with a purple Flood,
Of generous Wine (the Giant's blood,
As Poets feign) away I made,
For some refreshing verdant Shade;
Where musing on my Rambles strange,   535
And Fortune which so oft did change;
In midst of various Contemplations
Of Fancies odd, and Meditations,
I slumber'd long————————
Till hazy Night with noxious Dews,   540
Did Sleep's unwholsom Fetters lose:
With Vapours chil'd, and misty air,
To fire-side I did repair;
Near which a jolly Female Crew,
Were deep engag'd at *Lanctre-Looe;*   545
In Nightrails white, with dirty Mein,
Such Sights are scare in *England* seen:
I thought them first some Witches bent,
On Black Designs in dire Convent.
Till one who with affected air,   550
Had nicely learn'd to Curse and Swear:
Cry'd Dealing's lost is but a Flam,[39]
And vow'd by G-d she'd keep her *Pam.*[40]
When dealing through the board had run,
They ask'd me kindly to make one;   555
Not staying often to be bid,

38. Wild Turkies are very good Meat, and prodigiously large in *Maryland* (Cook's note).

39. Trick; delusion.

40. Jack of trumps.

I sat me down as others did:
We scarce had play'd a Round about,
But that these *Indian* Froes[41] fell out.
D—m you, says one, tho' now so brave,   560
I knew you late a Four Years Slave;
What if for Planters Wife you go,
Nature design'd you for the Hoe.
Rot you replies the other streight,
The Captain kiss'd you for his Freight;   565
And if the Truth was known aright,
And how you walk'd the Streets by night,
You'd blush (if one cou'd blush) for shame,
Who from *Bridewell* or *Newgate*[42] came.
From Words they fairly fell to Blows,   570
And being loath to interpose,
Or meddle in the Wars of Punk,[43]
Away to Bed in hast I slunk.
Waking next day, with aking Head,
And Thirst, that made me quit my Bed;   575
I rigg'd myself, and soon got up,
To cool my Liver with a Cup
Of *Succahana*[44] fresh and clear,
Not half so good as *English* Beer;
Which ready stood in Kitchin Pail,   580
And was in fact but *Adam's* Ale;
For Planters Cellars you must know,
Seldom with good *October* flow,
But Perry Quince and Apple Juice,
Spout from the Tap like any Sluce;   585
Untill the Cask's grown low and stale,
They're forc'd again to Goad[45] and Pail:
The soathing drought scarce down my Throat,

41. Fraus; women.
42. English prisons.
43. Prostitutes.
44. *Succahana* is Water (Cook's note).
45. A *Goad* grows upon an *Indian* Vine, resembling a Bottle, when ripe it is hollow; this the Planters make use of to drink water out of (Cook's note).

Enough to put a Ship a float,
With Cockerouse as I was sitting,   590
I felt a Feaver Intermitting;
A fiery Pulse beat in my Veins,
From Cold I felt resembling Pains:
This cursed seasoning I remember,
Lasted from *March* to cold *December;*   595
Nor would it then its *Quarters* shift,
Until by *Cardus*[46] turn'd a drift,
And had my Doctress wanted skill,
Or Kitchin Physick at his will,
My Father's Son had lost his Lands,   600
And never seen the *Goodwin-Sands:*
But thanks to Fortune and a Nurse
Whose Care depended on my Purse,
I saw myself in good Condition,
Without the help of a Physitian: 605
At length the shivering ill relieved,
Which long my Head and Heart had grieved;
I then began to think with Care,
How I might sell my *British* Ware,
That with my Freight I might comply,   610
Did on my Charter-party lie:
To this intent, with Guide before,
I tript it to the Eastern Shoar;
While riding near a Sandy Bay,
I met a *Quaker, Yea* and *Nay;*   615
A Pious Conscientious Rogue,
As e'er woar Bonnet or a Brogue,
Who neither Swore nor kept his Word,
But cheated in the Fear of God;
And when his Debts he would not pay,   620
By Light within he ran away.
With this sly Zealot soon I struck
A Bargain for my *English* Truck,
Agreeing for ten thousand weight,
Of *Sot-weed* good and fit for freight,   625

46. Thistle, used to heal fevers.

Broad *Oronooko* bright and sound,
The growth and product of his ground;
In Cask that should contain compleat,
Five hundred of Tobacco neat.
The Contract thus betwixt us made,   630
Not well acquainted with the Trade,
My Goods I trusted to the Cheat,
Whose crop was then aboard the Fleet;
And going to receive my own,
I found the Bird was newly flown: 635
Cursing this execrable Slave,
This damn'd pretended Godly Knave;
On due Revenge and Justice bent,
I instantly to Counsel went,
Unto an ambodexter *Quack*,[47]   640
Who learnedly had got the knack
Of giving Glisters,[48] making Pills,
Of filling Bonds, and forging Wills;
And with a stock of Impudence,
Supply'd his want of Wit and Sense;   645
With Looks demure, amazing People,
No wiser than a Daw in Steeple;
My Anger flushing in my Face,
I stated the preceding Case:
And of my Money was so lavish,   650
That he'd have poyson'd half the Parish,
And hang'd his Father on a Tree,
For such another tempting Fee;
Smiling, said he, the Cause is clear,
I'll manage him you need not fear;   655
The Case is judg'd, good Sir, but look
In *Galen*, No—in my Lord *Cook*,
I vow to God I was mistook:
I'll take out a Provincial Writ,
And Trounce him for his Knavish Wit;   660

47. This Fellow was an Apothecary, and turn'd an Attorney at Law (Cook's note).
48. Clysters; enemas.

Upon my Life we'll win the Cause,
With all the ease I cure the *Yaws*.[49]
Resolv'd to plague the holy Brother,
I set one Rogue to catch another;
To try the Cause then fully bent,   665
Up to *Annapolis*[50] I went,
A City Situate on a Plain,
Where scarce a House will keep out Rain;
The Buildings fram'd with Cyprus rare,
Resembles much our *Southwark* Fair: 670
But Stranger here will scarcely meet,
With Market-place, Exchange, or Street;
And if the Truth I may report,
'Tis not so large as *Tottenham Court*.
St. *Mary's* once was in repute,   675
Now here the Judges try the Suit,
And Lawyers twice a Year dispute:
As oft the Bench most gravely meet,
Some to get Drunk, and some to eat
A swinging share of Country Treat.   680
But as for Justice right or wrong,
Not one amongst the numerous throng,
Knows what they mean, or has the Heart,
To give his Verdict on a Stranger's part:
Now Court being call'd by beat of Drum,   685
The Judges left their Punch and Rum,
When Pettifogger Docter draws,
His Paper forth, and opens Cause:
And least I shou'd the better get,
Brib'd *Quack* supprest his Knavish Wit.   690
So Maid upon the downy Field,
Pretends a Force, and Fights to yeild:
The Byast Court without delay,
Adjudg'd my Debt in Country Pay;
In Pipe staves,[51] Corn, or Flesh of Boar,   695

---

49. The *Yaws* is the *Pox* (Cook's note).

50. The chief of *Maryland* containing about twenty four *Houses* (Cook's note).

51. There is a Law in this Country, the Plantiff may pay his Debt in Country pay, which consists in the produce of his Plantation (Cook's note).

Rare Cargo for the *English* Shoar:
Raging with Grief, full speed I ran,
To joyn the Fleet at *Kicketan*,[52]
Embarqu'd and waiting for a Wind,
I left this dreadful Curse behind.   700

    May Canniballs transported o'er the Sea   *prayer*
Prey on these Slaves, as they have done on me;
May never Merchant's, trading Sails explore
This Cruel, this Inhospitable Shoar;
But left abandon'd by the World to starve,   705
May they sustain the Fate they well deserve:
May they turn Savage, or as *Indians* Wild,
From Trade, Converse, and Happiness exil'd;
Recreant to Heaven, may they adore the Sun,
And into Pagan Superstitions run   710
For Vengence ripe————————
May Wrath Divine then lay those Regions wast
Where no Man's[53] Faithful, nor a Woman Chast.

    (1708?; 1708)   *American vernacular — American voice that indicts speaker who is a snob (British) — constructed as critique of British and satire of them.*

Bitter...

Similar to Chaucer

52. The homeward bound Fleet meets here (Cook's note). Now Hampton Roads, Virginia.
53. The Author does not intend by this, any of the *English* Gentlemen resident there (Cook's note).

Joel Barlow
(1754-1812)

JOEL BARLOW was Timothy Dwight's student at Yale and is commonly associated with him as a key member of the Connecticut Wits. Working within the same neoclassical conventions followed by Dwight, Barlow wrote *The Vision of Columbus* (1787), a long epic poem on the development and promise of the Americas, a work which he revised and expanded later as *The Columbiad* (1807). These epics demonstrate Barlow's poetic ambition and clarify his hopeful, democratic views—increasingly in opposition to Dwight's conservatism—but his shorter poems, especially "The Hasty Pudding" (1793) and "Advice to a Raven in Russia" (1812), give better evidence of his formal control and mastery of tone while remaining faithful to his humanistic values.

"The Hasty Pudding" is a mock-epic, celebrating in exalted language the simple pleasures of rural American life. Written while Barlow attended to one of his frequent extended business and diplomatic trips to Europe, it salutes democratic comforts as alternatives to the aristocratic excesses he saw in the Old World. He dedicated the poem to Martha Washington, urging her to encourage a healthful, simple life-style among Americans, even in presidential banquets. With its charming blend of humor, nostalgia, and instruction, "The Hasty Pudding" remains a classic work of early American poetry.

BIBLIOGRAPHIC NOTE

There is no complete modern edition of Barlow's work, but William K. Bottorff and Arthur L. Ford have edited a two-volume facsimile compilation of his prose and poetry: *The Works of Joel Barlow* (Gainesville, Fla.: Scholars' Facsimiles & Reprints, 1970). Books VII and VIII of *The Columbiad* and "The Conspiracy of Kings" appear in Vernon L. Parrington's anthology, *The Connecticut Wits* (New York: Thomas Y. Crowell Co., 1925; reprinted, 1969).

The best biography is by James Woodress: *A Yankee's Odyssey: The Life of Joel Barlow* (Philadelphia: J. B. Lippincott Co., 1958). Extended study of Barlow's life and writing can be found in Arthur L. Ford's book, *Joel Barlow*, Twayne's United States Authors Series (New York: Twayne Publishers, 1971), and Leon Howard's work, *The Connecticut Wits* (Chicago: University of Chicago Press, 1943). For a detailed analysis of "The Hasty Pudding," readers should consult Robert D. Arner's article, "The Smooth and Emblematic Song: Joel Barlow's *The Hasty Pudding*," *Early American Literature* 7 (1972): 76-91.

THE TEXT

This text of "The Hasty Pudding" follows the original New Haven edition of 1796 as reprinted in *American Literature: Tradition and Innovation*, ed. Harrison T. Meserole, Walter Sutton, and Brom Weber, vol. 1 (Lexington, Mass.: D.C. Heath and Company, 1969).

THE HASTY PUDDING

A POEM IN THREE CANTOS

Canto I

Ye Alps audacious, thro' the Heav'ns that rise,
To cramp the day and hide me from the skies;
Ye Gallic flags, that o'er their heights unfurl'd,
Bear death to kings, and freedom to the world,
I sing not you. A softer theme I choose,   5
A virgin theme, unconscious of the Muse,
But fruitful, rich, well suited to inspire
The purest frenzy of poetic fire.

[handwritten marginal note: Epic traditions]

364 Joel Barlow

Despise it not, ye Bards to terror steel'd,
Who hurl your thunders round the epic field;   10
Nor ye who strain your midnight throats to sing
Joys that the vineyard and the still-house bring;
Or on some distant fair your notes employ,
And speak of raptures that you ne'er enjoy.
I sing the sweets I know, the charms I feel,   15
My morning incense, and my evening meal,
The sweets of Hasty Pudding. Come, dear bowl,
Glide o'er my palate, and inspire my soul.
The milk beside thee, smoking from the kine,
Its substance mingle, married in with thine,   20
Shall cool and temper thy superior heat,
And save the pains of blowing while I eat.
    Oh! could the smooth, the emblematic song
Flow like thy genial juices o'er my tongue,
Could those mild morsels in my numbers chime,   25
And, as they roll in substance, roll in rhyme,
No more thy awkward unpoetic name
Should shun the muse, or prejudice thy fame;
But rising grateful to th' accustom'd ear,
All Bards should catch it, and all realms revere!   30
    Assist me first with pious toil to trace
Thro' wrecks of time, thy lineage and thy race;
Declare what lovely squaw, in days of yore,
(Ere great Columbus sought thy native shore)
First gave thee to the world; her works of fame   35
Have lived indeed, but lived without a name.
Some tawny Ceres,[1] goddess of her days,
First learn'd with stones to crack the well dried maize,
Through the rough sieve to shake the golden show'r,
In boiling water stir the yellow flour: 40
The yellow flour, bestrew'd and stirr'd with haste,
Swells in the flood and thickens to a paste,
Then puffs and wallops, rises to the brim,
Drinks the dry knobs that on the surface swim;

1. Roman goddess of agriculture.

The knobs at last the busy ladle breaks,   45
And the whole mass its true consistence takes.
    Could but her sacred name, unknown so long,
Rise, like her labors, to the son of song,
To her, to them, I'd consecrate my lays,
And blow her pudding with the breath of praise.   50
If 'twas Oella² whom I sang before
I here ascribe her one great virtue more.
Not through the rich Peruvian realms alone
The fame of Sol's sweet daughter should be known,
But o'er the world's wide clime should live secure,   55
Far as his rays extend, as long as they endure.
    Dear Hasty Pudding, what unpromised joy
Expands my heart, to meet thee in Savoy!
Doom'd o'er the world through devious paths to roam,
Each clime my country, and each house my home,   60
My soul is soothed, my cares have found an end,
I greet my long lost, unforgotten friend.
    For thee thro' Paris, that corrupted town,
How long in vain I wandered up and down,
Where shameless Bacchus, with his drenching hoard,   65
Cold from his cave usurps the morning board.
London is lost in smoke and steep'd in tea;
No Yankey there can lisp the name of thee;
The uncouth word, a libel on the town,
Would call a proclamation from the crown.   70
From climes oblique, that fear the sun's full rays,
Chill'd in their fogs, exclude the generous maize:
A grain, whose rich, luxuriant growth requires
Short gentle showers, and bright etherial fires.
    But here, though distant from our native shore,   75
With mutual glee, we meet and laugh once more,
The same! I know thee by that yellow face,

2. Incan goddess, said to be a daughter of the sun. With Manco Capac, she
brought the arts of agriculture and spinning to the Peruvian tribes. In Book II
of *The Vision of Columbus* (1787) and again in *The Columbiad* (1807), Barlow
celebrated these new-world mythic figures as examples of those who use the force
of reason to advance the welfare of the human community.

That strong complexion of true Indian race,
Which time can never change, nor soil impair,
Nor Alpine snows, nor Turkey's morbid air;   80
For endless years, through every mild domain,
Where grows the maize, there thou art sure to reign.
    But man, more fickle, the bold license claims,
In different realms to give thee different names.
Thee the soft nations round the warm Levant   85
Polanta call, the French of course *Polante.*
E'en in thy native regions, how I blush
To hear the Pennsylvanians call thee *Mush!*
Oh Hudson's banks, while men of Belgic spawn
Insult and eat thee by the name *Suppawn.*   90
All spurious appellations, void of truth;
I've better known thee from my earliest youth,
Thy name is *Hasty Pudding!* thus our sires
Were wont to greet thee fuming from their fires;
And while they argued in thy just defense   95
With logic clear, they thus explain'd the sense:—
"In *haste* the boiling cauldron o'er the blaze,
Receives and cooks the ready powder'd maize;
In *haste* 'tis serv'd, and then in equal *haste,*
With cooling milk, we make the sweet repast.   100
No carving to be done, no knife to grate
The tender ear, and wound the stony plate;
But the smooth spoon, just fitted to the lip,
And taught with art the yielding mass to dip,
By frequent journeys to the bowl well stored,   105
Performs the *hasty* honors of the board."
Such is thy name, significant and clear,
A name, a sound to every Yankey dear,
But most to me, whose heart and palate chaste
Preserve my pure hereditary taste.   110
    There are who strive to stamp with disrepute
The luscious food, because it feeds the brute;
In tropes of high-strain'd wit, while gaudy prigs
Compare thy nursling, man, to pamper'd pigs;
With sovereign scorn I treat the vulgar jest,   115

Nor fear to share thy bounties with the beast.
What though the generous cow gives me to quaff
The milk nutritious: am I then a calf?
Or can the genius of the noisy swine,
Though nursed on pudding, claim a kin to mine?   120
Sure the sweet song, I fashion to thy praise,
Runs more melodious than the notes they raise.
    My song resounding in its grateful glee,
No merit claims: I praise myself in thee.
My father lov'd thee thro' his length of days;   125
For thee his fields were shaded o'er with maize;
From thee what health, what vigor he possess'd,
Ten sturdy freemen from his loins attest;
Thy constellation rul'd my natal morn,
And all my bones were made of Indian corn.   130
Delicious grain! whatever form it take,
To roast or boil, to smother or to bake,
In every dish 'tis welcome still to me,
But most, my Hasty Pudding, most in thee.
    Let the green succotash with thee contend,   135
Let beans and corn their sweetest juices blend,
Let butter drench them in its yellow tide,
And a long slice of bacon grace their side;
Not all the plate, how fam'd soe'er it be,
Can please my palate like a bowl of thee.   140
Some talk of Hoe-Cake, fair Virginia's pride,
Rich Johnny-Cake, this mouth has often tri'd;
Both please me well, their virtues much the same,
Alike their fabric, as allied their fame,
Except in dear New England, where the last ⎫   145
Receives a dash of pumpkin in the paste,   ⎬
To give it sweetness and improve the taste. ⎭
But place them all before me, smoaking hot,
The big, round dumpling, rolling from the pot,
The pudding of the bag, whose quivering breast,   150
With suet lin'd leads on the Yankee feast,
The Charlotte brown, within whose crusty sides
A belly soft the pulpy apple hides;

The yellow bread whose face like amber glows,
And all of Indian that the bake-pan knows,— 155
You tempt me not—my fav'rite greets my eyes,
To that lov'd bowl my spoon by instinct flies.

Canto II

To mix the food by vicious rules of art,
To kill the stomach, and to sink the heart
To make mankind to social virtue sour, 160
Cram o'er each dish, and be what they devour;
For this the kitchen muse first fram'd her book,
Commanding sweats to stream from every cook;
Children no more their antic gambols tried,
And friends to physic wonder'd why they died. 165
Not so the Yankey—his abundant feast,
With simples furnish'd and with plainness drest,
A numerous offspring gathers round the board,
And cheers alike the servant and the lord;
Whose well-bought hunger prompts the joyous taste 170
And health attends them from the short repast.
While the full pail rewards the milk-maid's toil,
The mother sees the morning cauldron boil;
To stir the pudding next demands their care;
To spread the table and the bowls prepare; 175
To feed the household as their portions cool
And send them all to labor or to school.
Yet may the simplest dish some rules impart,
For nature scorns not all the aids of art.
Ev'n Hasty Pudding, purest of all food, 180
May still be bad, indifferent, or good,
As sage experience the short process guides,
Or want of skill, or want of care presides.
Whoe'er would form it on the surest plan,
To rear the child and long sustain the man; 185
To shield the morals while it mends the size,
And all the powers of every food supplies,
Attend the lesson that the muse shall bring,
Suspend your spoons, and listen while I sing.

But since, O man! thy life and health demand   190
Not food alone but labour from thy hand,
First in the field, beneath the sun's strong rays,
Ask of thy mother earth the needful maize;
She loves the race that courts her yielding soil,
And gives her bounties to the sons of toil.   195
When now the ox, obedient to thy call,
Repays the loan that fill'd the winter stall,
Pursue his traces o'er the furrow'd plain,
And plant in measur'd hills the golden grain.
But when the tender germ begins to shoot,   200
And the green spire declares the sprouting root,
Then guard your nursling from each greedy foe,
The insidious worm, the all-devouring crow.
A little ashes, sprinkled round the spire,
Soon steep'd in rain, will bid the worm retire;   205
The feather'd robber with his hungry maw
Swift flies the field before your man of straw,
A frightful image, such as school boys bring,
When met to burn the pope or hang the king.
Thrice in the season, through each verdant row   210
Wield the strong plow-share and the faithful hoe:
The faithful hoe, a double task that takes,
To till the summer corn, and roast the winter cakes.
Slow springs the blade, while check'd by chilling rains,
Ere yet the sun the seat of Cancer gains;   215
But when his fiercest fires emblaze the land,
Then start the juices, then the roots expand;
Then, like a column of Corinthian mould,
The stalk struts upward and the leaves unfold;
The busy branches all the ridges fill,   220
Entwine their arms, and kiss from hill to hill.
Here cease to vex them, all your cares are done:
Leave the last labors to the parent sun;
Beneath his genial smiles, the well-drest field,
When autumn calls, a plenteous crop shall yield.   225
Now the strong foliage bears the standards high,
And shoots the tall top-gallants to the sky;

The suckling ears their silky fringes bend,
And pregnant grown, their swelling coats distend;
The loaded stalk, while still the burden grows,   230
O'erhangs the space that runs between the rows;
High as a hop-field waves the silent grove,
A safe retreat for little thefts of love,
When the pledged roasting-ears invite the maid,
To meet her swain beneath the new-form'd shade;   235
His generous hand unloads the cumbrous hill,
And the green spoils her ready basket fill;
Small compensation for the twofold bliss,
The promised wedding, and the present kiss.
Slight depredations these; but now the moon   240
Calls from his hollow tree the sly raccoon;
And while by night he bears his prize away,
The bolder squirrel labors through the day.
Both thieves alike, but provident of time,
A virtue rare, that almost hides their crime.   245
Then let them steal the little stores they can,
And fill their gran'ries from the toils of man;
We've one advantage, where they take no part,—
With all their wiles they ne'er have found the art
To boil the Hasty-Pudding; here we shine   250
Superior far to tenants of the pine;
This envied boon to man shall still belong,
Unshar'd by them, in substance or in song.
At last the closing season browns the plain,
And ripe October gathers in the grain;   255
Deep loaded carts the spacious corn-house fill,
The sack distended marches to the mill;
The lab'ring mill beneath the burden groans
And show'rs the future pudding from the stones;
Till the glad house-wife greets the powder'd gold,   260
And the new crop exterminates the old.
[Ah, who can sing what every wight must feel,
The joy that enters with the bag of meal,
A general jubilee pervades the house,
Wakes every child and gladdens every mouse.]   265

Canto III

The days grow short; but tho' the falling sun
To the glad swain proclaims his day's work done,
Night's pleasing shades his various tasks prolong,
And yield new subjects to my various song.
For now, the corn-house fill'd, the harvest home,   270
The invited neighbors to the *Husking* come;
A frolic scene, where work, and mirth, and play,
Unite their charms to chace the hours away.
 Where the huge heap lies centered in the hall,
The lamp suspended from the cheerful wall,   275
Brown corn-fed nymphs, and strong hard-handed beaux,
Alternate rang'd, extend in circling rows,
Assume their seats, the solid mass attack;
The dry husks rustle, and the corncobs crack;
The song, the laugh, alternate notes resound,   280
And the sweet cider trips in silence round.
 The laws of Husking every wight can tell;
And sure no laws he ever keeps so well:
For each red ear a general kiss he gains,
With each smut ear he smuts the luckless swains;   285
But when to some sweet maid a prize is cast,
Red as her lips, and taper as her waist,
She walks the round, and culls one favored beau,
Who leaps, the luscious tribute to bestow.
Various the sport, as are the wits and brains   290
Of well pleas'd lasses and contending swains;
Till the vast mound of corn is swept away,
And he that gets the last ear wins the day.
 Meanwhile the house-wife urges all her care,
The well-earn'd feast to hasten and prepare.   295
The sifted meal already waits her hand,
The milk is strain'd, the bowls in order stand,
The fire flames high; and, as a pool (that takes
The headlong stream that o'er the mill-dam breaks)
Foams, roars, and rages with incessant toils,   300
So the vex'd cauldron rages, roars and boils.
 First with clean salt, she seasons well the food,

Then strews the flour, and thickens all the flood.
Long o'er the simmering fire she lets it stand;
To stir it well demands a stronger hand;   305
The husband takes his turn: and round and round
The ladle flies; at last the toil is crown'd;
When to the board the thronging huskers pour,
And take their seats as at the corn before.

    I leave them to their feast. There still belong   310
More useful matters to my faithful song.
For rules there are, tho' ne'er unfolded yet,
Nice rules and wise, how pudding should be ate.

    Some with molasses line the luscious treat,
And mix, like bards, the useful with the sweet,   315
A wholesome dish, and well deserving praise,
A great resource in those bleak wintry days,
When the chill'd earth lies buried deep in snow,
And raging Boreas drives the shivering cow.

    Blest cow! thy praise shall still my notes employ,   320
Great source of health, the only source of joy;
Mother of Egypt's god,—but sure, for me,
Were I to leave my God, I'd worship thee.
How oft thy teats these pious hands have prest!
How oft thy bounties prove my only feast!   325
How oft I've fed thee with my favorite grain!
And roar'd, like thee, to find thy children slain!

    Ye swains who know her various worth to prize,
Ah! house her well from winter's angry skies.
Potatoes, pumpkins, should her sadness cheer,   330
Corn from your crib, and mashes from your beer;
When spring returns, she'll well acquit the loan,
And nurse at once your infants and her own.

    Milk then with pudding I should always choose;
To this in future I confine my muse,   335
Till she in haste some further hints unfold,
Good for the young, nor useless to the old.
First in your bowl the milk abundant take,
Then drop with care along the silver lake
Your flakes of pudding; these at first will hide   340

Their little bulk beneath the swelling tide;
But when their growing mass no more can sink,
When the soft island looms above the brink,
Then check your hand; you've got the portion due,
So taught our sires, and what they taught is true.   345
  There is a choice in spoons. Though small appear
The nice distinction, yet to me 'tis clear.
The deep bowl'd Gallic spoon, contrived to scoop
In ample draughts the thin diluted soup,
Performs not well in those substantial things,   350
Whose mass adhesive to the metal clings;
Where the strong labial muscles must embrace,
The gentle curve, and sweep the hollow space.
With ease to enter and discharge the freight,
A bowl less concave, but still more dilate,   355
Becomes the pudding best. The shape, the size,
A secret rests, unknown to vulgar eyes.
Experienc'd feeders can alone impart
A rule so much above the lore of art.
These tuneful lips that thousand spoons have tried,   360
With just precision could the point decide.
Though not in song; the muse but poorly shines
In cones, and cubes, and geometric lines;
Yet the true form, as near as she can tell,
Is that small section of a goose egg shell,   365
Which in two equal portions shall divide
The distance from the center to the side.
  Fear not to slaver; 'tis no deadly sin:—
Like the free Frenchman, from your joyous chin
Suspend the ready napkin; or like me,   370
Poise with one hand your bowl upon your knee;
Just in the zenith your wise head project,
Your full spoon, rising in a line direct,
Bold as a bucket, heed no drops that fall,
The wide mouth'd bowl will surely catch them all!   375

  (1793; 1796)

INDEXES

Index of Poets and Titles

377

Index of First Lines